Future Directions in Distance Learning and Communication Technologies

Timothy K. Shih
Tamkang University, Taiwan

Jason C. Hung
Northern Taiwan Institute of Science and Technology, Taiwan

IDEA GROUP PUBLISHING
Hershey • London • Melbourne • Singapore

Acquisitions Editor: Michelle Potter
Development Editor: Kristin Roth
Senior Managing Editor: Jennifer Neidig
Managing Editor: Sara Reed
Copy Editor: Larissa Vinci
Typesetter: Cindy Consonery
Cover Design: Lisa Tosheff
Printed at: Integrated Book Technology

Published in the United States of America by
Information Science Publishing (an imprint of Idea Group Inc.)
701 E. Chocolate Avenue
Hershey PA 17033
Tel: 717-533-8845
Fax: 717-533-8661
E-mail: cust@idea-group.com
Web site: http://www.idea-group.com

and in the United Kingdom by
Information Science Publishing (an imprint of Idea Group Inc.)
3 Henrietta Street
Covent Garden
London WC2E 8LU
Tel: 44 20 7240 0856
Fax: 44 20 7379 0609
Web site: http://www.eurospanonline.com

Library of Congress Cataloging-in-Publication Data

Future directions in distance learning and communications technology / Timothy Shih and Jason C. Hung, editors.
p. cm.
Summary: "This book summarizes theoretical studies and practical solutions for engineers, educational professionals, and graduate students in the research areas of e-learning, distance education, and instructional designs. Readers will find solutions and research directions in this interesting book"--Provided by publisher.
ISBN 1-59904-376-9 (hardcover) -- ISBN 1-59904-377-7 (softcover) -- ISBN 1-59904-378-5 (ebook)
1. Instructional systems--Design. 2. Distance education. 3. Multimedia systems. 4. Teaching--Aids and devices. 5. Educational technology. I. Shih, Timothy K., 1961- II. Hung, Jason C., 1973-
LB1028.38.F87 2007
371.35--dc22
2006018827

British Cataloguing in Publication Data
A Cataloguing in Publication record for this book is available from the British Library.

Future Directions in Distance Learning and Communication Technologies

Table of Contents

Section III: Intelligent Technologies

Preface

Distance education or distance learning is an important direction to current high level education. With the blooming of Internet and Web technologies, the popularity of distance learning programs enforces us to think about what advanced technologies can help traditional education. In general, the new era of distance education needs several types of people to work together. Educational professionals are the main players as usual. The design of high-quality contents is the most important factor toward the success of a distance learning program. It is also important that clear presentation/lecture is delivered, both from educational (e.g., clear writing and organization) and technological (e.g., high quality video) perspectives. To ensure the quality and friendliness of contents, digital art designers may assist educational professionals to ensure that multimedia technologies are properly applied to contents. Especially, if Web-based channel is the main delivery media, a visually pleasant design of interface for friendly browsing is necessary. In order to support efficient delivery, a distance learning program also needs technical persons to operate network and computer systems to ensure that video or Web-based contents can be accessed smoothly. Thus, an administrative office needs to gather different types of professionals, include teachers, art designers, and technicians. The administrative office also needs to develop curricula and maintain records for students and accounting, and to ensure that the operation is running smoothly.

The organization of a distance learning program needs a number of professionals. On the other hand, the need of advanced computer and network technologies are essential toward a smooth operation of the program. In fact, advanced technologies for distance learning is still a challenge research area, with several interesting problems not yet discovered and solved. This book collects a few best revised papers from the *International Journal of Distance Education Technologies*, in additional to several invited papers. The book is organized into five sections. The first section includes a paper which addresses several challenge issues from both sociological and technological perspectives. The article also includes a collection of questions and answers found in panel discussions in international conferences. This article will help new students who are interested in distance education technologies. Section II to Section IV includes 13 articles, which addresses research results from communication, intelligence, and educational perspectives. These three aspects are also the themes of the *International Journal of Distance Education Technologies*. The last section points out a few interesting research issues in a chapter. Especially, advanced multimedia and communication technologies are discussed. The readers of this book can start from the first chapter to have a glance of technical issues of distance learning. Depending on his or her research interest, one can choose Section III to Section V for detailed issues. We give an overview of these thirteen chapters in the next paragraphs. For graduate students in computer engineering or computer science departments who are looking for research issues, the final chapter is recommended.

Communication technologies include new network infrastructures, real-time protocols, broadband and wireless communication tools, quality-of-services issues, multimedia streaming technology, distributed systems, mobile systems, multimedia synchronization controls, and other technologies of distance education. Recently, with the blooming of wireless communication technologies, outdoor distance learning can be achieved base on devices such as PDA or cellular phones. In Chapter II, an e-learning system called TDeLS uses a top-down method, which was proposed in the Information Processing Society of Japan in 1999. The system uses XML-based contents that can be delivered on cellular phones. Whether the contents are delivered on personal computers or mobile devices, the use of privacy and security issues associated with e-learning is an essential need. Chapter III discussed a number of existing privacy enhancing technologies, including methods for network privacy, policy-based privacy/security management, and trust systems. In Chapter IV, a network protocol based on distributed topology construction protocol (DTCP) is discussed. The protocol can be used to improve communication efficiency of mobile devices for distance learning. To support students study in traditional university campuses, Chapter V discusses an agent-based system on cellular phone which is able to provide four types of services: campus navigation, news, login states of students, and online web information. The system was used by several users in a university in Japan with a reasonable satisfaction. Communication technologies can be used not only in distance learning. But, good communication systems are essentially important toward the success of distance leaning programs.

Intelligent technologies include intelligent tutoring, individualized distance learning, neural network or statistical approaches to behavior analysis, automatic FAQ reply methods, copyright protection and authentication mechanisms, soft computing, visual computing, and other technologies of distance education. Computer science and computer engineering foundations usually play an important role. Chapter VI presents an essential technique based on the TAOML language (an extension of XML), from a software engineering perspective. An experimental courseware called the Growing Book is also presented by using the technology. Reusability is one of the focuses in this chapter. A mediator-based architecture is proposed in Chapter VII. The architecture brings help from a service provider to a service requester, through the actions of an agent which is able to allocate proper learning resources via a definition of ontology. TutorFinder, an online tool for students and lecturers to locate suitable tutors, is also included in Chapter VII. In addition, Chapter VIII presents an approach of using adaptive hypermedia for a particular learner based on the profile or records of the learner. The chapter also addresses an advanced assessment technique, called the concept effect model. Students can benefit from the system of knowing what portion of study the individual should further enhance, by following suggestions from the outcome of a test. With a slightly different focus, Chapter IX presents a virtual lab for students to learn DSP (i.e., digital signal processing). A prototype of VDSPL has been implemented by using the IBM Aglet system and Java native interface for DSP experimental platforms. Experimental results demonstrate that the system has received many positive feedbacks from both students and teachers. In general, intelligent technologies have no specific underlying model to achieve one of the challenge issues in e-learning — intelligent tutoring.

Educational technologies include practical and new learning models, automatic assessment methods, effective and efficient authoring systems, and other issues of distance education. Even with a less emphasis of educational technologies in the *International Journal of Distance Education Technologies*, recently, we found several interesting articles with computational mechanisms based on educational technologies. An interesting approach to improve student memory retention by using distance learning tool is proposed in Chapter X. Communication preference and learning style of students were analyzed. Conclusively, the WISDeM's interactive system is likely to make a significant improvement to student learning and remembering. The scaffolding theory is used in Chapter XI. By using visualized domain ontology, an authoring environment based on resource description framework/resource description framework schema (RDF/RDFS) was used to construct domain ontology of mathematics at a secondary school level. The authoring tool is further extended to a content repository management system (CRMS). Another study and experiments of using live audio-video delivery, text chat and document annotations of a lecture presentation are presented in Chapter XII. Using Nanyang Technological University, Singapore as a test-bed, the authors recommends a few development stages of e-learning in a university. In Chapter XIII, grid computing and a grid engine (Globus Toolkit 3.2) were used to develop a SCORM-based ubiquitous learning environment. The environment is able to support learning on different devices such as PC, Laptop, Tablet PC, PDA, and mobile phones. A study of using such a system for English teaching is presented. And finally, Chapter XIV presents an interesting system on the Web to teach students how to write Chinese characters.

The expected great success of distance learning and the virtual university paradise is still not coming. Even if technology can support such an operation, there still remain some sociological and methodological problems. It is questionable, whether it is political, or technical, for the society to approve virtual university degrees. However, distance learning is now very active in mission-based instruction, and in community-based lifelong education. We hope the academia, the government, the engineers, and the society can work tightly toward the great success of distance education.

Timothy K. Shih
Tamkang University, Taiwan

Jason C. Hung
Northern Taiwan Institute of Science and Technology, Taiwan

Section I
Introduction

Chapter I

A Survey of Distance Education Challenges and Technologies

Timothy K. Shih[1], Tamkang University, Taiwan

Jason C. Hung,
Northern Taiwan Institute of Science and Technology, Taiwan

Jianhua Ma, Hosei University, Japan

Qun Jin, University of Aizu, Japan

Abstract

Distance education, e-learning, and virtual university are similar terms for a trend of modern education. It is an integration of information technologies, computer hardware systems, and communication tools to support educational professionals in remote teaching. This chapter presents an overview of distance education from the perspective of policy, people, and technology. A number of questions frequently asked in distance learning panel discussions are presented, with the suggested answers from the authors. The survey presented in this chapter includes communication, intelligent, and educational technologies of distance education. Readers of this chapter are academic researchers and engineers who are interested in new research issues of distance education, as well as educators and general participants who are seeking for new solutions.

History, Trend, and Elements of Distance Education

With the growing popularity of multimedia and Internet technologies, distance education programs have become popular and thus, importance of the related technologies are realized by educational professionals and information technology researchers. However, distance education is not totally new. The use of computer and information technologies in education has a long history. Ever since Thomas Edison predicted that motion pictures would replace textbooks for learning in 1922, the use of video was popular in training. Especially, in the World War II, the U.S. Army used video tapes to train employees. Shortly after WWII, video technology and television were used for training and demonstration. In this period, instruction was broadcasted in a single direction. There is no **interaction** between audiences and the instructor. However, the advantage is, the number of participants to the program can be larger than the traditional classroom education, especially when satellite communication was integrated with video broadcasting. **Efficiency** of video training was the first reason for education to use modern technology. The use of computers follows video technology as the second phase of modern education. Computer-based training (CBT) and computer-assisted instruction (CAI) use information technologies and educational theory to develop interactive software. The solution allows students to interact with their instructor (i.e., a computer) in a limited way. Mostly, CBT was limited to drill and practice. However, CBT and CAI were the first attempt to use computers for teaching, which enrich a new instruction delivery style — the **automation**. In spite of this advantage, CBT and CAI software had a problem in the '70s and the '80s — lack of **stability**. In that stage, computer hardware, operating systems, and system programs evolved dramatically and quickly. A CBT program is hardly used for several years due to the change of its supporting environments. Stability was a main consideration for computer-based modern education. Since the early '90s, the third period of modern education was stimulated by the invention of multimedia and Internet technologies. Multimedia presentations as CD ROM titles for education, Web-based distance-learning programs, and even online video conferencing based on ISDN, ADSL, and broadband communication channels became popular. With the new millennium and beyond, computer and communication technologies will be integrated with

Contents (i.e., the integration of 3Cs). Distance education is certainly one of the potential activities rely on this integration. However, new technologies can be further investigated. For instance, real-time protocols, broadband and wireless communication technologies, multimedia streaming algorithms, intelligent tutoring, behavior analysis of students, copyright protection and authentication mechanisms, visual computing, and new learning models, as well as other issues of distance education still need researchers, engineers, and participants to work together, to make the third revolution stage of modern education successful. The *International Journal of Distance Education Technologies* (JDET) is a primary forum for disseminating practical solutions to the automation of open and distance learning. We hope the journal will look at some of these problems from the technology perspective, and contribute solutions to the third stage of modern education.

We begin with the presentation on categories of distance learning, which include distance learning programs in conventional universities and virtual universities, as well as e-learning portals. Elements of distance learning including policy, people, and technology needs toward the success of distance education are also presented, followed by some highlights of challenge issues. In Section II, we collect 18 questions which were frequently asked in several panel discussions in distance education related international conferences, with some suggested answers from the authors or panelists. Then, we present a survey of distance education technologies, which are divided into three categories according to the theme of JDET.

Categories of Distance-Learning Programs

Distance learning is widely available in **conventional universities**, as regular and continuous education programs. Types of courses offered include general education, management and business administration, engineering, language education, and others. Most courses taught in classroom are possible for distance learning, except a few cases which require lab experiments (e.g., chemistry). Degrees or certificates offered including bachelor, master, and even doctorate levels. Supporting systems or tools used in this type of distance-learning programs can be divided into two types:

- **Traditional tools:** Videotape (S-VHS), cable/public television, satellite video conferencing, tele-conferencing, textbook

- **Computer-assisted and network tools:** CD-ROM titles, Web browser, Whiteboard, Chat room, Real player, Quicktime, Windows Media Player, broadband video conferencing, WebCT, LearningSpace, Blackboard

Note that, textbooks are still widely used, even it is possible to publish their electronic versions on the Internet. Proprietary communication tools are developed to support online discussion, either in a limited bandwidth environment (e.g., chat room) or in a broadband communication facility (e.g., video conferencing). A few integrated systems such as WebCT are commercially available. These systems provide functions ranging from administration, courseware creation and management, communication, assessment, and some even provide course contents. It is interesting to see how a traditional university evaluates performance of distance-learning students. Some rely on fax, e-mail, or even surface mail to collect reports and homework. In some cases, secure online quizzes and chat room participations are counted as evaluation criteria. However, personally-proctored examinations are commonly found in this type of distance education (i.e., distance-learning programs in conventional universities).

With a similar functionality but different audience target, **virtual universities** are also widely available for continuous education programs. University of Phoenix and Athabasca University are one of the largest virtual universities in U.S. and Canada, respectively. Virtual universities allow students to take the flexibility of time and location. Students who have their industrial career will be able to complete their higher level education without sacrificing their business. In some cases, a distance-learning course in virtual university can be completed in five to six weeks. And, it is possible to shorten the number of years to gain a diploma (as compared to four years of study for an undergraduate degree). Software systems and student evaluation strategies in virtual universities are similar to traditional universities. Even some virtual universities aim to provide a 100% remote learning based on Internet, to get a degree, some residential requirements are necessary, especially for a higher level degree.

E-learning portal is another style of distance learning. It is similar to virtual university, but with a different emphasis on the kind of audiences and courses. E-learning portals aim to provide a solution to small or middle size companies, which like to have their employee training or customer service on the Internet. Practical courses instead of theory studies are welcome in e-learning portals. In some cases, customized course contents can be built to satisfy the needs of individual companies. Usually, e-commerce facility is incorporated with an e-learning portal to provide additional services (e.g., book selling).

Elements of Distance Learning

In spite of the slight difference among the three categories of distance-learning programs, the fundamental elements of distance education are similar. These elements (shown in Figure 1) are the essential components which affect the development of distance-learning programs.

From the policy perspective, the evaluation criteria of distance-learning programs affect the instructional quality and performance of students, which has an influence to how the industry trusts distance education. On the other hand, the approval of diploma is an important factor of attraction to students who wish to join a virtual university. If the government or a university establishes a high requirement, less number of students will enroll. Thus, standard evaluation criteria should be established. The overall evaluation may include teaching evaluation to instructors and the review of course contents, as well as the performance evaluation of students. The standardization of courseware format and platform (e.g., SCORM) (Dodds, 2002) will ease the exchange of course materials. It is time consuming to create high quality distance-learning courseware. Courseware exchange has become one of the possible solutions to reduce the load of a courseware designer. But, each courseware has a copyright. Who should own the intellectual property (IP) is an issue of policy. In some cases, the IP belongs to the virtual university. But, this is definitely different from the IP of a textbook. The IP issue is different depending on different institutes and countries. Moreover, different traditional universities have different focuses and strengths. The focuses of virtual universities are different as well. Other policy issues are related to sociological behavior of students, such as how an individual trusts a friend in the virtual world. We will discuss some of these issues in Section II.

Figure 1. Elements of distance education

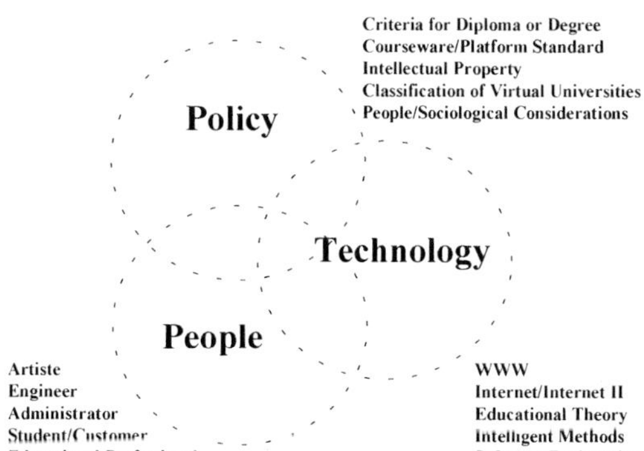

From the perspective of who should work for a distance-learning program, there are several types of experts. To create a high quality distance-learning courseware, educational professionals, engineers, and art designers should work together. Distance-learning platforms should be maintained by an engineer or an instructor. The administrator should review and manage distance-learning courses as well as the curriculum schedule. Sometimes, it is hard to divide the boundary. An instructor can maintain the distance-learning platform by himself or herself, as well as handling the schedule. The organization of human resource in a distance-learning program also affects the success of the program.

This journal focuses on the technology perspective of distance education. We will discuss some technical challenges of distance education in the next section. We should point out that, technology should be used by people. That is, an investigation of automatic mechanism to build a better distance-learning system must consider the need of an end user. But, the development of a good software system also affects the decision of a policy, which affects the end user again. Therefore, policy, technology, and people are strongly related in the life-cycle of distance education.

Challenges and Issues of Distance-Learning Technologies

Several advantages make distance learning become popular and important. Convenience and flexibility are some of the main reasons. With the growing number of Internet users, Web-based distance-learning programs enable lifelong education anytime at any location. Scalability of participants is another advantage. With a proper support of network infrastructures and computer systems, a large number of students can join distance-learning programs together. Moreover, timely update of course contents and online discussion give students the benefit of acquiring firsthand information, which is precisely presented by using computer software. All of these advantages accelerate the development of distance education.

However, challenges and issues must be investigated from different perspectives, including sociological, policy, and technical issues. Even sociological and policy issues are less related to technology, in the next section, we present some questions and answers. From the technique perspective, we highlight some research issues as the following:

- **Course and user management:** An administration system should provide efficient management tools for administrators, instructors, and students. If online course materials are provided on the Web, a friendly interface and supporting tools are required. For instance, an online student service center helps students to find references, suitable courses, and answers to general questions.
- **Efficient courseware development tools:** It is time consuming for a course designer to develop high quality courseware. A friendly courseware tool helps instructors to design or customizes course materials from reusable course components. In addition, a question database and exam composition tool may help an instructor to design an examination easily.
- **Instance hints and intelligent tutoring:** While a student is navigating an online course, an intelligent agent is able to analyze his or her behavior, and provides real-time and useful suggestions. In some cases, an agent program will guide the student through different learning topology depending on the behavior of the student.
- **FAQ summarization and automatic reply:** It is also time consuming for an instructor to answer questions from students' e-mails. An auto-reply system should be able to use information retrieval techniques to summarize frequently asked questions, and reply to new questions with proper answers.
- **Unbiased examination and student assessment:** It is difficult to ensure the behavior of students while an online examination is under processing but without a human monitor. A surveillance tool can randomly take a snapshot of on-the-spot screen while the examination proceeds. Also, in some distance-learning programs, chat room participation will be counted as an evaluation criterion. An intelligent tool should be able to check if a student has devoted himself or herself in a discussion.
- **Individualized quizzes:** Some distance-learning systems are able to generate different test questions for each individual student on the basis of a similar difficulty level. This type of system will ensure an unbiased examination as well.
- **Privacy of student:** Personal information of a student should be hid from another student, the administrator, and even the instructors. Unless it is necessary to assess student performance from his or her personal data (such as answers to an assignment or exam), privacy should be enforced.
- **Broadband and real-time communication:** For online discussion using video conferencing, quality-of-services should be guaranteed with the support of broadband and real-time communication facilities.

- **Universal and mobile accessibility:** Students and instructors should be able to access the distance-learning Web site from any location with different devices, such as PDAs or cellular phones. Wireless communication techniques may be incorporated in a distance-learning system.
- **Scalability:** As the number of students enrolled becomes larger, distributed Web services should be able to re-direct requests of students to different Web servers to share bandwidth and hardware load.
- **Remote lab and simulation:** Domain specific remote labs connected to Internet need to be developed to support online experiments. If remote labs are not available, online simulation tools (i.e., virtual lab) should be provided.
- **Multilingual support:** Since distance education can be accessed from anywhere in the world, distance education platform and systems should consider multilingual support for the international society.
- **Evaluation standard of distance education:** Standard criteria and questionnaires should be setup to allow teaching evaluation, evaluation of courseware, student performance evaluation, and the evaluation of a distance-learning program.

Some of the previous issues had been solved, as we will discuss in Section III. Before the survey of these solutions, we present some questions and answers frequently occurred in distance-learning related panel discussions.

Problems and Discussions

According to software engineering principles, verification and validation are two key methods to ensure the quality of a software system. Verification means to check whether a software system meet the requirement of a specification. Most importantly, validation checks whether a software system meets the needs of users. A software system not used by any user will lose its value. Thus, it is important to know "what the users need" before any distance-learning system is developed. In addition, methodological and sociological issues of distance education may influence what the users need. It is important to realize these fundamental issues, before we consider any software specification of a distance-learning system.

We collect questions frequently asked in panel discussions of international conferences related to multimedia computing, distributed systems, communication, and database systems. These panel discussions focus on distance learning or virtual society. Some of the panelists are authors of this chapter. We also circulate these questionnaires among experts, either as system developers, or as end users of distance-learning systems. We summarize suggestions and answers[2] from the international society, which is presented next.

1. Who is interested in distance-learning courses? What motivates the students to take distance-learning courses?
   - Adult working students are interested (Shih, Dow, Chee, Jin, Asirvatham, Leong, Arndt)
   - Intercampus courses for university students or geographically isolated students (Dow, Li, Arndt)
   - Professional training for career (Li, Asirvatham, Leong)
   - To get the first degree (Chee)
   - Flexibility in time and location (Shih, Dow, Li, Jin, Leong, Arndt)
   - Can save money (Arndt)
2. What is the role of student service center (i.e., TAs, Curriculum Advisors, and Administrators)? Is the center a success reason to attract students?
   - Education is a service (i.e., the center is a requirement) (Shih, Jin, Asirvatham)
   - Student Service Center is a successful reason (Shih)
   - TA's in Student Service Center help students (Li, Lin, Leong, Arndt)
   - Provide vital human element in learning is necessary (Chee)
   - Korea adult students seem to be independent. Seventy percents of students choose DL program without the help from a tutor (Jung, quoted by Shih)
3. What is the minimal requirement for admission? Will GRE, GMAT, and TOEFL be taken into the considerations?
   - TOEFL Should be considered for courses in English for international students (Shih, Li, Lin, Leong)
   - Basic language and literacy skills is necessary (Chee, Arndt)
   - Working experiences should be considered (Asirvatham)
   - May not be necessary (wide-entrance and narrow-exit, allowing better financial support to the organization) (Jin, Asirvatham, Leong, Arndt)

4. What types of courses are suitable for distance learning?
    - Lab facility is a consideration (Shih, Lin, Jin, Chee, Asirvatham, Arndt)
    - Courses with less update of contents (e.g., English grammar, math, etc.) (Shih)
    - Popular courses (for efficiency) (Dow)
    - Courses which can benefit from hypermedia and multimedia technologies (Li)
    - Knowledge-oriented courses (i.e., literature, language) (Chee, Leong)
    - Courses of high degree interaction may be restricted due to facility (Leong)
5. What types of instructors are suitable for distance learning?
    - Instructors who like to have online interactions and to try distance learning tools (Li, Chee, Jin, Leong, Asirvatham)
    - Instructors who wants to reuse course materials (Li, Asirvatham)
    - Instructors who appreciate the flexibility of distance learning (Arndt)
6. What levels of distance programs are realistic (e.g., colleague education vs. elementary education)?
    - College level is suitable (Shih, Li, Lin, Chee, Jin, Asirvatham, Leong, Arndt)
    - K-12 (Shih, Jin, Arndt)
    - Adults and job training (Jin)
7. Is the classification of virtual universities necessary (i.e., university ranking for different purposes)?
    - Virtual universities may have different missions and focuses (Shih, Li, Chee, Jin, Asirvatham, Leong, Arndt)
8. Can students learn from each other? Is group discussion less efficient in distance education?
    - Student can learn from each other if a better communication facility is provided (Shih, Chee, Jin, Asirvatham, Leong)
    - Discussion using chat room tools will be efficient as well. And, discussion should be a requirement (Dow, Li, Asirvatham, Leong, Arndt)
    - Communication techniques should be considered (i.e., human to human and human to computer interactions) (Jin)
    - Conflicts with different view points in an off-line discussion may be higher than those proceeded online or face-to-face (Leong)

9. Does student need grade in a virtual university? Does virtual university need to operate the same as a traditional university (i.e., quiz and exam)?
   - Need grade to gain a trust from the society (Shih, Lin, Chee, Asirvatham, Leong)
   - Need grade to enforce and encourage students (Dow, Li, Asirvatham)
   - Grade can be used as a feedback from students (Dow)
   - May not need grade (let the society to make the justification) (Shih, Chee, Jin, Leong)
   - Virtual university should support both graded and non-graded (i.e., audit) options (Arndt)
10. Do traditional and virtual university students behave differently in different Culture? For instance, oriental students are shy to ask questions in class. But, they will ask questions using e-mail.
    - Sending e-mail for question is common everywhere (Shih, Jin, Arndt)
    - Distance education may benefit oriental students in off-line discussions (Li, Dow, Asirvatham, Leong)
11. Will the sociological behavior of students be different in virtual university? For instance, will a colleague student have a difficulty to find girl (or boy) friend in a virtual university?
    - Students can still make some virtual friends (Shih, Dow, Li, Lin, Jin)
    - Sociological behavior could be different (Chee, Asirvatham)
    - Easy to find a friend, but hard to gain trust (Jin, Leong)
    - Face-to-face interaction in the beginning will facilitate further discussion (Arndt)
12. Does the industrial society trust the quality of distance education?
    - The reputation of a virtual university may depend on its founding university (a conventional university) (Shih, Jin, Asirvatham, Leong)
    - Good quality of service and contents will gain trust (Dow, Li, Lin, Jin)
13. Who should design the course material (i.e., the instructor vs. the book author)?
    - A generic course content can be designed by the book author, while allowing each instructor to edit the content as needed (Shih, Dow, Jin, Leong)
    - The instructor should design the content. Copyright of the textbook should be considered (Li, Lin, Chee, Asirvatham, Arndt)

14. What about the intellectual property and legal issues of the course material? Should the course material belong to the instructor, or to the university (and for how long)?
    - Belong to the instructor, but commercial profit should be shared with the university (Dow, Asirvatham)
    - Belong to the university (Li, Lin)
    - To be decided by different government and situation (Chee, Jin, Arndt)
15. Will there be a threat from "the big professor" and "the super university"?
    - Yes (Shih, Dow, Li, Chee, Jin, Asirvatham, Leong)
    - Yes, but still need a large number of instructors for online tutoring to fit individual needs (Leong, Arndt)
16. How does distance learning impact high-level education in the near future?
    - Distance learning will affect high-level education, for instance, in continued education and profession education (Dow, Li, Lin, Jin, Asirvatham)
    - Combining traditional lecture and distance learning (Asirvatham, Leong)
    - Will bring a higher degree of competition among universities (Arndt)
17. How does distance learning impact the industry?
    - Distance learning can be used in training and customer service (Dow, Li, Chee, Jin, Asirvatham, Leong, Arndt)
    - The industry can provide feedback to university (Li)
18. Yet another "dotcom" issue (i.e., not so optimistic)?
    - No (Shih, Dow, Li, Lin, Jin, Asirvatham, Leong, Arndt)
    - Distance learning will be used as a supplement to traditional university. Thus, it will last. (Shih, Jin)

The previous questions and answers indicate some problems, mostly related to sociological and policy issues. However, from the perspective of technology, there are a few issues which can result in better situations if automatic mechanisms are developed. It is the hope that, educational professionals, researchers, software developers, and even students can work together to seek out new and useful automatic tools, to make distance education easier and successful. For instance, the role of student service centers is considered important in most answers. But, teaching assistants should be incorporated. A good tool will help TAs to locate questions and answers, which can be annotated to satisfy a particular situation while help is requested. If the list of questions and answers can be properly stored in a database, with advanced information retrieval technology, the system can possibly reply to frequently asked questions automatically. In addition, if a remote lab is hard to build, a virtual lab (i.e., simulation) should be developed ss that chemistry and other experiments can be implemented. Also, advanced communication tools will certainly help group discussion. Regarding the development of courseware, a word processor for typesetting textbooks should be integrated with an authoring tool, such that Web-based courseware can be automatically or semi-automatically created. Image and video watermark techniques will help copyright protection of online courseware. And, secure payment mechanisms developed for E-commerce can be used in distance education. These examples encourage us to develop good distance-learning systems, which should fit the need of instructors, administrators, as well as students.

But, how should a virtual university operate? According to a traditional university, instruction delivery is the most important activity. In order to realize the main activity smoothly, administration is required. A traditional university usually has some student activities and organizations, which need to be properly supported by the university's infrastructure. These are some of the important operation factors of a traditional university. A virtual university also focuses on instruction delivery. But, due to the geographical difference, communication tools should be efficient enough to realize instruction. Communication efficiency points out an important factor: the awareness impact. Awareness indicates how strong an individual feels the existence of another person in the communication. For instance, when two persons have an eye contact, the awareness is high. When people are located in different cities and are talking on the phone, the awareness is lower. Sending postal mail has the lowest awareness among these three communication channels. Since a virtual university is distributed geographically, how to use computer networks to guarantee a reasonable awareness is one of the considerations. Awareness certainly affects instruction quality. On the other hand, a virtual university needs administration, which includes activities such as registration, course selection, accounting, and so on. Furthermore, a university needs to ensure that students are learning in order to meet some evaluation standard. This step is to guarantee the quality of education. A virtual university is different to a traditional university in that assessment is difficult. Conclusively, we believe that, a well-considered virtual university supporting system needs to meet the following three criteria:

- **The administration criterion:** A virtual university environment needs to have administration facilities to keep admission records, transcripts, accounting records, and so on. These administration tools should be available to administrators, instructors, and students (e.g., checking transcript information).

- **The awareness criterion:** Distance learning is different from traditional education. Since instructors and students are separated spatially, they are sometimes hard to "feel" the existence of each other. A virtual university supporting environment needs to provide reasonable communication tools such that awareness is satisfied.
- **The assessment criterion:** Assessment is the most important and difficult part of distance education. Tools to support the evaluation of student learning should be sophisticated enough to avoid unbiased assessment.

In the next section, we summarize automatic mechanisms which can be applied in the development of distance education systems. We divide the mechanisms according to the themes of this journal, which are communication, intelligent, and educational technologies for distance education.

Distance Education Technologies

As we have mentioned before, the purpose of JDET is to publish research contributions for the development of automatic tools to be used in distance learning. In the past few decades, computer technologies such as deductive reasoning, neural networks, and statistical analysis mechanisms can be used to develop intelligent tutoring or individualized learning tools. Information retrieval techniques can help the implementation of a precise search engine for seeking after class references. Network technologies ensure real-time interaction in a synchronized distance-learning session, and improve the quality of presentation services. Mobile and wireless communication systems allow distance learning on PDAs and even on cellular phones. On the other hand, educational technologies had been used in different levels of schools to improve the efficiency of instruction delivery and student assessment. Learning models need to be incorporated with new authoring tools to improve the quality of instructions. We present a few success examples in this section, according to communication, intelligent, and educational technologies.

Communication Technologies

Communication and network technologies can be divided into several levels. According to the ISO standard, network architectures can be divided into seven layers. However, other new technologies, such as ATM, use a different architecture. From the perspective of communication tools that are used in distance education, we focus on the network application level, which includes integrated systems rely on other lower level technology, such as those for real-time media streaming. In addition, the communication technologies we discuss here are not from the perspective of human interaction, either are they related to human-computer interactions.

Related to broadband communication technologies, there are a few articles. In Fernandez et al. (2001), distance-learning applications were tested over an IPv6/ATM-based broadband facility. The conclusion states that, users must understand the consequences of QoS differentiation, and the cost they paid. Another ATM-based conference system (Bai, He, Liao, & Lin, 2000) supports multicasting and point-to-point communication. The chapter also discusses an application for distance learning based on this technology. On the other hand, an agent-based architecture (i.e., mStar) to support the development of real-time communication is discussed (Parnes, Synnes, & Schefstrom, 2000). In the article, a bandwidth manager agent determines how bandwidth should be utilized. The strategy adapted considers the number of users, as well as the number of media used. In Maly et al. (1997), an interactive learning system supports two-way video, on-the-fly interaction, and application sharing is implemented on a high speed network. A prototype configuration, based on ATM network, for courses on-demand was developed at Stanford University (Harris & DiPaolo, 1996). Experiences including system integration, educational effectiveness, and economics are also discussed. Wang and Su (2000) also proposed a real-time communication tool to teach speaking skills. A real-time interactive Web-based teaching system for engineering students was developed in Hong Kong (Chu, 1999). Another real-time interactive virtual classroom tool is presented in Deshpande and Jenq-Neng (2001). New coding algorithm is used to enhance the quality of handwritten text video. A set of tools were also developed to record live classroom sessions. The use of operational user profile and the control of end-user QoS are suggested in Vouk, Bitzer, and Klevans (1999). The conclusion suggests a range of user-level delays, which is acceptable by most users. The chapter also recommends a number of facilities for the developers of distance education systems, to make the systems effective. A low-bandwidth streaming technology focuses on the application layer QoS is discussed in Fong and Hui (2001). A hybrid architecture using an exchange server is able to avoid the conflicting requirements, and to allow efficient point-to-point transfer. From the above discussions, we realize that real-time media streaming technology, with the control of quality of services, will be important for interactions in distance learning.

In addition to network-based tools, middleware systems to support distance education, or to enable the integration of tools are widely found in the literature. A set of distance-learning tools (Shih, 2001a), including a shared whiteboard and a chat room tool, are integrated to a distance-learning environment, which provides a complete platform for distance education. Another distance lecture supporting system (Chen, 1999) for streaming video clips and dynamically loaded HTML course content is developed, based on a synchronization framework known as WSML (Web-based synchronized multimedia lecture). Huang (2000) also uses Windows media streaming technology to integrate a distance system, which supports both real-time communication and on-demand-based media production. A distance-learning system (Duran-de-Jesus, Villacorta-Calvo, & Izquierdo-Fuente, 2000) for real-time teaching and interactive course is proposed. Parameters for the measurement of QoT (quality of teaching) are also defined in Duran-de-Jesus et al. (2000). A distance-learning system (Lee, 1997) based on Java is implemented to facilitate communication, management, and the evaluation of distance learning. This system is designed to work on a heterogeneous environment to support PCs and workstations. Another Java-based network educational system (Foster & MacGregor,, 1999) is also developed to support tele-teaching applications. For communication, a mechanism to control who to speak in a distributed virtual environment is proposed (Keh, Shih, Deng, Liao, & Chang, 2001). The control mechanism can be used for multimodal, multichannel, and multi-user communications. A client-server distributed environment (Benetazzo, 2000) to support virtual lab, using commercially standard components, is discussed. The system is tested by a class of students learning electrical measurements in different connections and operating conditions. Another Web-based remote laboratory (Ko, Chen, Jianping, Zhuang, & Chen Tan, 2001) for the experiments on a coupled tank apparatus was developed at the National University of Singapore. Video conferencing technique is used to provide audio and video feedback. A Web-based interactive simulation tool for electronics was developed in Scotland (Masson, 1999).

In a larger scale, a number of distance projects (Castro, 2001) to improve the technology of collaboration and communication were discussed. Experiences of building a virtual community for enriching e-learning experience and humanizing learning process are discussed in Carver (1999). In addition, Multimedia Micro-University (Chang, Hassanein, & Hsieh, 1998) is a project arms to support the management and operation of distance education of a small academic institution. A virtual library tools and an intelligent system are implemented to support online tutoring. Skill requirements to build efficient virtual community are presented. The experience of using satellite-based digital video, Web technology, and Internet-based interactions is also discussed in Brackett (1998). Lecture recording and playback systems using video and PowerPoint presentation are presented (Deng & Shih, 2002a; Latchman, Salzmann, Gillet, & Kim, 2001). A suite of Internet multimedia tools support both synchronized and asynchronized collaboration is presented in Peden, Burleson, and Leonardo (2000). The SimulNet (Anido et al., 2001b) distance-learning platform includes a few tools, such as authoring and communication tools. A set of synchronous distance education tools is also proposed in Pullen and Benson (1999). A system supports both synchronous and asynchronous mode of collaboration is proposed in Peden (2000). The system is used in a VLSI chip design course. A system allows video conferencing, interactive classroom, Web-based instruction, and traditional lecture is proposed in Siddiqui and Zubairi (2000). Mobile agent technologies were used in a distributed distance-learning system (Deng, 2002b), which allow students to have persistent personal data while they are accessing a centralized distance-learning server from different locations.

In addition to the communication tools used in a virtual community, Virtual Reality (VR) is a good medium, in distance learning, for making abstract concepts concrete, for example to touch or to manipulate virtual geodesic domes and to observe theirs symmetries (Sala, 2002). The difficulty of understanding scientific concepts is well-researched (Garnett & Treagust, 1999). Zoller (1990) has affirmed: *"Students' misunderstandings and misconceptions in school sciences at all levels constitute a major problem of concern to science educators, scientist-researchers, teachers, and, of course, students"* (p. 1054). Virtual reality can also help constructivist learning (Winn, 1993). Virtual reality modelling language (VRML) can help to create virtual objects in the cyberspace.

Intelligent Technologies

Artificial intelligence (AI) has been studied since many decades ago. In general, there are two directions of AI research: computational logic and neural network. The former has symbolic representation of knowledge. Using deductive reasoning and searching techniques, the former method tries to compute conclusions, which may represent new knowledge. On the other hand, there is intelligence which is hard to have a symbolic representation. The use of neural network relies on network of nodes, which encapsulate the second type of intelligence. Training is applied to the network, with modification to thresholds among these nodes. The resulting network is able to recognize the subsequent queries with proper suggestions. Whether the intelligent technology has a symbolic representation, it is possible to build autonomic systems, which help or guide students in an online learning session. Research issues of these systems include intelligent tutoring (Shih, 1997), individualized learning (Ha, Bae, Sung-Min, & Park, 2000), behavior analysis, auto-reply to frequently asked questions, and so on. We give some examples of intelligent technologies in distance education.

IMMPS (Shih, 1997) is an integration of a multimedia presentation design system and a back end intelligent system. The author is able to design rule-based knowledge for each presentation window, with different layout and multimedia references. An instructor can use the system to design individualized course materials. A learning control strategy based on neural network is presented in Si and Yu-Tsung (2001). The mechanism learns from mistake of user through the reinforcement signal, and tries to improve the user's future performance. Positive reinforcement is also learned by the system. A path analysis technique (Ha et al., 2000) is used for customized education. The discovery of Web page association rues is also used to analyze knowledge structure. The information collected will help the designer to develop a more efficient courseware. Another system and framework for Web content customization is proposed in Ochi, Yano, and Wakita (2000). The system supports resource customization, sharing, and searching. Using personal agents, a virtual classroom environment (Trajkovic, Davcev, Kimovski, & Petanceska, 2000) serves as a bridge between students and a virtual professor. An active video control and selection mechanism is proposed in Kameda, Ishizuka, and Minoh (2000). The mechanism is based on dynamic object detection, and a human intrinsic time constraint. The implemented system is used in distance-learning courses between UCLA and Kyoto University. An online assessment mechanism using Web technology is presented (Chetty, 2000). The system is for students of control engineering, in the practice of answering several questions, before an experiment is actually carried.

Educational Technologies

Educational theory and technologies has a great impact to the development of distance-learning systems. A software system will be useless if no one use it. Relying on educational theories and experiences for professionals, the design of any distance-learning system should consider its usability as the first step. A few articles look at distance-learning system from both educational (Jun & Gruenwald, 2001; Schar & Krueger, 2000) and engineering (Shih, 2000) perspectives. A formal model that evaluates interactivity and motivation of students is proposed in Jun et al. (2001). The model is tested on several Web-based instruction courses. And, experiences are discussed. In addition, five major factors for the development of computer-aided learning were proposed in Schar et al. (2000). The factors include theories for learning, multimedia didactic, learning technologies, information models in human-computer interaction, and user acceptance. Criteria of how distance education software systems are developed are presented in Shih (2000). The discussion includes administration, communication, and assessment tools that should be developed for distance education.

In addition to these guidelines, educational and software technologies were used to build distance education systems. Educational theory such as student-problem chart is used in the development of an assessment system (Chang, 2002), which supervise students via automatic generated Web tutorial. The system is able to incorporate user interactions. Thus, each tutorial generated is based on the individual behavior of student. On the other hand, to develop better courseware, a revised influence diagram method is proposed in Shih (2002) for courseware designs. The diagram helps the designers to construct a more efficient learning topology for students. A quantitative analysis is given to each course topology designed. Thus, comparison is made between different course structures. Moreover, a paradigm supports the development of Web documents is proposed in Shih, Chang, Tsai, Ma, and Huang (2001b). The paradigm can be extended to support courseware designs. Metrics of Web documents are also defined.

Summary

We point out challenges of distance education, as well as important research issues in this article. Experiences in the literature show that, distance education has a great impact not only to high-level education, but also to industrial training. A study report and the discussion of a distance-learning center established in MIT are discussed in Penfield and Larson (1996). A complete report of this study is available at http://www-evat.mit.edu/report/. The impact of information technology to high-level education is also discussed in Beckett (1996). Experiences of using multimedia and distance education tools in online teaching and conventional classrooms are discussed in Latchman, Salzmann, Gillet, and Bouzekri (1999). The analysis of distance-learning issues in U.S., UK, Canada, Australia, and New Zealand is reported in Stein and Harman (2000). The "learning-by-doing" (Anido, Llamas, & Fernandez, 2001a) paradigm for distance leaning in traditional university and life long training was also proposed. The access of real equipments using Internet and the use of Java-based simulation tools are compared, with several analytical parameters presented to the readers. But, what are the basic requirements to make a successful system? Two factors make instructors and students to use online distance-learning tools, such as video-based lectures are, firstly, the production process must be easy, and secondly, there must be advantages to overcome in-class teaching. The paper (Anderson et al., 2000) points out these reasons. A comparison of two sections of students enrolled in technical writing class, one in a conventional class and the other in a Web-based environment, is presented in Mehlenbacher, Miller, Covington, and Larsen (2000). Although no significant difference of student performance is found, there are small differences of learning style and attitudes. Moreover, a complete report known as "The No Significant Difference Phenomenon" (http://teleeducation.nb.ca/nosignificantdifference/) collects a set of quotations back to 1928. The report surveys 355 references.

The above reports and experiences show that, distance learning seems to be promising. But, what will be the future of distance education? Will e-learning be another "dotcom" issue? That is, will the impact of e-learning decreases or even vanishes? Perhaps we do not have an answer today. However, from the development of new technologies, we see a few issues of future distance education:

- **Bring outdoors to indoors:** Virtual reality-based communication and situated learning use augmented panorama and real-time communication technologies in a distance-learning CAVE. Students can feel and experience with outdoor facilities inside the classroom.
- **Bring indoors to outdoors:** Wireless communication for encyclopedia and E-books will be available. Outdoor students can participate to a lecture, use online references, or read class notes.
- **Edutainment:** Education will be easier and more interesting. It is possible to use game technologies in education, to attract students and to increase their motivation.
- **E-commerce:** E-learning will be a commercial activity. Knowledge is for sale in the future.
- **E-inequality:** Each virtual university has its own uniqueness and focus. But, it is possible that a virtual university dominates a particular area of distance-learning courses.
- **E-problem:** It will be a less people-centric natural of learning. With a large number of project-oriented courseware available, an individual student will choose a focus for training. That is, students will adapt to course sequences more as compared to course sequences are designed for students.

The expected great success of distance learning and the virtual university paradise is still not coming. Even if technology can support such an operation, there still remains some sociological and methodological problems. It is questionable, whether it is political, or technical, for the society to approve virtual university degrees. However, distance learning is now very active in mission-based instruction, and in community-based lifelong education. We hope the academia, the government, the engineers, and the society can work tightly toward the great success of distance education.

References

Anderson, D., Harvel, L., Hayes, M., Ishiguro, Y., Jackson, J., & Pimentel, M. (2000). Internet course delivery — Making it easier and more effective. *2000 IEEE International Conference on Multimedia and Expo, ICME 2000, 1*(1), 84-87.

Anido, L., Llamas, M., Caeiro, M., Santos, J., Rodriguez, J., & Fernandez, M. J. (2001b). An update on the SimulNet educational platform. Towards standards-driven E-learning. *IEEE Transactions on Education, 44*(2), 194.

Anido, L., Llamas, M., & Fernandez, M. J. (2001a). Internet-based learning by doing. *IEEE Transactions on Education, 44*(2), 193.

Bai, J., He, X., Liao, Q., & Lin, X. (2000). An ATM-based multimedia communication system and its application in distance learning. *Proceedings of International Conference on Communication Technology (WCC-ICCT 2000)* (Vol. 2, pp. 1383-1386).

Beckett, J. (1996). The impact of IT on education. *Engineering Science and Education Journal, 5*(4), 185-189.

Benetazzo, L., Bertocco, M., Ferraris, F., Ferrero, A., Offelli, C., Parvis, M., & Piuri, V. (2000). A Web-based distributed virtual educational laboratory. *IEEE Transactions on Instrumentation and Measurement, 49*(2), 349-356.

Brackett, J. W. (1998). Satellite-based distance learning using digital video and the Internet. *IEEE Multimedia, 5*(3), 72-76.

Carver, C. (1999). Building a virtual community for a tele-learning environment. *IEEE Communications Magazine, 37*(3), 114-118.

Castro, M., Lopez-Rey, A., Perez-Molina, C. M., Colmenar, A., de Mora, C., Yeves, F., Carpio, J., Peire, J., & Daniel, J. S. (2001). Examples of distance-learning projects in the European Community. *IEEE Transactions on Education, 44*(4), 406-411.

Chang, F. (2002). Intelligent assessment of distance learning. *Information Science: An International Journal* (Special Issue on Interactive Virtual Environment and Distance Education), *140*, 105-126.

Chang, S., Hassanein, E., & Hsieh, C. (1998). A multimedia micro-university. *IEEE Multimedia, 5*(3), 60-68.

Chen, H., Chen, G., & Hong, J. (1999, June). Design of a Web-based synchronized multimedia lecture system for distance education. *IEEE International Conference on Multimedia Computing and Systems, 2*, 887-891.

Chetty, M. (2000). A scheme for online Web-based assessment. *Engineering Science and Education Journal*, *9*(1), 27-32.

Chu, K. C. (1999). The development of a Web-based teaching system for engineering education. *Engineering Science and Education Journal*, *8*(3), 115-118.

Deng, L. Y., & Shih, T. K. (2002a, July 2-4). Implementing a distributed lecture-on-demand multimedia presentation system. *Proceedings of the 4th International Workshop on Multimedia Network Systems and Applications (MNSA2002)*, Vienna, Austria.

Deng, L. Y., Shih, T. K., Huang, T., Liao, Y., Wang, Y., & Hsu, H. (2002b, July). A distributed mobil agent framework for maintaining persistent distance education. *Journal of Information Science and Engineering* (Special Section on Parallel and Distributed Systems), *18*(4), 489-506.

Deshpande, S. G., & Jenq-Neng, H. (2001). A real-time interactive virtual classroom multimedia distance-learning system. *IEEE Transactions on Multimedia*, *3*(4), 432-444.

Dodds, P. (2002). *ADL sharable courseware object reference model (SCORM), advanced distributed learning.* Retrieved from http://www.adlnet.gov/scorm/index.cfm

Duran-de-Jesus, J., Villacorta-Calvo, J. J., & Izquierdo-Fuente, A. (2000). Complete system for distance learning over IP. *IEEE International Conference on Multimedia and Expo (ICME 2000)*, *1*(1), 27-30.

Fernandez, D., Garcia, A. B., Larrabeiti, D., Azcorra, A., Pacyna, P., & Papir, Z. (2001). Multimedia services for distant work and education in an IP/ATM environment. *IEEE Multimedia*, *8*(3), 68-77.

Fong, A. C. M., & Hui, S. C. (2001). Low-bandwidth Internet streaming of multimedia lectures. *Engineering Science and Education Journal*, *10*(6), 212-218.

Foster, A., & MacGregor, K. J. (1999). The use of a Java implementation of SLP in a tele-teaching application. Distributed computing systems. *Proceedings of the 7th IEEE Workshop on Future Trends* (pp. 273-278).

Garnett, P. J., & Treagust, D. F. (1999). Conceptual difficulties experienced by senior high school students of electrochemistry: Electrochemical (Galvanic) and electrolytic cells. *Journal of Research in Science Teaching*, *29*(10), 1079-1099.

Ha, S., Bae, S., & Park, S. (2000). Web mining for distance education. *Proceedings of the 2000 IEEE International Conference on Management of Innovation and Technology (ICMIT2000)* (Vol. 2, pp. 715-719).

Harris, D. A., & DiPaolo, A. (1996). Advancing asynchronous distance education using high-speed networks. *IEEE Transactions on Education, 39*(3), 444-449.

Huang, S., & Hu, H. (2000). Integrating Windows streaming media technologies into a virtual classroom environment. *Proceedings of International Symposium on Multimedia Software Engineering* (pp. 411–418).

Jun, W., & Gruenwald, L. (2001). An evaluation model for Web-based instruction. *IEEE Transactions on Education, 44*(2), 9.

Kameda, Y., Ishizuka, K., & Minoh, M. (2000). A live video imaging method for capturing presentation information in distance learning. *2000 IEEE International Conference on Multimedia and Expo (ICME 2000), 3*(3), 1237-1240.

Keh, H., Shih, T. K., Deng, L. Y., Liao, I., & Chang, R. (2001, April 16-19). Using the floor control mechanism in distributed multimedia presentation system. *Proceedings of the 3rd International Workshop on Multimedia Network Systems (MNS2001)*, AZ.

Ko, C. C., Chen, B. M., Jianping, C., Zhuang, Y., & Chen Tan, K. (2001). Development of a Web-based laboratory for control experiments on a coupled tank apparatus. *IEEE Transactions on Education, 44*(1), 76-86.

Latchman, H., Salzmann, C., Gillet, D., & Kim, J. (2001). Learning on demand-a hybrid synchronous/asynchronous approach. *IEEE Transactions on Education, 44*(2), 208-214.

Latchman, H. A., Salzmann, C., Gillet, D., & Bouzekri, H. (1999). Information technology enhanced learning in distance and conventional education. *IEEE Transactions on Education, 42*(4), 247-254.

Lee, K., Chang, K., Yu, S., Chang, I., Shia, C., Chen, W., & Huang, J. (1997). Design and implementation of important applications in a Java-based multimedia digital classroom. *IEEE Transactions on Consumer Electronics, 43*(3), 264-270.

Maly, K., Abdel-Wahab, H., Overstreet, C. M., Wild, J. C., Gupta, A. K., Youssef, A., Stoica, E., & Al-Shaer, E. S. (1997). Interactive distance learning over intranets. *IEEE Internet Computing, 1*(1), 60-71.

Masson, A. M. (1999). Web-based simulations for computer-assisted learning in the higher education sector. *Engineering Science and Education Journal, 8*(3), 107-114.

Mehlenbacher, B., Miller, C. R., Covington, D., & Larsen, J. S. (2000). Active and interactive learning online: A comparison of Web-based and conventional writing classes. *IEEE Transactions on Professional Communication, 43*(2), 166-184.

Ochi, Y., Yano, Y., & Wakita, R. (2000). Development of Web customize system for sharing educational resources. *Proceedings of the 1st International Conference on Web Information Systems Engineering* (Vol. 2, pp. 173 -178).

Parnes, P., Synnes, K., & Schefstrom, D. (2000). mStar: Enabling collaborative applications on the Internet. *IEEE Internet Computing*, *4*(5), 32-39.

Peden, J., Burleson, W., & Leonardo, C. (2000). The multimedia online collaboration architecture: Tools to enable distance learning. *2000 IEEE International Conference on Multimedia and Expo (ICME 2000)* (Vol. 2, pp. 593-596).

Penfield, P. Jr., & Larson, R. C. (1996). Education via advanced technologies. *IEEE Transactions on Education*, *39*(3), 436-443.

Pullen, J. M., & Benson, M. (1999). ClassWise: Synchronous Internet desktop education. *IEEE Transactions on Education*, *42*(4), 19.

Sala, N. (2002). Virtual reality as an educational tool. *Proceedings International Conference on Computers and Advanced Technology Education (CATE)* (pp. 415-420). Cancun, Mexico.

Schar, S. G., & Krueger, H. (2000). Using new learning technologies with multimedia. *IEEE Multimedia*, *7*(3), 40-51.

Shih, T. K. (2000). Criteria of virtual university operation. The *24th Annual International Conference on Computer Software and Applications, COMPSAC 2000* (pp. 284-285).

Shih, T. K. (2001a, September 30-October 5). Software systems for virtual university operations. *Proceedings of the 2001 ACM Multimedia Conference*, Ottawa, Ontario, Canada.

Shih, T. K., Chang, S., Tsai, J., Ma, J., & Huang, R. (2001b, December) Supporting well-engineered web documentation development — A multimedia software engineering approach toward virtual university courseware designs. *Annals of Software Engineering* (Vol. 12, 139-165). Special Volume on Multimedia Software Engineering.

Shih, T. K., & Davis, R. E. (1997, April-June). IMMPS: A multimedia presentation design system. *IEEE Multimedia, 4*(2), 67-78.

Shih, T. K., & Hung, R. (2002, August 26-29). Multimedia courseware development using influence diagram. *Proceedings of the 2002 IEEE International Conference on Multimedia and Expo (ICME2002)*, Lausanne, Switzerland.

Si, J., & Yu-Tsung, W. (2001). Online learning control by association and reinforcement. *IEEE Transactions on Neural Networks*, *12*(2), 264-276.

Siddiqui, K. J., & Zubairi, J. A. (2000). Distance learning using Web-based multimedia environment. *Proceedings of Academia/Industry Working Conference on Research Challenges* (pp. 325-330).

Stein, S., & Harman, B. (2000). Distance learning — The global challenge. *Proceedings of International Workshop on Advanced Learning Technologies (IWALT2000)* (pp. 197-200).

Trajkovic, V., Davcev, D., Kimovski, G., & Petanceska, Z. (2000). Web-based virtual classroom. *Proceedings of 34th International Conference on Technology of Object-Oriented Languages and Systems (TOOLS 34)* (pp. 137-146).

Vouk, M. A., Bitzer, D. L., & Klevans, R. L. (1999). Workflow and end-user quality of service issues in Web-based education. *IEEE Transactions on Knowledge and Data Engineering, 11*(4), 673-687.

Wang, Y., & Su, C. (2000). Synchronous distance education: Enhancing speaking skills via Internet-based real time technology. *Proceedings of the 1st International Conference on Web Information Systems Engineering* (Vol. 2, pp. 168-172).

Winn, W. (1993). *A conceptual basis for educational applications of virtual reality*. (HITL Tech. Rep. No. TR-93- 9). Seattle, WA: Human Interface Technology Laboratory. Retrieved from http://www.hitl.washington.edu/publications/r-93-9

Zoller, U. (1990). Students' misunderstandings and misconceptions in college freshman chemistry (general and organic). *Journal of Research in Science Teaching, 27*(10), 1053-1065.

Endnotes

1 Except the first author, the co-authors are sorted by last names.

2 Answers for each question are cited by the last name of authors in between brackets, to distinguish the answers from paper citations.

Section II
Communication Technologies

Chapter II

An E-Learning System Based on the Top-Down Method and the Cellular Models

Norihiro Fujii, Hosei University, Japan

Shuichi Yukita, Hosei University, Japan

Nobuhiko Koike, Hosei University, Japan

Tosiyasu L. Kunii,
IT Institute of Kanazawa Institute of Technology, Japan

Abstract

As the broadband connectivity to the Internet becomes common, Web-based e-learning and distance learning have come to play the central roles for self-learning, where learners are given much flexibility in choosing the place and time to study. However, the learners still have to spend a lot of time before reaching the learning goal. This discourages the learner to continue their studies and diminishes their motivations. To overcome this problem and to let the learners keep focusing on their primary interests, we propose a top-down e-learning system called TDeLS. The TDeLS can offer learners the learning materials based on the top-down (i.e., goal-oriented) method, according to the learners' demands and purposes. Moreover, the TDeLS can distribute them to the learners through the Internet, and manage the database for learning materials. In order to share learning materials among learners through the Web, these learning materials are wrapped in XML with a specially designed vocabulary for TDeLS. We employed the cellular models that ensure the consistency among design modules and support a top-down design methodology. In this chapter, we present the TDeLS for hardware logic design courses based on the cellular models. The primary goal is to design complex logic circuits in VerilogHDL which is an industrial-standard hardware description language. This chapter also presents the basic XML vocabulary designed to describe hardware modules efficiently, and a brief introduction to the structure and functions of the proposed system, which implements the TDeLS.

Introduction

We present a new top-down e-learning system (Abe, Yukita, & Kunii, 2003; Fujii et al., 2003; Fujii, Yukita, Koike, & Kunii, 2003) called TDeLS. The TDeLS provides the functions for dynamic and efficient retrieval of suitable learning materials across the network such as the Internet. It dynamically generates appropriate courseware according to the learner's needs, and assists the learner to achieve the learning target efficiently. Using the TDeLS equipped with these functions, students can keep focusing on their primary interests to achieve their goals successfully.

With the rapid progress of Web technologies, one of the most important requirements for an e-learning system is easy and efficient accessibility in the Semantic Web environment (Stojanovic, Staab, & Studiers, 2001). One solution is to represent the structure of courseware in some XML vocabularies. Furthermore, the top-down method is required for the efficient and robust development of the courseware. We adopt the cellular models (Kunii, 1999; Kunii & Kunii, 2001; Ohmori & Kunii, 2001; Yukita & Kunii, 2003) in order to ensure the consistency and also to maintain the conformance among the learning contents data. The contents are stored in the cellular database for efficient data link manipulation.

In a modern logic circuit design classroom, the use of hardware description languages (HDLs) is becoming very popular. They contribute to reduce both design effort and design time. With these HDLs we can share designed sub-circuit logic modules among learners and educators. However, without the help of such an e-learning system such as we propose, it would be very difficult to keep the learners' interests and motivations to lead them to the final goal. It would result in students' dropout before reaching the final goal. To show the effectiveness of our approach, we choose an example of courseware for the design of an 8 bits CPU (called TinyCPU) that processes four operation codes.

The TDeLS monitors the learner's achievements and navigates the learner. The learning material selection is determined based on the learner's skill, achievement, and degree of interest. Just selecting the learning materials is not sufficient. It is necessary to offer the learning materials in an appropriate order, which is expected to yield a better and shorter path to the goal. We show the algorithm for obtaining a much better order, and give an example of the generation of courseware for the top-down study.

This chapter is organized as follows:

- **Section 2:** We explain the top-down method, the cellular models and the cellular data structure.
- **Section 3:** We describe a common cell and the transformation of the cellular data into XML document are described.
- **Section 4:** The e-learning contents for hardware logic circuit design are described.
- **Section 5:** The transformation of VerilogHDL (The IEEE Verilog standard #1364, 2001) model into XML is described.
- **Section 6:** The structure of e-learning materials using the cellular models is shown.
- **Section 7:** We explain the courseware generation algorithm to generate learning contents and courseware.
- **Section 8:** The structure and the function of the TDeLS are shown.
- **Section 9:** Finally this chapter concludes with the current status and future work.

Use of the Top-Down Method and the Cellular Models for E-Learning

We employed the methodology of the courseware generation based on the top-down method and on the cellular models so that learners can walk through the courseware effectively without loosing their sight of the goals, and that the courseware designers can reduce the complexity of design process (Abe et al., 2003; Yukita & Kunii, 2003; Fujii, Yukita, Koike, & Kunii, 2003; Fujii et al., 2003).

Top-Down Method

Recently, the importance of the curriculum organization, especially in the computer science education field, based on the top-down method, is recognized (Information Processing Society of Japan, 1999). The educational curriculum based on the top-down method is employed by several domestic and foreign universities and showed its effectiveness (Kunii, 1993).

The goal-oriented method (Haiya, Horai, & Saeki, 2002) is similar to a top-down method. In goal-oriented methods, we pursue the top-level final goal in the goal hierarchy and go downward. Hence, the goal-oriented methods are a type of top-down approaches in the goal hierarchy. An analogous approach is found in Hayashi, Yamasaki, Ikeda, and Mizoguchi (2003). However, our approach is unique in focusing on the cellular structures.

We take advantage of the top-down educational methods to enhance the learning process. The top-down education maintains learner's willingness to learn and improves the efficiency to achieve the final target. It shows the way to the final target clearly, and offers the optimized courseware to reach the goal.

Cellular Theory and Cellular Models for E-Learning

The cellular models are data models that are based on the cellular theory (Kunii, 1999). Because the cellular models adopt the hierarchy of the incremental modular abstraction concepts, they can accommodate the characteristics of existing various data models. The cellular models are formulated by introducing the concepts of cells and pre-cells (Yukita & Kunii, 2003) (see Figure 1). A pre-cell connects a cell associated with the cell_id. Each cell has a cell_id in the cell definition.

Figure 1. Cell and pre-cells

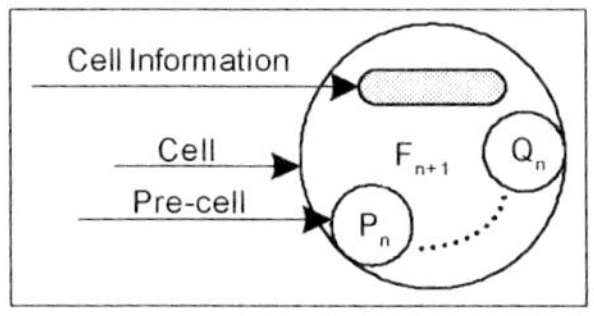

Figure 2. Connected situation of pre-cell

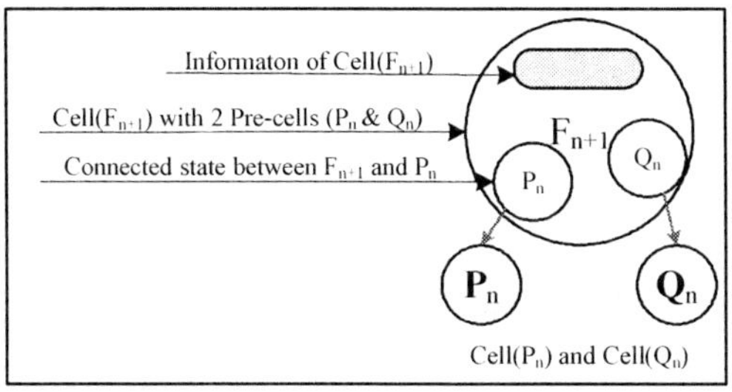

Cellular Data Structure

The cell_id and the pre-cell are used to specify the connection. Figure 2 shows connected situation of three cells using two pre-cells. Cell P_n and pre-cells P_n in cell F_{n+1}, and Cell Q_n and Pre-cell Q_n in cell F_{n+1} are connected. In this case, cells are connected from the higher dimensional cell to the lower dimensional cell belonging to the pre-cell information shown.

In Figure 3, 4-dimensional cell (A_4) which has the highest dimension in this cellular database and contains the pre-cell information (pre-cell B_3), is connected to a 3-dimensional cell (B_3). In the same way, the B_3 cell is connected to F_2, E_2 and Z_2. In this way, cells are connected to each other and the cellular structure is organized.

Figure 3. Cellular data structure

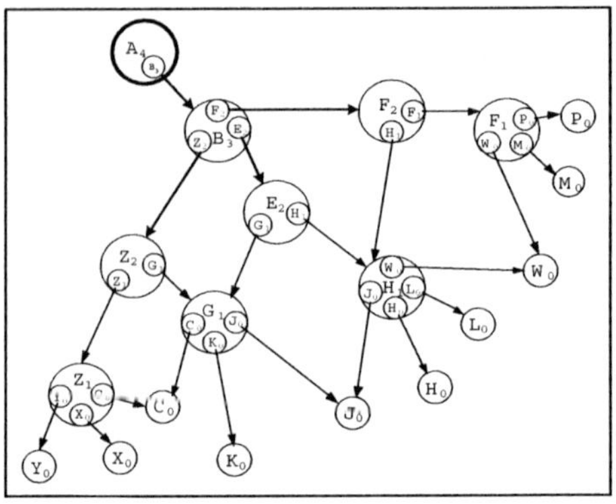

Common Cell and the Transformation of the Cellular Data into XML Document

Semantic Web

In the top-down education, as previously explained, it is necessary to retrieve the learning materials arranged in a cellular database, to clarify the learning goal, and to achieve it efficiently. Also, the education system should make an educator design the courseware and prepare the learning materials easily. To make the learning materials open to the public on the Web, the use of XML in the Semantic

Table 1. The tag composition of common cell with XML

Tag Name	Meaning of Tag
cell_id	Cell identification number
Dimension	The weight of cellular data
cell_label	Description of cell
Background	The information (date, author, path) about this cell
Date	The date that generated this cell.
author_path	The URL of Author who generated this cell.
detail_path	The URL for showing an additional explanation for this cell.
Boundary	The boundary information (pre-cell, path, title) about this cell
pre-cell	Describes about the cell that the pre-cell indicates.
cell_title	A short explanation of the cell that the pre-cell indicates.
Path	The URL of the cell that the pre-cell indicates.
Contents	The detail of this cellular information
Path	A URL that indicates the content of this cell.

Web environment is effective. It is possible to organize well structured and robust learning materials by applying the cellular models to build the XML data structure.

Common Cells with XML

Those cells containing the following tag names as shown in the Table 1 are called the common cells. Figure 4 shows the XML document, expressed by making use of a common cell in XML.

Learning Contents

Hardware Logic Design Class

In a modern logic design classroom, hardware description languages such as VerilogHDL and VHDL are mostly used to describe circuits for FPGAs. For designing the digital circuit on PC, the design process follows the sequence of function test, design synthesis, and timing simulation. Furthermore, the designed

Figure 4. XML Document of common cell

```
<cell:celldata>
  <cell:cellmodule>
  <!-- cell_id = moduleID -->
   <cell:cell_id>3321</ cell:cell_id>
   <cell:dimension>4</ cell:dimension>
   <cell:cell_label>Tiny CPU</ cell:cell_label>
   <cell:background>
      <cell:cell_date>2003- 05- 17</ cell:cell_date>
      <cell:author>
        <cell:path>" file:\ \ d:\ VerilogHDL\ authorlist\ hKatsumata.html" </ cell:path>
      </ cell:author>
      <cell:detail_path>
        <cell:path>" file:\ \ d:\ VerilogHDL\ cell_data\ 3321_detail.html" </ cell:path>
      </ cell:detail_path>
   </ cell:background>
   <cell:boundary>
      <cell:pre_cell>
        <cell:websiteTitle>ALU</ cell:websiteTitle>
        <cell:path>file:\ \ d:\ VerilogHDL\ cell_data\ 3222.html</ cell:path>
      </ cell:pre_cell>
      <cell:pre_cell>
        <cell:websiteTitle>Latch</ cell:websiteTitle>
        <cell:path>file:\ \ d:\ VerilogHDL\ cell_data\ 3572.html</ cell:path>
      </ cell:pre_cell>
   </ cell:boundary>
  </ cell:cellmodule>
  <cell:contents>
   <cell:path>file:\ \ d:\ VerilogHDL\ cell_contents\ 3321_content.html</ cell:path>
  </ cell:contents>
</ cell:celldata>
```

circuit can be actually implemented on FPGA or CPLD attached to the PC, and can be tested by running the hardware. These CAD tasks were usually performed by central servers in a time-sharing fashion. Nowadays, PCs become powerful enough to perform such tasks locally without the servers. So, each student can design hardware independently. Students can even get data and know how to design the circuits through the Internet. Thus, the logic circuit design course is a suitable area to adopt the TDeLS.

Hardware Description Language

The logic circuit can be designed by using the hardware description language (HDL). HDL is a programming language designed to describe behavior of logic circuits. As the gate size of FPGA becomes very large, the schematic entry method becomes impractical and the use of HDL has become popular. Thanks to the recent advancement in logic synthesis tools, obtained circuit quality is comparable with human design. The generated circuits by the logic synthesis tools are verified their correctness through logic simulations. The circuit described by HDL consists of a hierarchical combination of modules. The behavior of each circuit module is described in the form of input/output signals and internal module functions. Complicated larger circuit module can be designed by a combination of less complicated smaller modules. The circuit module is then converted into a net-list, where the circuit is described in the form of the connection of components.

Circuit Design Using Hardware Description Language

In this section, the method of decomposing the circuit specification into a collection of modules is described. At first, the design specification of the circuit is described, and then it is decomposed into the circuit of modules, which perform independent functions. Next, each module is designed according to its specification. When already designed module is again attempted to be designed, the system find the designed module description and reuse it, instead of duplicating the design.

As an example of VerilogHDL, Figure 5 shows the example of a circuit development and mounting. The target circuit is decomposed into two modules: Module A and B. These modules are further implemented separately and then combined to implement the desired circuit module.

The hardware description language, such as VerilogHDL or VHDL, allows us to employ the top-down design method or top-down development method. Figure 5 shows a typical design procedure in accordance with the top-down design

Figure 5. Sample of hardware design procedure by HDL

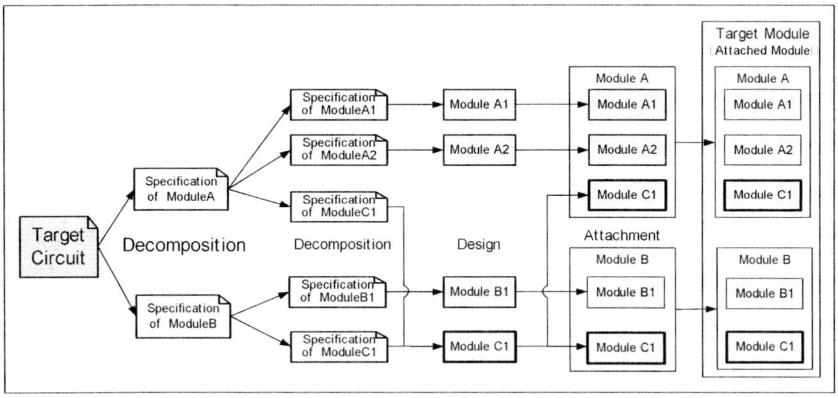

method. According to the specification of this target circuit, it is decomposed into two module specifications (Module A and B). After that, Module A and B are further decomposed into the detailed modules.

Finally, the target circuit is implemented by the combination of decomposed modules (Module A1, A2, A3, B1, and C1). It is important to note that the module C1 is denoted as a common module. As C1 appears both in Module A and Module B, duplicated design is avoided and their design can be shared by using this common module notation.

The Contents for Hardware Logic Design

As an example of the circuit design with VerilogHDL, an 8 bits CPU (Module name: TinyCPU) is employed for the final target circuit. Figure 6 shows the block

Figure 6. Block diagram of the TinyCPU

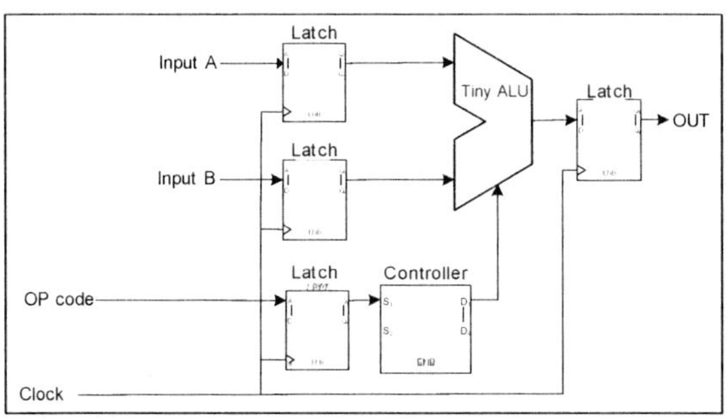

Figure 7. Module structure for the TinyCPU

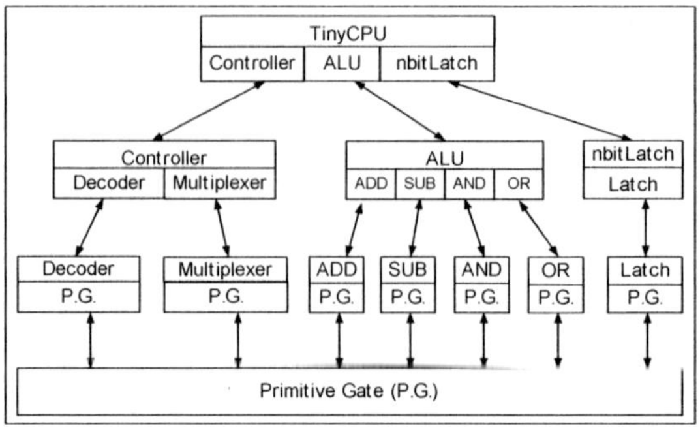

Figure 8. Top module

```
// Top Module
// Module TinyCPU.TinyCPU.TinyCPU
// Created:
//          by -  khiro (KATSUMATA)
//          at -  12:32:27 05/ 17/ 03
`resetall
`timescale 1ns/ 10ps
module TinyCPU( A, B, OPCODE, OUT, CLK );
                parameter WIDTH = 4;
                input [WIDTH- 1:0] A,B;
                input [1:0] OPCODE;
                input CLK;
                output [WIDTH- 1:0] OUT;
                // internal wire
                wire [WIDTH- 1:0] A_i,B_i,R_i;
                wire [1:0] OP_i;
              ALU alu( .A(A), .B(B), .FUNC(OP_i), .R(R_i) );
              xbitLatch a_latch( .IN(A), .OUT(A_i), .CLK(CLK) );
              xbitLatch b_latch( .IN(B), .OUT(B_i), .CLK(CLK) );
              xbitLatch r_latch( .IN(r_i), .OUT(OUT), .CLK(CLK) );
              xbitLatch op_latch( .IN(OPCODE), .OUT(OP_i), .CLK(CLK) );
endmodule
```

diagram of an 8 bits TinyCPU circuit and Figure 7 shows the composition module structure of this TinyCPU.

Figure 8 shows the top module description of a TinyCPU. It contains two module A (see Figure 9) and module B (see Figure 10). These modules' source codes are described with VerilogHDT. L.he module A shows the ALU of TinyCPU and the module B shows xbitLatch.

The TinyCPU is composed of an arithmetic logic unit (ALU) and an xbitLatch, as shown in Figure 7. It shows the layered structure. The arithmetic logic unit further consists of ALU={ADD, SUB, AND, OR}. Also, the xbitLatch can be composed in similar fashion as the ALU. Figure 11 shows the ADD module which is one of the composition modules of the ALU.

Figure 9. Module A (ALU)

```
// Module A
// Module TinyCPU.ALU.ALU
// Created:
//        by - khiro (KATSUMATA)
//        at - 13:00:32 05/17/03
`resetall
`timescale 1ns/10ps
module ALU( A, B, OPCODE, R );
        parameter WIDTH = 4;
        input [WIDTH-1:0] A,B;
        input [3:0] OPCODE;
        output [WIDTH-1:0] R;
        AND func_and( .IN1(A), .IN2(B), .OUT(and_out) );
        ADD func_add( .IN1(A), .IN2(B), .OUT(add_out) );
        SUB func_sub( .IN1(A), .IN2(B), .OUT(sub_out) );
        OR func_or(  .IN1(A), .IN2(B), .OUT(or_out) );
        MUX mux(     .IN1(and_out),
                     .IN2(add_out),
                     .IN3(sub_out),
                     .IN4(or_out),
                     .SEL(OPCODE)  );
endmodule
```

Figure 10. Module B (xbitLatch)

```
// Module B
// Module TinyCPU.xbitLatch.xbitLatch
// Created:
//        by - khiro (KATSUMATA)
//        at - 13:04:21 05/17/03
`resetall
`timescale 1ns/10ps
module xbitLatch( D, CLK, Q );
        parameter WIDTH = 4;
        input [WIDTH-1:0] D;
        input CLK;
        output [WIDTH-1:0] Q;
        Latch latch(D,CLK,Q);
endmodule
```

Figure 11. Module A1 (ADD)

```
// Module A1
// Module TinyCPU.ADD.ADD
//
// Created:
//        by - khiro.UNKNOWN (KATSUMATA)
//        at - 13:08:00 05/17/03
//
`resetall
`timescale 1ns/10ps
module ADD( IN1, IN2, OUT );
        parameter WIDTH = 4;
        input [WIDTH-1:0] IN1,IN2;
        output [WIDTH-1:0] OUT;
        assign OUT = IN1 + IN2;
endmodule
```

Figure 12. XML document of VerilogHDL

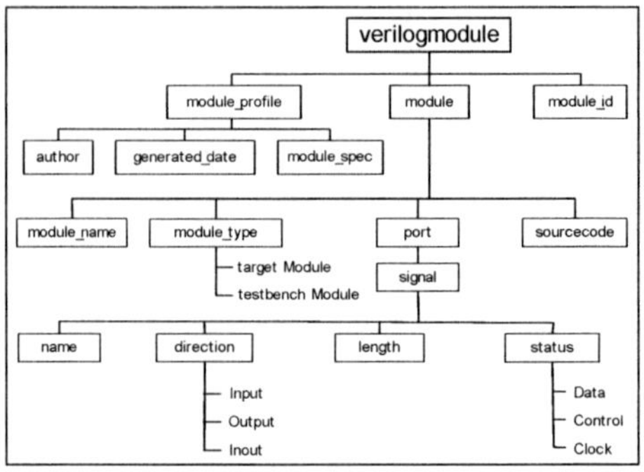

Table 2. XML document tag definitions

Tag Name	Meaning of Tag
module_id	Unique ID of Module
module_profile	The profile of this module
module_spec	Outline specification of Module
generated_date	Date that this cell generated
author	Author name
module	Details of this VerilogHDL module
module_name	Module name
module_type	Indicate Target module or Simulation module
port	Port Specification of Module
signal	About the input-output port
name	Port name
direction	Input, Output, Inout
length	Bandwidth of Port
status	Kind of Signal (Data, Control, Clock)
sourcecode	HDL Source Code
sentence	Source Code

Expression of Logic Circuit Module Packed with XML

The use of cellular models with XML document is explained in this section. The details of the tags are described in Figure 12 and Table 2. An attribute is added to compose the cellular models. Using this attribute, each module can be combined with the cellular database. Also, the circuit module can be uniquely specified on the Web.

Figure 13. XML document of ALU Module

```
<verilogmodule xmlns=" file:/ / D:/ VerilogHDL/ cell_dataXML/ hdl" >
<module_id>3222</ module_id>
<module_profile>
   <module_spec>ALU,ADD,SUB,AND,OR</ module_spec>
   <submitted>2003- 05- 17</ submitted>
   <author>Hiromitsu Katsumata</ author>
</ module_profile>
   <module>
      <modulename>alu</ modulename>
      <moduletype>target</ moduletype>
      <port>
              <signal>
                 <name>A</ name>
                 <direction>input</ direction>
                 <length>8</ length>
                 <status>data</ status>
              </ signal>
              <signal>
                 <name>B</ name>
                 <direction>input</ direction>
                 <length>8</ length>
                 <status>data</ status>
              </ signal>
              <signal>
                 <name>OPCODE</ name>
                 <direction>input</ direction>
                 <length>4</ length>
                 <status>control</ status>
              </ signal>
              <signal>
                 <name>R</ name>
                 <direction>output</ direction>
                 <length>8</ length>
                 <status>data</ status>
              </ signal>
      </ port>
         <sourcecode> <!- - Source Code for ALU - - > </ sourcecode>
   </ module>
</ verilogmodule>
```

Figure 14. XML Document of Testbench

```
<module>
     F
  <moduletype>testbench</moduletype>
        F
     <sourcecode>
       F// Describe source code of a test bench at here.
     </sourcecode>
</module>
```

Figure 13 shows an XML document of the ALU module. A module named testbench is also needed for the simulation of the designed circuit. The testbench generates the test patterns. Figure 14 shows the testbench used to simulate the target module.

The Organization of Learning Materials Using the Cellular Models

Figure 15 shows the outline of learning material using the cellular models. The header of a learning material identifies a cell and its pre-cells information. The pre-cells have inter-cell connecting information. This header also provides information of common cells (refer to 3.2 Common Cells with XML) for hardware logic design. The content has specifications and a source code of circuits, and a testbench for simulation in VerilogHDL (refer to 4.5 Logic Circuit Module packed with XML).

Figure 15. Outline of learning material using cellular models

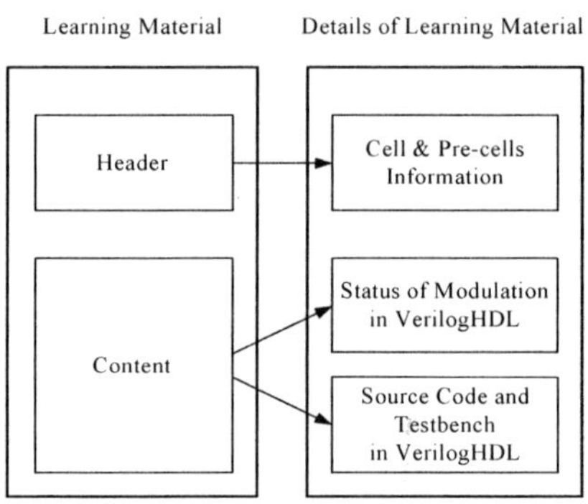

Figure 16. The structure of courseware

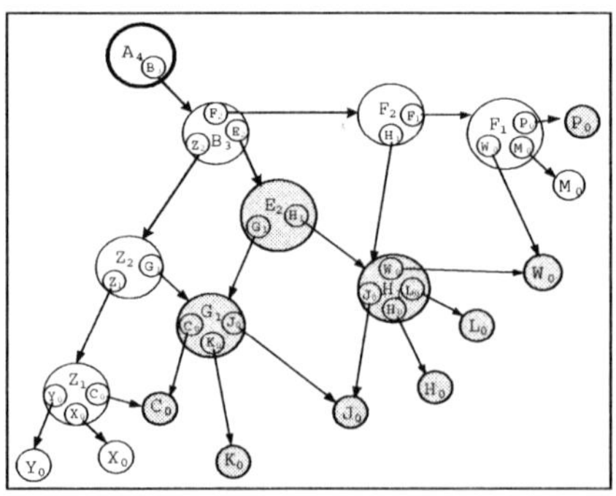

The Courseware Generation Algorithm

The courseware is generated in three stages. The first stage is to build the data structure including the learning materials, which are aimed at the learning goal. The second stage is to extract all lower dimensional cells, which include necessary and sufficient related materials (we call this processing *optimization*). Finally, the optimized courseware is serialized by the Navigation Path Generation (we refer this as *serialization* hereafter).

Building of the Data Structure

It is necessary to retrieve the cellular data from the cellular database, and extract necessary cellular data. The learning material cell implements the TDeLS (see Figure 19). It uses information on the pre-cell and the lower dimensional cell, in order to prepare the courseware selection function.

These functions are as follows:

1. **Cell search function:** To search the learning materials in the cellular database
2. **Cell attaching function:** To attach the cellular data with pre-cell information. Figure 16 shows the data structure of courseware after the build

The Courseware Optimization

Figure 17 shows the optimized courseware (A) and the unnecessary courseware (B) after optimized. It also shows the study route and the learning material cellular structure. The TDeLS accumulates the learning history data including the learning evaluation into the database. This history data is utilized to optimize the attached materials.

The Navigation Path Generation

The learning content is presented in a hierarchical order according to the learner's demand. The serialization (Yukita & Kunii, 2003) is to decide and to offer the order of the learning materials in the learning contents. For the serialization, three kinds of methods are employed to investigate the learning material cellular structure and to decide the order.

Figure 17. Optimized courseware (A) and needless courseware (B)

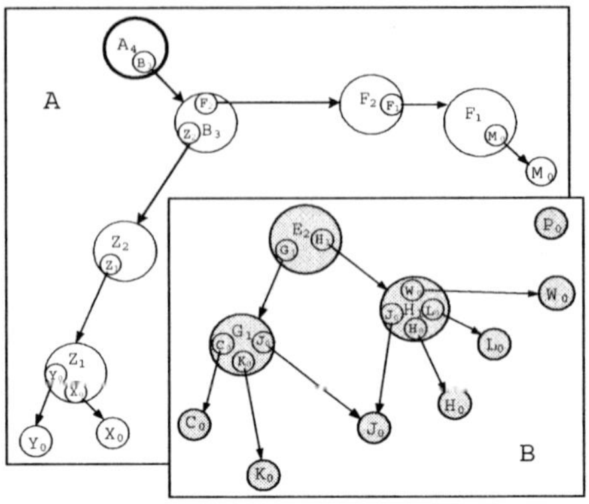

The on-demanding serialization is offered first, according to the learner's current study order history. If it is not accepted, the second alternative is offered, determined by the automatic study ordering.

- **On demanding serialization:** The TDeLS can offer the courseware according to the learner's demand. The learner is requested to decide which to be selected as a learning material among them when there are two or more learning materials candidates
- **Automatic serialization:** This is a method that the TDeLS automatically generates the order of offering the learning material according to the following serializing algorithm

Serialization is the act of deciding the order of the learning material in the learning contents. We have examined the following three methods for automatic serialization that makes full use of the optimized courseware example in Figure 17-A. The first two kinds of the serializing methods are the Breadth-First type (BF Type) and the Depth-First type (DF Type). Other one method is Combined Type (Combine BF type and DF type).

1. **The Breadth-First type (BF type):** The TDeLS pays attention to the dimension which is one of cell information and offers the learning material of the same dimension. Higher dimensional cells have higher priority than the lower ones in the serialization, like in the breadth first algorithm. From Figure 17-A, the serialized order of cells is A_4->B_3->Z_2->F_2->Z_1->F_1->Y_0->X_0->M_0. <> means the serialized order

Serialized Order=$<A_4, B_3, Z_2, F_2, Z_1, F_1, Y_0, X_0, M_0>$

2. **The Depth-First type (DF type):** The TDeLS offers the learning material of the lower dimension than the current dimension. Cells are ordered in the depth first way from Figure 17-A, the following two kinds of serialized order are obtained

Ser1=$<A_4, B_3, Z_2, Z_1, X_0, Y_0>$
Ser2=$<B_3, F_2, F_1, M_0>$

The TDeLS composes these two serialized orders.

Serialized Order = $<$Ser1, Ser2$>$
= $<A_4, B_3, Z_2, Z_1, X_0, Y_0, B_3, F_2, F_1, M_0>$

It is shown that Ser1 and Ser2 have derived from the B3 cell in Figure 17-A. It is necessary to judge which cell should be selected for serialization. Offered top-down e-learning tools is decided according to learner's information.

3. **The Combined type:** This is a serialize method which uses the BF type together with the DF type. The learner can switch the DF type and BF type search at any point of navigation in the courseware.

In this example, the learner switches from the BF type to the DF type after reaching cell Z_1. After this choice, the learner visits all the related subordinated cells below cell Z_1, then comes back to the BF search.

Ser1=$<A_4, B_3, Z_2, F_2>$
Ser2=$<Z_1, Y_0, X_0>$
Ser3=$<F_1, M_0>$

The Ser1 is serialized using the BF type. The Ser2 and Ser3 are the results of the serialization by processing of the DF type. It becomes the following order when it is serialized by this method.

Serialized Order = <Ser1, Ser2, Ser3>

$$=\langle A_4, B_3, Z_2, F_2, Z_1, Y_0, X_0, F_1, M_0 \rangle$$

The Navigation Path Generation Example

This section shows an example (Figure 18) of the navigation path generation (NPG). Roughly speaking, the first task of NPG is to select the needed learning materials in the database. The next task is to build the courseware ready to be delivered to learners in an appropriate order. Details are given in the following.

- **1st Stage - Building of the data structure:** The TDeLS searches the learning materials (cellular data) in the learning materials database (cellular database) and then attach them with connecting information (pre-cell).
- **2nd Stage - The courseware optimization:** The TDeLS accumulates the learning history data including the learning evaluation into the database. This history data is utilized to optimize the attached materials.
- **3rd Stage - The navigation path generation:** This sample employed DF Type to serialize methods and is executed. The following two kinds of serialized order are obtained.

Figure 18. A sample of the generating courseware

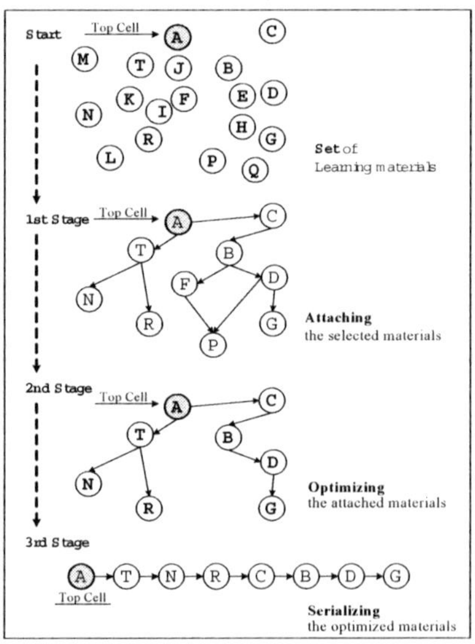

Ser1 = <A, T, N, R>

Ser2 = <C, B, D, G>

The e-learning system composes these two serialized orders.

Serialized Order = <Ser1, Ser2>

= <A, T, N, R, C, B, D, G>

Finally, TDeLS can offer the materials to the learners via the Web, according to the order: A, T, N, R, C, B, D, and G.

Top-Down E-Learning System

System Outline

Figure 19 shows top-down e-learning system (TDeLS) outline.

1. **Web server block:** This block is Web base processing to offer the learning materials and the production of the learning materials.
2. **Authoring block:** It is a learning contents producing site.
3. **Navigation block:** This block has a navigating function, whose sub-functions are to register the learner, to analyze the learner's needs, learning

Figure 19. Outline of TDeLS

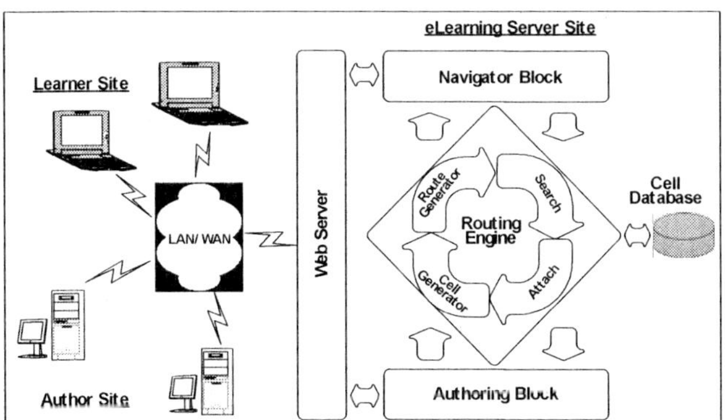

Table 3. The function of the routing engine

Block	Function
Searching	To search the learning materials in the cellular database.
Attaching	To attach the learning materials
Route Generator	To decided the courseware based on the learning history and learner information.
Cell Generator	A new learning material becomes a cellular data and is registered in the database.

history, and the level of understanding, to determine the information to be fed to the Web server.

4. **Routing engine block:** It is a courseware search engine to offer the best learning contents for learners. Table 3 shows the functions that the routing engine operates. And it plays an ancillary role for the learner to select the learning contents. This routing engine has also the function of the serialization function as previously mentioned.
5. **Cellular database block:** This block decides the best courseware based on learner's demand and learning history.

System Design

We are developing top-down e-learning systems (TDeLS) based on MVC (model-view-controller) (Burbeck, 1992; Sun Microsystems, 2002) model. MVC model is the design pattern suitable for developing a large-scale Web application and interactive applications like our e-learning system as shown in Figure 20. We,

Figure 20. System design

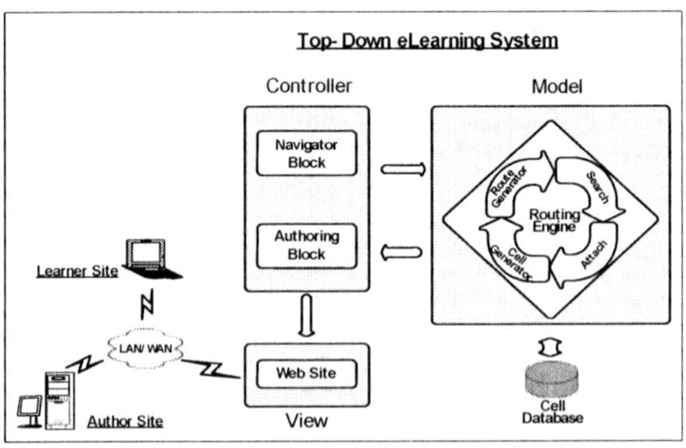

therefore, employed MVC model for the implementation of our e-learning system. MVC model organizes an interactive application into three separate modules as follows.

- **Model:** The model contains the core of the application's functionality. The model encapsulates the state of the application.
- **View:** The view provides the presentation of the model. It is the *look* of the application. The view can access the model getters, but it has no knowledge of the setters. In addition, it knows nothing about the controller. The view should be notified when changes to the model occur.
- **Controller:** The controller reacts to the user input. It creates and sets the model.

Forms on Browser

In order to show how the TDeLS acts, the following four browser forms are shown as examples: the Learner's Background Form, the Query Form, the Learning history Form, and the Learning Material Form.

Figure 21. Learner's background form

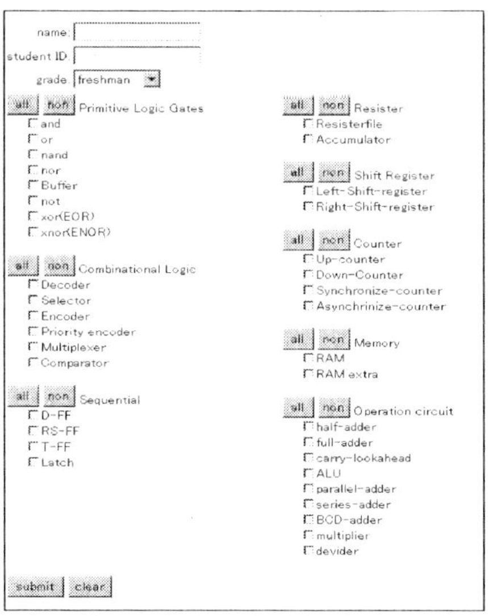

Figure 22. Query form

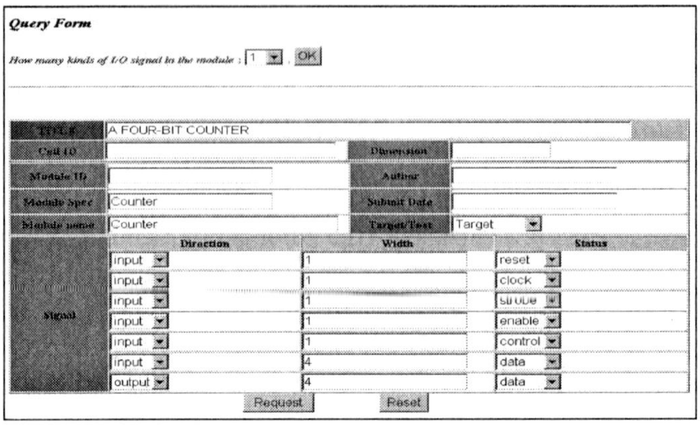

Learner's Background Form

The information retrieved from the background form as shown in Figure 21 is used to analyze the learner's understanding level regarding the logic circuit.

Query Form

Learner can set data of the goal of learning using this query form (Figure 22) to search the first learning material of logic circuit module in VerilogHDL. Input items are title, module specification, module name, input/output signal name, and so on. The result of the searching defines the first learning material shown as the Top Cell A_4 in Figure 16.

Learning History Form

This learning history form (Figure 23) displays the learning history. Using this screen, the learner can confirm one's learning history. This screen shot shows the list of the available learning materials to study and the contents that the learner has already learned.

Figure 23. Learning history form

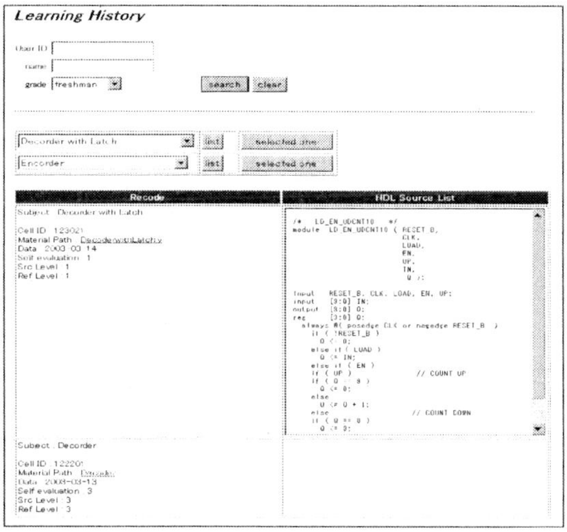

Figure 24. Learning material form

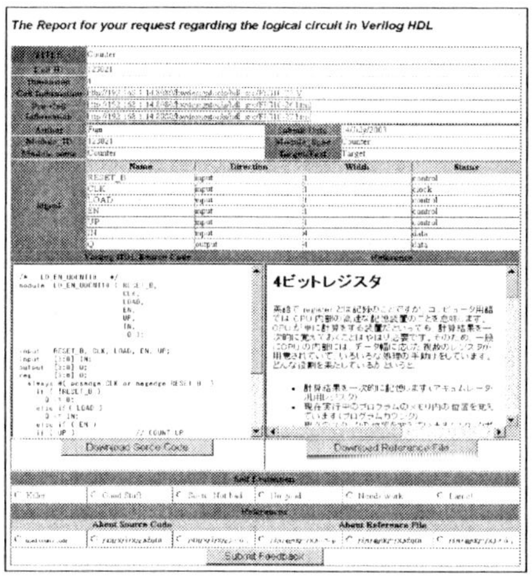

Learning Material Form

The Learning Material Form (Figure 24) displays the Verilog HDL source code, the references about circuits, and the details of material. The learner registers one's self-evaluation in the learning history file.

Conclusion

The effectiveness of the proposed TDeLS is demonstrated with an example of an 8 bits ALU design. It is shown that the learners are offered an appropriate learning material selected by the serialization process.

Learning materials are organized as the cell data, in order to be compiled as a cellular database and to be utilized as a Web-based courseware. The system automatically selects the contents and dynamically generates and proposes an appropriate learning courseware based on the learner's learning history, his or her learning ability and study-needs. The system finds the suitable material from already learned materials or from new learning materials. We proposed three priority rules to perform the serialization.

It is scheduled that a large-scale circuit such as 32 bits CPU will be included as a learning target.

The verification of TDeLS functionalities and the evaluations of the ability whether an appropriate learning materials can be offered, are planned.

We expect the following benefits by employing the top-down method and the e-learning system. It is possible to build an e-learning system which allows two-way communication between learners and educators. The learning material selection can be determined based on the learner's skill, achievement, and degree of interest. The TDeLS keeps the learners' interests and motivations, to lead them to the final goal efficiently. Because of the generality of the cellular model, we expect this system to be useful for other applications such as a software programming course or distributed computation course. This architecture is applicable not only to hardware but also to software.

References

Abe, T., Yukita, S., & Kunii, T. L. (2003, November 5-8). Top-down learning navigator based on the cellular models. *Proceedings of Frontiers in Education Conference 2003*, Boulder, Colorado.

Burbeck, S. (1992). *How to use model-view-controller.* Retrieved January 7, 2004, from http://st-www.cs.uiuc.edu/users/smarch/st-docs/mvc.html

Fujii, N., Imai, A., Abe, T., Suzuta, N., Yukita, S., Kunii, T. L., & Koike, N. (2003, November 5-8). Top-down education for digital logic design course based on cellular methods. *Proceedings of Frontiers in Education Conference 2003*, Boulder, Colorado.

Fujii, N., Yukita, S., Koike, N., & Kunii, T. L. (2003, December 3-5). Top-down e-learning tools for hardware logic design. *Proceedings of International Conference on Cyberworlds (CW2003),* Singapore.

Haiya, H., Horai, H., & Saeki, M. (2002). AGORA: Attributed goal-oriented requirements analysis method. *IEEE Joint International Conference on Requirements Engineering (RE2002)*.

Hayashi, Y., Yamasaki, R., Ikeda, M., & Mizoguchi, R. (2003). An ontology-aware design environment for learning contents. *Journal of Information Processing Society of Japan, 44*(1), 195-208. (In Japanese). Retrieved January 7, 2004, from http://www.ei.sanken.osaka-u.ac.jp/pub/hayashi/

The IEEE Verilog standard #1364. (2001). An IEEE working group was established in 1993 under the Design Automation Sub-Committee to produce the IEEE Verilog standard #1364. Verilog became IEEE Standard #1364 - 1995. It has recently been revised and standardized as IEEE standard #1364-2001.

Information Processing Society of Japan. (1999). *Curriculum of computer science education for information system subject of faculty of science and engineering of university*. J97 Version 1.1, September. ipsj-iDesigner-hayashi.pdf.

Kunii, T. L. (1993). *Computer science curriculum. Bit separate volume.* Kyoritsu Shuppan Co.

Kunii, T. L. (1999). Valid computational shape modeling: Design and modeling. *International Journal of Shape Modeling, 5*(2), 123-133.

Kunii, T. L., & Kunii, S. H. (2001). *A cellular Web model — For information management on the Web.* September 14, 2001. Corrected and Revised: September 18-20.

Ohmori, K., &Kunii, T. L. (2001). Shape modeling using homotopy in shape modeling and applications. SMI 2001. *IEEE Computer Society Press*, 126-133.

Stojanovic, L., Staab, S., & Studer, R. (2001). eLearning based on the Semantic Web. *WebNet2001—World Conference on the WWW and Internet*, Orlando, Florida.

Sun Microsystems. (2002). *Java BluePrints model-view-controller.* Retrieved January 7, 2004, from http://java.sun.com/blueprints/patterns/MVC-detailed.html

Yukita, S., & Kunii, T. L. (2003, November 5-8). Development of topdown courseware and cellular models. *Proceedings of Frontiers in Education Conference 2003*, Boulder, Colorado.

Chapter III

Privacy and Security in E-Learning[1]

George Yee, Institute for Information Technology, Canada

Yuefei Xu, Institute for Information Technology, Canada

Larry Korba, Institute for Information Technology, Canada

Khalil El-Khatib, Institute for Information Technology, Canada

Abstract

For a variety of advantages, universities and other organizations are resorting to e-learning to provide instruction online. While many advances have been made in the mechanics of providing online instruction, the needs for privacy and security have to-date been largely ignored. This chapter examines privacy and security issues associated with e-learning. It presents the basic principles behind privacy practices and legislation. It investigates the more popular e-learning standards to determine their provisions and limitations for privacy and security. Privacy requirements for e-learning systems are explored with respect to the "privacy principles." The capabilities of a number of existing privacy enhancing technologies, including methods for network privacy, policy-based privacy/security management, and trust systems, are reviewed and assessed.

Introduction

One of the key characteristics of our information economy is the requirement for lifelong learning. Industrial and occupational changes, global competition, and the explosion of information technologies have all highlighted the need for skills, knowledge, and training. Focused on attracting and retaining staff, companies have placed an emphasis on training to bolster soft and hard skills to meet new corporate challenges. In many cases, career training has been placed in the hands of employees, with the understanding that employees must be able to keep ahead of technological change and perform innovative problem solving. One way of meeting the demand for these new skills (especially in information technology) is through online e-learning, which also offers the potential for continuous learning. Moreover, e-learning provides answers for the rising costs of tuition, the shortage of qualified training staff, the high cost of campus maintenance, and the need to reach larger learner populations.

From the corporate perspective, employee training is an approach to increase the level and variety of competencies in employees, for both hard and soft skills. Online learning has become an important tool to implement corporate learning objectives. Indeed, specific e-learning courseware may be used to target specific corporate needs pertaining to strategic directions. Key trends for corporate e-learning, germane to privacy and e-learning include (Hodgins, 2000):

- Learners may access courseware using many different computing devices and from different locations, via different networks.
- E-learning technology will overtake classroom training to meet the needs for "know what" and "know how" training.
- E-learning will offer more user personalization, whereas courseware will dynamically change based on learner preferences or needs. In other words, e-learning applications of the future will be intelligent and adaptive.
- Corporate training is becoming knowledge management. This is the general trend in the digital economy. With knowledge management, employee competencies are assets which increase in value through training. This trend has pushed the production of training that is more task specific than generic. Changes in corporate strategic directions are often reflected as changes in e-learning requirements prompted by the need to train staff for those new directions.
- E-learning is moving toward open standards.

Most e-learning innovations have focused on course development and delivery, with little or no consideration to privacy and security as required elements. However, it is clear from the previous trends that there will be a growing need for high levels of confidentiality and privacy in e-learning applications, and that security technologies must be put in place to meet these needs. The savvy of consumers regarding their rights to privacy is increasing, and new privacy legislations have recently been introduced by diverse jurisdictions. It is also clear that confidentiality is vital for information concerning e-learning activities undertaken by corporate staff. While corporations may advertise their learning approaches to skills and knowledge development in order to attract staff, they do not want competitors to learn the details of training provided, which could compromise their strategic directions.

In this chapter, we investigate the problem of privacy and security for distributed mobile e-learning systems. These kinds of e-learning systems provide service mobility, where the learner can access the learning content from anywhere using any suitable device (e.g., desktop computer at home or work, PDA with wireless connection). We focus on the protection of personal information of a learner in an e-learning system. While it is an important issue in e-learning, we do not consider security issues related to copyright protection of course material. An overall theme of the chapter is to highlight the privacy requirements for e-learning systems based on the so called "privacy principles" (Department of Justice, n.d.). We explore the area of standards for e-learning systems and describe their deficiencies with respect to these privacy requirements. Finally, we describe several security and privacy enhancing technologies that can be applied to e-learning systems to satisfy the e-learning privacy requirements identified earlier. We do not claim that these technologies are the best fit to the requirements, only that they are *candidate* technologies to fulfill the requirements. We are currently engaged in research to identify the best fit (see Section 6).

The remainder of this chapter is organized as follows: the second section, "Privacy Principles," describes key privacy principles that underpin privacy practices and legislation. The third section, "Privacy and Security in Current E-Learning Standards," investigates privacy and security issues among available e-learning standards. The fourth section, "Privacy and Security Requirements for E-Learning," examines e-learning system requirements for privacy and security using an architectural model for e-learning. The fifth section, "Candidate PET for E-Learning," evaluates the more common privacy enhancement technologies (PET), including W3C's P3P, network privacy approaches, policy-based technologies, and trust mechanisms. The last section offers conclusions and recommendations.

Privacy Principles

Incidents of privacy violation have led governments worldwide to raise privacy awareness for their citizens and to develop privacy legislation and policies to prevent exploitation of personal information. In countries where there is privacy legislation, individual control is required for the use of personal information, including the collection, use, disclosure, retention, and disposal of personal data by organizations that may handle that information. Privacy principles have been developed to expose the implications of either privacy laws or privacy policy adopted by online organizations. One way of assessing how well an application meets privacy requirements is to assess the application in light of the privacy principles. Table 1 briefly describes the 10 privacy principles incorporated in the *Personal Information Protection and Electronic Documents Act* of Canada (Department of Justice, n.d.). We will refer to these privacy principles in our analysis of the applicability of potential privacy enhancing technologies (PET) for e-learning applications. Generally speaking, while these principles are

Table 1. The 10 privacy principles used in Canada

Principle	***Description***
1. Accountability	An organization is responsible for personal information under its control and shall designate an individual or individuals accountable for the organization's compliance with the privacy principles.
2. Identifying Purposes	The purposes for which personal information is collected shall be identified by the organization at or before the time the information is collected.
3. Consent	The knowledge and consent of the individual are required for the collection, use, or disclosure of personal information, except when inappropriate.
4. Limiting Collection	The collection of personal information shall be limited to that which is necessary for the purposes identified by the organization. Information shall be collected by fair and lawful means.
5. Limiting Use, Disclosure, and Retention	Personal information shall not be used or disclosed for purposes other than those for which it was collected, except with the consent of the individual or as required by the law. In addition, personal information shall be retained only as long as necessary for fulfillment of those purposes.
6. Accuracy	Personal information shall be as accurate, complete, and up-to-date as is necessary for the purposes for which it is to be used.
7. Safeguards	Security safeguards appropriate to the sensitivity of the information shall be used to protect personal information.
8. Openness	An organization shall make readily available to individuals specific information about its policies and practices relating to the management of personal information.
9. Individual Access	Upon request, an individual shall be informed of the existence, use, and disclosure of his or her personal information and shall be given access to that information. An individual shall be able to challenge the accuracy and completeness of the information and have it amended as appropriate.
10. Challenging Compliance	An individual shall be able to address a challenge concerning compliance with the above principles to the designated individual or individuals accountable for the organization's compliance.

challenging to realize in any sector, they do offer a means for critiquing the appropriateness of different technologies (*Privacy Technology Review*, 2001).

These principles may be implemented in computer systems to varying degrees due to the nature of each principle. For example, Principle 1 is largely manual but portions of it can still be implemented to facilitate its compliance. The following suggests ways in which each principle may be "implemented":

1. **Accountability:** The name and contact information of the person who is accountable can be clearly advertised in the organization's online system.
2. **Identifying purpose:** The purpose is clearly identified by the organization's online system and can be retrieved at will.
3. **Consent:** The person's consent is obtained by the organization's online system in the form of a signed certificate to guarantee authentication and non-repudiation.
4. **Limiting collection:** The organization's system keeps secure logs of its data collection so that it can prove that it has complied with this principle if challenged; in addition, the organization's system identifies how it will collect the information to show that the collection will be fair and lawful.
5. **Limiting use, disclosure, and retention:** The organization's system keeps secure logs of its uses, disclosures, or retention of the data so that it can prove that it has complied with this principle if challenged.
6. **Accuracy:** The system of the collecting organization can (a) ask the individual providing the data to verify the data and sign-off on its accuracy and completeness, (b) periodically request the individual to update his personal information, and (c) run rule-based checks on the data to identify inconsistencies.
7. **Safeguards:** Security safeguards such as authentication and encryption can be implemented.
8. **Openness:** The organization's online system can advertise its policies and practices relating to the management of personal information as well as provide easily accessible links to this information.
9. **Individual access:** The organization's online system can provide facilities for the individual to perform all access functions required by this principle.
10. **Challenging compliance:** The organization's online system can provide a facility for the individual to address a compliance challenge to the person who has been identified as accountable by Principle 1.

Privacy and Security in Current E-Learning Standards

Emerging standards for distance learning and education will influence the development of online learning systems in a major way. Standardization and compatibility are vital for both e-learning vendors and end users to be able to sell or purchase portable content and inter-changeable components on the market. They are also very important where different e-learning systems must interact with one another.

There are currently a number of working groups seeking to develop industry-wide standards, including IEEE Learning Technology Standards Committee (IEEE LTSC) (IEEE Learning Technology Standards Committee, n.d.), IMS Global Learning Consortium (IMS GLC) (IMS Global Learning Consortium, n.d.), Aviation Industry CBT (computer-based training) Committee (AICC) (Aviation Industry CBT Committee, n.d.), Alliance of Remote Instructional Authoring and Distribution Networks for Europe (ARIADNE) (Alliance of Remote Instructional Authoring and Distribution Networks for Europe, n.d.), and advanced distributed learning sharable content object reference model (ADL-SCORM) (Advanced Distributed Learning, 2004). Although these proposed standards mostly concern sharable components and learning objects, some of the suggested infrastructures and concepts are related to privacy and security requirements in e-learning systems. In the following subsections, we briefly review these standards for their privacy and security concerns and implications.

IEEE P1484

The IEEE P1484 is a series of standards for learning technology proposed by the Learning Technology Standards Committee (LTSC) of the IEEE Computer Society. The specification of public and private information (PAPI) for learners (P1484.2) (IEEE P1484.2/D7, 2000) outlines the syntax and semantics as well as the privacy and security of learner's information, which may be created, stored, retrieved, used, etc., by learning systems, individuals, and other entities. It defines the elements for recording descriptive information related to a learner's learning process, including personal contact information, learner relationships, learner preferences, learner performance, and portfolios. It categorizes the security and privacy concerns from the point of view of different stakeholders, such as developer, institution, regulator, and user. Table 2 briefly shows the security related features of this standard.

Table 2. Security features defined in IEEE P1484.2

Model	Specification	Model	Specification
Session-View Security Model	D	Non-Repudiation Model	I
Security Parameter Negotiation Model	D	Repudiation Model	I
Security Extension Model	D	Privacy Model	N
Access Control Model	D	Confidentiality Model	N
Identification Model	I	Encryption Model	N
Authentication Model	O	Data Integrity Model	N
De-identification Model	O	Validation of Certificates	N
Authorization Model	I	Digital Signature Model	N
Delegation Model	I		

D - Defined: the model and/or requirements are defined or provided.
I - Implementation-dependent: the detailed methods are dependent on implementations.
O - Outside the scope: the methods are outside the standard.
N - Non-specified: the standard doesn't specify the model and requirements.

As for privacy concerns, the P1484.2 does not specify a detailed model or technologies. It states that the implemented security techniques, including physical security, confidentiality, etc. can all be used to provide privacy. As well, it does not specify any particular privacy policy. The institutional administrators and users may act as privacy policy-makers to mandate policies, which are implemented via a variety of security techniques, technologies, processes, and procedures. A meaningful feature facilitating privacy protection is defined in the standard, which is called logical division of learner information. Using this feature, learner information may be de-identified, partitioned, and compartmentalized. Effectively, many privacy concerns for the learner may be addressed by virtue of this feature.

IMS LIP

The IMS Global Learning Consortium (IMS GLC) is another organization working on developing open specifications for distributed learning. It addresses key problems and challenges in distributed learning environments with a series of reference specifications, including meta-data specifications, enterprise specification, content & packaging specification, question & test specification, simple sequencing specification, and learner information package specification. Among these, the IMS learner information package (IMS LIP) specification addresses the interoperability of learner information systems with other systems that support the Internet learning environment. It covers ways of organizing learner information so that learning systems can be more responsive to the specific needs of each user. Learner information is defined as the collection of information about a learner or learning producer. The typical sorts of learner information include education record, training log, professional development record, life-long learning record, and community service record (e.g., work and training experience).

The mechanisms for maintaining privacy and security of the learner information are enabled in the IMS LIP specification. A learner information server is responsible for exchanging learner's data with other information servers or other systems (e.g., a delivery system). The server will support an information owner defining what part of the information is shared with other systems. The packages that can be used to import data into and extract data from the learner information server are described in the specification.

The IMS LIP treats data privacy and integrity as essential requirements. However, the standard does not define any details of implementation mechanisms or architectures that could be employed to support learner privacy protection. The IMS LIP final specification V1.0 (IMS Global Learning Consortium, 2001) does provide the following structures to support the implementation of "any suitable architecture" for learner privacy protection:

- **Privacy and data protection meta-structure:** Within a learner information tree structure, each tree node and leaf has an associated set of privacy description, which defines the concerns of privacy level, access rights, and data integrity. The granularity of information is the smallest set of data where there is no further breakdown of independent privacy data.
- **"SecurityKey" data structure:** The security keys for the learner include password, public key, and digital signatures. In this structure, the password and security codes are used for communication. The structure can allow for public key encryption, data authenticity, and password-based access control on learner information.

Other E-Learning Standards

There are other standards or industry organizations working on specifications applicable for distance learning systems. These were mentioned at the beginning of this section and are: the Aviation Industry CBT (computer-based training) Committee (AICC), the Alliance of Remote Instructional Authoring, and Distribution Networks for Europe (ARIADNE), and the Advanced Distributed

Learning-sharable content object reference model (ADL-SCORM). However, most of them are focusing on content management, meta-data specification, or other areas with little reference to security and privacy. For example:

- The AICC focuses on practicality and provides recommendations on e-learning platforms, peripherals, digital audio, and other implementation aspects.
- The ARIADNE focuses mainly on meta-data specification of electronic learning materials with the goal of sharing and reusing these materials.
- ADL-SCORM (advanced distributed learning-sharable content object reference model) is concerned with how to aggregate, describe, and sequence learning objects, as well as defining run-time communication and the data to be tracked for learning objects.

Privacy and Security Requirements for E-Learning

The roles of security include the following: user authentication /authorization, protection of private information from unintended access, and protection of data integrity (guarding against data corruption by attackers). We focus on requirements for privacy and data integrity. We begin by describing an architectural model for e-learning, taken from IEEE P1484.1/D9: the learning technology systems architecture (LTSA) (IEEE LTSC, 2001). We analyze this model as it applies to mobile, distributed e-learning with respect to the privacy principles and derive requirements for privacy and data integrity.

Figure 1. LSTA system components

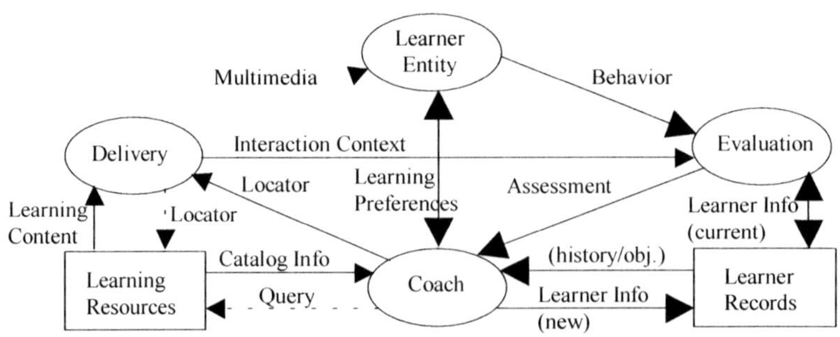

LTSA Architectural Model for E-Learning

The LTSA prescribes processes, storage areas, and information flows for e-learning. Figure 1 shows the relationships between these elements. The solid arrows represent data flows (the thick arrows are explained below); the dashed arrows represent control flows. The overall operation is as follows: *Learning Preferences,* including the learning styles, strategies, methods, etc., are initially passed from the *learner entity* to the *Coach* process; the *Coach* reviews the set of incoming information, such as performance *history*, future *objectives*, and searches *Learning Resources*, via *Query*, for appropriate learning content; the *Coach* extracts *Locators* for the content from the *Catalog Info* and passes them to *Delivery*, which uses them to retrieve the content for delivery to the learner as *multimedia*; *multimedia* represents learning content, to which the learner exhibits a certain *behaviour*; this behaviour is evaluated and results in an *Assessment* and/or *Learner Information* such as performance; *Learner Information* is stored in *Learner Records*; *Interaction Context* provides the context used to interpret the learner's behavior.

Fundamental Privacy Requirements

The Safeguards Principle requires security safeguards be placed on any e-learning system component that is associated in anyway with private information. These components are highlighted with thick lines in Figure 1 and they are:

- The transmission channels between the Learner entity and both the Evaluation and Coach modules
- The transmission channel between the Evaluation module and the Coach module
- The transmission channel between Evaluation and Learner Records (service provider link)
- The transmission channels between Coach and Learner Records (service provider link)
- The Learner Records themselves

In case the learning content contains sensitive information, the transmission channels between Learner Entity, Delivery, Learning Resources, and Coach would also need to be protected leaving the Interaction Context channel as the only unprotected channel (one could argue that the Locator channels, the Catalog

Info channel, and the Query channel may not need protection). Also in this case, the Learning Resources would have to be protected.

Network Privacy Requirements

With the open structure of the Internet and the readily available, easy-to-use tools for monitoring network activity, it is possible for a relative novice to extract vital information simply by analyzing the traffic patterns between the communicating entities. Some may consider that technologies such as secure sockets layer or virtual private networks would provide all of the safeguards one may require for network privacy. While these technologies may protect the data transferred between parties from network snoopers relatively well, a number of passive attack techniques can reveal sensitive information about the participating communicators (Raymond, 2000). Timing and communication pattern attacks, for example, extract information about the timing of communications, the locations of the communicating parties, and the amount of information being shared. By examining the pattern, timing, and origin and destination of communications, a snooper can deduce relationships between parties. For some activities in an organization, it is vital to safeguard this information. For instance, a company may have secretly chosen a new strategic initiative wherein specialized training is required for several key members of a development team. As per a recent trend, the company may have chosen to purchase a course from an online training company. In order to maintain confidentiality concerning the new strategic direction, the company would want to ensure that it would be very difficult for anyone to determine that it even has a relationship with the online training company. Indeed, the e-learning company itself may wish to distinguish its offerings from the competition by providing customers with the option of allowing students and employers to keep their network interactions confidential.

Referring again to Figure 1, all transmission channels that are used for communicating the *Learning Preferences, Behavior*, and *Multimedia* may be subject to traffic analysis and therefore counter-measures need to be in place to protect against these types of attacks. When the *Evaluation* process resides on the learner's machine, a protected transmission channel between the *Learner Entity* and the *Coach* can be used for both learning preferences and assessment information. The channel between the *Learner Entity* and the *Evaluation* process would not need protection any more.

Location Privacy Requirements

While some e-learning systems give learners the freedom to select the time and learning content according to their preferences and convenience, service mobility in e-learning offers learners additional freedom: a learner (see learner entity in Figure 1) can access the e-learning service anywhere using any available device. Wireless communication and device mobility compliment service mobility by delivering e-learning content to mobile computing devices, such as personal digital assistants (PDA) and Internet-enabled cellular phones. Using these mobile devices, learners can receive e-learning content anywhere at any time, while traveling, commuting, or waiting in line.

Location privacy is of particular importance for mobile e-learning systems. With the convenience of delivering e-learning content to mobile devices, there is the potential of jeopardizing the location privacy of the learner. Some learners might be reluctant to reveal the location from which they are accessing e-learning content and consider this information private. Compiling this location information may provide useful information about the mobility pattern of the learner, which could be useful for a third party interested in the mobility of the learner.

Candidate PET for E-Learning

In this section, we examine and critique a number of PET that can potentially satisfy privacy and security requirements for e-learning systems. We begin by looking at the P3P (Platform for Privacy Preferences Project, n.d.), followed by approaches for network privacy. We next examine policy-based approaches for privacy/security management and go on to look at trust mechanisms. We end the section by describing the application of secure distributed logs.

Platform for Privacy Preference (P3P)

While a learner is using online learning services from an Internet website, he or she always has concerns about his or her privacy, such as:

- What information does the e-learning website gather and for what purpose
- Can the learner have access to the information related to his or her privacy
- How long is this information kept
- Is this information revealed to other companies and for what purpose

The Platform for Privacy Preferences Project (P3P), developed by the World Wide Web Consortium (W3C), provides a solution for answering these questions to some extent. It enables websites to express their privacy policies in a standard format that can be automatically retrieved and interpreted by software acting on behalf of or under the control of a user (i.e., a user agent). P3P defines a machine-readable format (XML) for privacy policies. Websites can post their privacy policies, and users can specify their privacy preferences in P3P format. APPEL is a P3P exchange language that allows a user to express his or her preferences (rules) over the P3P policies. Based on these preferences, a user agent can make automated or semi-automated decisions regarding the acceptability of machine-readable privacy policies from P3P enabled websites. This allows P3P-enabled client software or user agents to retrieve Website privacy policies and to compare them against the user's privacy preferences. If the user's privacy preferences are satisfied by the privacy policy of the website, then the user may proceed with the service; otherwise, the user might be warned that the website does not conform to his or her privacy preferences.

Although P3P allows websites to express their privacy policy and notify users in a standard format, it is very limited with respect to current and emerging privacy practices and protection requirements. P3P falls short in fully supporting the Privacy Principles presented in Table 1 for the following reasons:

a. **Limited coverage of privacy protection:** As mentioned in Section 2, the Personal Information Protection and Electronic Documents Act (Department of Justice, n.d.) describes privacy rights with respect to personal information which are expressed as Privacy Principles. Regarding the Privacy Principles , P3P supports only the following three principles reasonably well:

   - **Identifying purposes:** The purposes for which personal information is collected are identified at or before the time the information is collected through the Web browser.
   - **Consent:** The individual's collection, use, or disclosure of personal information are acknowledged. Consent is implicitly given when the user accepts the stated guidelines for a Web site.
   - **Openness:** Web site privacy policies on use and disclosure practices are open to public review.

   The other seven principles, including accountability, limiting collection, limiting use/disclosure/retention, accuracy, safeguards, individual access, challenging compliance, are not addressed at all or are dealt with in a very weak manner in the P3P specification.

b. **Lack of privacy policy enforcement:** P3P specification 1.0 states that it only provides a mechanism for ensuring that users can be informed about privacy policies before they release personal information. It does not provide a technical mechanism for ensuring that sites act according to their policies. The real guarantees on privacy are outside the scope of the P3P specification and depend upon specific implementations.

c. **Weak model for privacy and security protection:** Technically, P3P is a standardized set of multiple-choice questions. It is built upon the "notice and choice" privacy approach. Users are given notice of the privacy practice. If they do not like it, their choice is to leave the website. This is a weak model for privacy and security protection.

The W3C's efforts on P3P are a positive contribution and a good beginning for privacy protection in the online environment. But P3P alone does not ensure strong privacy practices due to the weaknesses described above. Additional technical measures are needed to give people better control over the collection and use of personal information.

Approaches for Network Privacy

A number of approaches have been developed to provide the level of safeguarding for network privacy that is required in the company example above, in which the company needs to keep its relationship with the online training company hidden. One approach for Web-based training is to use a proxy to redirect Web requests (Anonymizer Web Service, n.d.; The Lucent Personalized Web Assistant, n.d.). When used in combination with secured communication channels, this approach may offer some privacy protection against casual attacks but it does have its drawbacks. It is vulnerable to timing and pattern attacks. As well, the access logs of these privacy services would provide a rich source of information concerning all users of the privacy service. Also, keeping all these logs in one location tempts hackers. Many organizations also may not want to trust a single proxy third party to protect its confidentiality and privacy. Other technologies have been developed to provide more robust privacy, such as onion routing (Goldschlag, Reed, & Syverson, 1999), MIX networks (Chaum, 1981), DC-Net (Chaum, 1988; Waidner, 1989), crowds (Reiter, & Rubin, 1998) as well as commercial networks like the Freedom Network (Boucher, Shostack, & Goldberg, 2000). These approaches involve the deployment of a network of elements such as Chaum mixes (Chaum, 1981) for routing information between communicating parties. A single mix generally uses cryptographic packet tailoring techniques to hide the correlation between incoming and outgoing messages. A chain of mixes can be used to provide a more robust network privacy protection. Using a chain of mixes requires that routing at intermediate nodes be pre-determined statically by the source node, such as in the case of onion routing, or probabilistically by each intermediate node, as in the case of crowds. An advantage of using multiple mixes is that these mixes are usually distributed under the control of multiple administrations in different jurisdictions so no single mix can compromise the user's privacy and collusion between mixes is not an easy task.

While network privacy techniques provide the required degree of anonymity, it achieves this with a certain cost. Techniques like onion routing incur setup overhead for each established connection. A larger delay for the data transfer is also incurred since the data is transferred along a path that may be different from the shortest path. This delay increases with the number of intermediate nodes along the path from the sender to the receiver. Cryptographic functions applied to the data in transit add more delay. This total additional delay may not affect the perceived quality of asynchronous applications such as e-mail or file transfer, but it is an issue for interactive applications such as video-conferencing. A balance needs to be established between the degree of anonymity and the perceived quality of the session.

Figure 2 illustrates two different situations. Figure 2a depicts the situation wherein a user connects over the public Internet to a service using a conventional secured connection (VPN or SSL). Queries or data from the user are routed through various routers to a service. It is clear that at any point along the route, various attack techniques may be used to determine the location (IP address) of the two parties and the nature of the interactions themselves.

In the case of a confidentiality network (Figure 2b), proxies at the user and service sides modify the exchanged data so as to hide information using both cryptographic and traffic management techniques. The octagonal boxes in the network cloud represent MIX nodes that provide the cryptographic and traffic management functions. In this case, examining the traffic between any individual node pairs within the network cloud will reveal nothing about the nature and identity of the users or service.

a. In this case, only exchanges between a user and a service are encrypted. Unfortunately, communication patterns between users and a service may be attacked through traffic and timing analysis to reveal the nature and Internet addresses of the participants.

b. In the case of a MIX network, traffic and data from different users are mixed at each intermediate mix node so as to make it difficult to determine the origin and destination of messages and the nature of the interactions.

Figure 2. The operation of a secured connection: (a) Conventional connection using VPN or SSL and (b) confidentiality network using MIX nodes

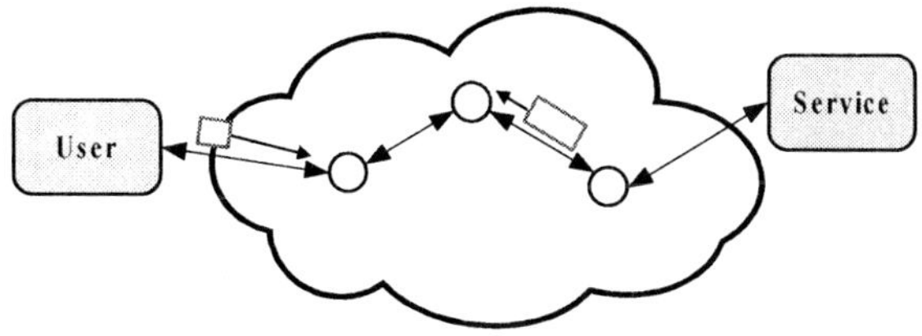

a) In this case, only exchanges between a user and a service are encrypted. Unfortunately, communication patterns between users and a service may be attacked through traffic and timing analysis to reveal the nature and Internet addresses of the participants.

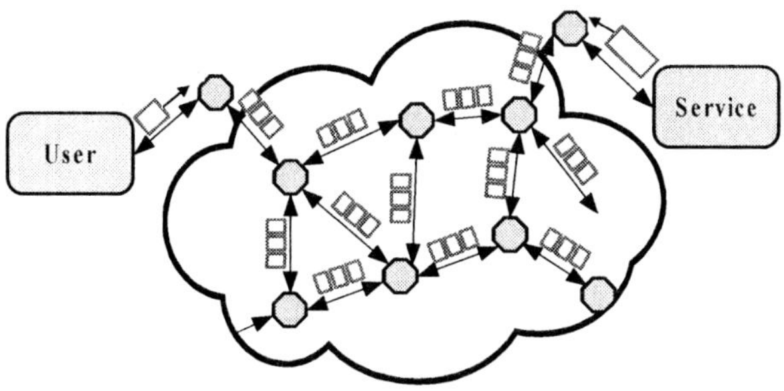

b) In the case of a MIX network, traffic and data from different users are mixed at each intermediate Mix node so as to make it difficult to determine the origin and destination of messages and the nature of the interactions.

It is clear that not all e-learning clients will require the degree of privacy safeguarding offered by technologies such as onion routing. There will likely be varying degrees of requirements. Certainly, according to the privacy principles, network privacy is an important safeguard. However, offering a secure channel for exchange of information between the e-learning provider and the client may be adequate in most cases. Protecting network transmissions in a manner that would conceal location specific information and the nature of the online activities will be an important consideration for companies as they become more reliant upon third party e-learning vendors. In the near future, providing network privacy approaches will be a differentiating factor among the offerings from different e-learning vendors.

Policy-Based Approach for Privacy/Security Management

Policy-based management approaches have been used effectively to manage and control large distributed systems. In most policy-based management systems, policies are used to change the behavior of systems. Policies are usually expressed in terms of authorization and obligation imperatives over subject and object entities: authorization policies define the authorized and unauthorized actions of a subject over an object; obligation policies specify the positive and negative obligations of a subject toward an object.

As in any other distributed system, e-learning may also use a policy-based framework to manage the security and privacy aspects of operations upon objects in the system. To conform to the privacy principles introduced in Section 2, policies can be used to specify: limiting collection and individual access. Obligation policies can be used to specify: identifying purpose, consent (acquiring the user's consent for collecting data), supplying proof for limiting collection, limiting use/disclosure/retention, safeguards, and openness.

In a policy-based e-learning system, the system administrator might specify some basic policies for the general operation of the system, and additional policies might be added based on the preferences of the entities. There would be sets of policies for each of the entities in the system (administrator, teacher, student, course material...) as well as for the interaction between these entities. In addition, governments and other regulatory bodies may have privacy laws or regulations (*Privacy Technology Review*, 2001). These may be translated into electronic policies and added to the general policies (Korba, 2002). Conflicts might occur between these many policies. To streamline online activities, some sort of mechanism should be in place to detect policy conflicts and to resolve them. Thus, a facility for policy specification and negotiation would be beneficial for e-learning systems, where the e-learner and e-learning provider can identify policy conflicts and negotiate a resolution.

Interestingly, while a policy-based approach makes it possible to specify and manage privacy aspects of system operation, there is a challenge in implementing the actual controls within or around the objects themselves. Consider the principle of limiting collection. This principle may be readily expressed as obligation policies. Unfortunately, in implementation, limiting the extent of collection of personal information is difficult, if not impossible. For instance, an organization may specify that it will only collect names of students strictly for the purpose of managing record keeping during course execution. Yet it is difficult to imagine a system that would prevent collection of other information regarding the students' behavior during course execution, or the data mining of other information sources for further information about the user for any purpose the organization chooses. Indeed, especially for the principles of limiting collection and limiting use, trust and audit approaches are the most obvious recourse.

Trust Mechanisms

Like traditional face-to-face education, "trust" is an important concern in e-learning systems. In the context of networking and distributed applications, one system needs to be trusted to access another underlying system or service. Trusted interaction forms the underlying requirement between users and providers. For example, a service provider must trust that a learner truly has credentials that are not forged and is authorized to attend the course, or is limited to accessing only some services. On the other hand, the learner must trust the services. More importantly, the learner must believe the service provider will only use his/her private information, such as name, address, credit card details, preferences, and learning behavior in a manner expressed in the policy provided for the e-learning system user. The most common trust mechanisms are related to digital certificate-based approaches and are found in trust management systems as follows.

a. **Digital certificate-based mechanisms:** These are based on the notion that "certificates represent a trusted party." The key concept behind these mechanisms is the digital certificate. A certification authority issues a digital certificate to identify whether or not a public key truly belongs to the claimed owner. Normally a certificate consists of a public key, the certificate information, and the digital signature of the certificate authority. The certificate information contains the user's name and other pertinent identification data; the digital signature authenticates the user as the owner of the public key. The most common approaches in use today are based on X.509/PKIX and PGP.

X.509/PKIX (Public-Key Infrastructure, n.d.) defines a framework for the provision of authentication services. This is a hierarchically structured PKI, and is spanned by a tree with a root certificate authority (RCA). In this structure, the trust is centered at the root, and then transferred hierarchically to all the users in the network via certificate authorities (CA).

PGP (An Open Specification for Pretty Good Privacy, n.d.) presents a way to digitally sign and encrypt information "objects" without the overhead of a PKI infrastructure. In PGP, anyone can decide whom he or she trusts. Unlike X.509/PKIX certificates, which come from a professional CA, PGP implements a mechanism called "Web of Trust," wherein multiple key-holders sign each certificate attesting the validity of the certificate.

The trust mechanisms based upon digital certificates, like X.509/PKIX and PGP, provide a series of systematic and comprehensive methods to define, verify, and manage trusted parties. These mechanisms have been proven to be good ways to establish one entity's credentials when doing transactions on the Internet. However, in these mechanisms, the user's confidence and trust depends on the authenticity of the public key. There are still however many uncertainties and risks that challenge certificate-based mechanisms (Ellison & Schneier, 2000). For example, why and how can we trust a PKI vendor? There are also questions related to a vendor's authentication rules before issuing a certificate to a customer. In practice, this kind of mechanism needs to be adjusted to offer different types of security and privacy protection depending on the application, for both the user side and the service provider side. Some examples of such mature applications are PGP mail encryption and SSL-enabled connections based on PKI.

b. **Trust management systems:** Trust management systems have the goal of providing standard, general-purpose mechanisms for managing trust. Examples of trust management systems include KeyNote (Blaze, Feigenbaum, Ioannidis, & Keromytis, 1999) and REFEREE (Chu, 1997). Both are designed to be easily integrated into applications.

KeyNote provides a kind of unified approach to specifying and interpreting security policies, credentials, and relationships. There are five key concepts or components in this system:

- **Actions:** The operations with security consequences that are to be controlled by the system
- **Principals:** The entities that can be authorized to perform actions
- **Policies:** The specifications of actions that principals are authorized to perform
- **Credentials:** The vehicles that allow principals to delegate authorization to other principals
- **Compliance checker:** A service used to determine how an action requested by principals should be handled, given a policy and a set of credentials

REFEREE (rule-controlled environment for evaluation of rules and everything else) is a trust management system for making access decisions relating to Web documents, developed by Yang-Hua Chu based on PolicyMaker (Blaze, Feigenbaum, & Lacy, 1996). It uses PICS labels (Resnick, & Miller, 1996), which specifies some properties of an Internet resource, as the "prototypical credential." It introduces the idea of "programmable credentials" to examine statements made by other credentials and fetch information from the network before making decisions.

Trust management systems provide a number of advantages for specifying and controlling authorization, especially where it is advantageous to distribute (rather than centralize) trust policy. Another advantage is that an application can simply ask the compliance checker whether a requested action should be allowed or not. However, although these trust management systems provide a more general solution to the trust management problem than public key certificate mechanisms, they mainly focus on establishing trust in resource access and possibly service provision. They still do not comprehensively cover the entire trust problem, and especially not the privacy concerns mentioned in Section 1. In e-learning, more tailored solutions or mechanisms are needed to fulfill the privacy and security requests from the learner and service provider.

Secure Distributed Logs

Secure distributed logs allow a record to be kept of transactions that have taken place between a service user and a service provider. The logs are distributed by virtue of the fact that they may be stored by different applications operating on different computers. Details of the transaction including the time of its occurrence, would be "logged" and the resulting record secured using cryptographic techniques, to provide assurance that their modification, deletion or insertion would be detectable. For e-learning, the use of secure distributed logs has important implications for privacy. In fact they support the privacy principles of accountability, limiting use/disclosure/retention, and challenging compliance. In the case of accountability and limiting use/disclosure/retention, the existence of a secured record of transactions allows verification that conformance to each principle has been maintained. In the case of challenging compliance, the existence of a record is very useful for possibly showing where compliance has wavered.

Conclusion and Current Research

We have examined the privacy principles and investigated current e-learning standards for their privacy and security provisions. The privacy principles provide a basis for analyzing potential PET in terms of their capabilities to provide required privacy and security for e-learning. Current e-learning standards only treat privacy and security superficially, if at all. The LTSA architectural model for e-learning, IEEE P1484.1/D9, provides a high-level model of the components of an e-learning system. Together with the privacy principles, this model assists in identifying which components of an e-learning system require privacy or security safeguards. We identified such components in Section 4.2. We also looked at the requirements for network and location privacy. Existing technologies such as SSL or VPN fail to prevent traffic analysis attacks. Mobility for e-learners may lead to the need for location privacy.

We next examined a number of candidates PET for e-learning. As mentioned in the Introduction, these are only candidate PET and are not necessarily the best fit for the requirements. We are continuing our research to identify the best fit. Although P3P has some serious weaknesses with respect to privacy and security, it is a good starting point for online privacy protection. We overviewed a number of technologies for network privacy, including Onion Routing and mixed networks, which offer protection from traffic analysis attacks. Not all e-learning applications will require the stringent privacy offered by these privacy-enhancing networking techniques, but such levels of privacy are becoming increasingly important for more companies as they rely increasingly on third party e-learning vendors. We also looked at the policy-based approach for privacy and security management and identified how such an approach can satisfy the privacy principles. Finally, we examined trust mechanisms and described the use of secure distributed logs. Trust mechanisms provide for trusted interactions between a service user and a service provider. For e-learning, a trust management system can be used to set up authorizations for course access and learner privacy safeguards via policies, in conjunction with a policy-based approach to privacy and security management.

Table 3 provides a summary of our assessment of a variety of PET and indicates the degree to which they address the privacy principles.

We are continuing our research and development to improve privacy and security technologies for e-learning. Our focus is on the following areas:

- **Network privacy:** Technologies such as Onion Routing to protect from traffic analysis attacks

Table 3. Privacy principles and potential PET that may be developed for e-learning applications

	Technology			
Principles	***Network Privacy***	***Privacy Policy Negotiation***	***Trust Mechanisms***	***Secure Distributed Logs***
1. Accountability	*N*	*D*	*I*	*D*
2. Identifying Purposes	*N*	*D*	*N*	*I*
3. Consent	*N*	*D*	*N*	*I*
4. Limiting Collection	*I*	*I*	*N*	*I*
5. Limiting Use, Disclosure, and Retention	*N*	*I*	*N*	*D*
6. Accuracy	*N*	*N*	*I*	*I*
7. Safeguards	*I*	*I*	*I*	*I*
8. Openness	*N*	*D*	*D*	*I*
9. Individual Access	*I*	*I*	*I*	*I*
10. Challenging Compliance	*N*	*I*	*D*	*D*

D - Direct support of a principle

I - Indirect or partial support of a principle

N - No support of a principle

- **Location privacy:** Technologies to ensure location privacy for mobile e-learners
- **Policy-based approach for privacy and security management:** How to apply this approach to e-learning to satisfy the privacy principles; policy specification and negotiation mechanisms
- **Trust mechanisms:** How to apply this to e-learning to satisfy the privacy principles

References

Advanced Distributed Learning. (2004). *Sharable content object reference model (SCORM) 2004* (2nd ed.). Retrieved April 24, 2006, from http://www.adlnet.gov/downloads/70.cfm

Alliance of Remote Instructional Authoring and Distribution Networks for Europe. (n.d.). *ARIADNE Foundation for the European knowledge pool.* Retrieved April 24, 2006, from http://www.ariadne-eu.org

Anonymizer Web service. (n.d.). *Anonymizer*. Retrieved April 1, 2002, from http://www.anonymizer.com/

Aviation Industry CBT Committee. (n.d.). Retrieved March 3, 2002, from http://aicc.org

Blaze, M., Feigenbaum, J., & Lacy, J. (1996). Decentralized trust management. *Proceedings of the 17th IEEE Symposium on Security and Privacy* (pp. 164-173). IEEE Computer Society.

Blaze, M., Feigenbaum, J., Ioannidis, J., & Keromytis, A. D. (1999). *The KeyNote Trust-Management System Version 2, Request For Comments (RFC) 2704*. Retrieved February 22, 2002, from http://www.ictf.org/rfc/rfc2704.txt?number=2704

Boucher, P., Shostack, A., & Goldberg, I. (2000). *Freedom Systems 2.0 Architecture*. Retrieved October 3, 2001, from http://www.freedom.net/info/whitepapers/Freedom_System_2_Architecture.pdf

Chaum, D. (1981). Untraceable electronic mail, return address, and digital pseudonyms. *Communications of the ACM, 24*(2), 84-88.

Chaum, D. (1988). The dining cryptographers problem: Unconditional sender and recipient untraceability. *Journal of Cryptology, 1*(1), 65-75.

Chu, Y. (1997). *REFEREE: Trust management for Web applications*. Retrieved April 1, 2002, from http://www.w3.org/PICS/TrustMgt/presentation/97-04-08-referee-www6/

Department of Justice. (n.d.). *Privacy provisions highlights*. Retrieved April 4, 2002, from http://canada.justice.gc.ca/en/news/nr/1998/attback2.html

Ellison, C., & Schneier, B. (2000). Ten risks of PKI: What you're not being told about public key infrastructure. *Computer Security Journal, XVI*(1), 1-7.

Goldschlag, D., Reed, M., & Syverson, P. (1999). Onion Routing for anonymous and private Internet connections. *Communication of the ACM, 42*(2), 39-41.

Hodgins, H. W. (2000). *Into the future: A vision paper, commission on technology & adult learning*. Retrieved April 1, 2002, from http://www.learnativity.com/download/MP7.PDF

IEEE Learning Technology Standards Committee. (n.d.). Retrieved March 3, 2002, from http://ltsc.ieee.org/index.html

IEEE LTSC. (2001, December 30). *IEEE P1484.1/D9, Draft Standard for Learning Technology - Learning Technology Systems Architecture (LTSA)*. Retrieved April 24, 2006, from http://ltsc.ieee.org/wg1/files/IEEE_1484_01 _D09_LTSA.pdf

IEEE P1484.2/D7. (2000, December 28). *IEEE P1484.2/D7, Draft Standard for Learning Technology — Public and Private Information (PAPI) for*

Learners (PAPI Learner). Retrieved April 24, 2006, from http://ltsc.ieee.org/wg2/papi_learner_07_main.pdf

IMS Global Learning Consortium. (2001). *Final Specification of IMS Learner Information Package Information Model, Version 1.0*. Retrieved March 3, 2002, from http://imsproject.org

IMS Global Learning Consortium. (n.d.). Retrieved March 3, 2002, from http://imsproject.org

Korba, L. (2002, January 7-11). Privacy in distributed electronic commerce. *Proceedings of the 35th Hawaii International Conference on System Science (HICSS)*.

The Lucent Personalized Web Assistant. (n.d.). Retrieved April 1, 2002, from http://www.bell-labs.com/projects/lpwa

An Open Specification for Pretty Good Privacy (openpgp). (n.d.). Retrieved January 22, 2002, from http://www.ietf.org/html.charters/openpgp-charter.html

Platform for Privacy Preferences (P3P) Project. (n.d.). Retrieved February 12, 2002, from http://www.w3c.org/P3P

Privacy Technology Review. (2001). Retrieved April 24, 2006, from http://www.hc-sc.gc.ca/hcs-sss/pubs/ehealth-esante/2001-priv-tech/index_e.html

Public-Key Infrastructure (X.509) (pkix). (n.d.). Retrieved January 22, 2002, from http://www.ietf.org/html.charters/pkix-harter.html

Raymond, J. (2000). Traffic analysis: Protocols, attacks, design issues, and open problems. *Volume 2009 of Lecture Notes in Computer Science* (pp. 10-29). Springer-Verlag.

Reiter, M. K., & Rubin, A. D. (1998). Crowds: Anonymity for Web transactions. *ACM Transactions on Information and System Security*, *1*(1), 66 92.

Resnick, P., & Miller, J. (1996). PICS: Internet access controls without censorship. *Communications of the ACM*, *39*(10), 87-93.

Waidner, M. (1989, April). Unconditional sender and recipient untraceability in spite of active attacks. *Eurocrypt'89*.

Endnote

[1] NRC Paper Number: NRC 48120

Chapter IV

Bluetooth Scatternet Using an Ad Hoc Bridge Node Routing Protocol for Outdoor Distance Education

Yao-Chung Chang, National Taitung University, Taiwan

M. T. Lin, National Dong Hwa University, Taiwan

Han-Chieh Chao, National Dong Hwa University, Taiwan

Jiann-Liang Chen, National Dong Hwa University, Taiwan

Abstract

In recent years, the prevalence of Internet and wireless technology has promoted mobile communications as a major research area. For the future distance education purposes (Instructional Technology Council), to be able to access the course materials anytime and everywhere will become a key issue. Especially when students are out of classroom and are within a museum or a field investigation process, using Ad Hoc mechanism to access the real time brief or introduction can definitely improve their learning interests greatly. One of the topics is IEEE802.11, which includes the wireless LAN and mobile ad hoc network (MANET) infrastructure (Perkins, 2000). MANET has no fixed infrastructure, but capable of dynamic changing network architectures, such as PDAs, cellular phones, and mobile computers. Bluetooth (The Official Bluetooth SIG) possesses a smaller radio range, low power, and low costs. The Bluetooth Scatternet is a specific case of MANET (IETF MANET Working Group). In this chapter, we propose a bridge node routing protocol (BNRP) based on a revised distributed topology construction protocol (DTCP), which a shortcut mechanism is added into it for better performance. The BNRP uses bridge nodes to preserve effective transmissions and achieve better Bluetooth Scatternet performance, and it can apply for outdoor distance education environment anytime and everywhere.

Bluetooth Scatternet and MANET

Distance Education

The process of extending learning, or delivering instructional resource-sharing opportunities, to locations away from a classroom, building or site, to another classroom, building or site by using video, audio, computer, multimedia communications, or some combination of these with other traditional delivery methods. Defined by ICT (Instructional Telecommunications Council).

Hence, the distance education is growing and more and more schools are using distance learning to assist teachers and students in study. Distance education can be divided into synchronous and asynchronous by time; video, radio and data by teaching mediums. Several kinds of distance education are shown in Table 1.

Table 1. Classifications of distance education

	Synchronous	Asynchronous
Video	Videoconferencing	Videotape, Broadcast video
Radio	Audio-conferencing	Audiotape, Radio
Data	Internet chat, Desktop videoconferencing, Web	E-mail, CD-ROM, Web

For the future distance education purposes, the ability to access the course materials anytime and everywhere will become a key issue. One scenario is that when the teacher is outdoors teaching with his notebook, all other students are using PDA or mobile devices to access the materials from the teacher's notebook. This kind of scenario extends the usage of distance education, especially when students are out of a classroom and are within a museum or a field investigation process. Using the ad hoc mechanism of MANET to access the real time brief or introduction can definitely improve their learning interests greatly.

Bluetooth Scatternet and MANET

Bluetooth Scatternet is the specific case of MANET. Bluetooth Scatternet is associated with several Piconets; each Master Node of Piconets coordinates all communication in its Piconet. Two Bluetooth devices must form a Master-Slave pair to connect each other, it's quite different from the MANET connection operations.

Figure 1 shows the difference among three network architectures: infrastructure mobile network, ad hoc mobile network, and Bluetooth Scatternet.

The main properties of the Bluetooth are low-cost and low-power radio transceiver. The goal of Bluetooth is to replace cable connection between electrical equipments and provide short-range communication in the Personal Area Network (IEEE 802.15 Working Group for WPANsTM). Therefore, the conventional routing protocols designed on MANET are not suitable for Bluetooth

Figure 1. (a) Infrastructure mobile network, (b) ad hoc mobile network, and (c) Bluetooth Scatternet

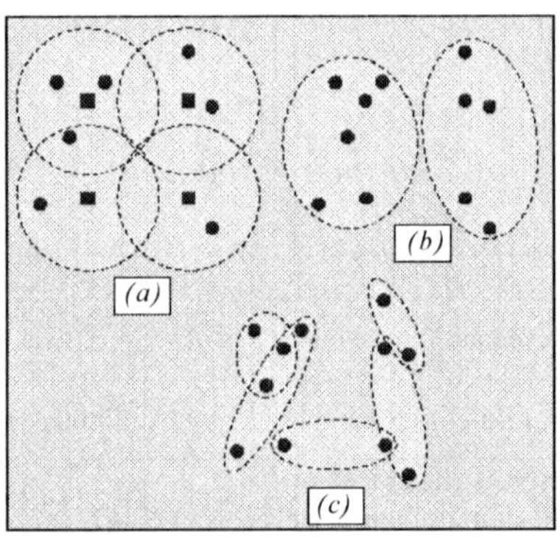

Scatternet environment. Because of the variable characteristic of the Scatternet architecture, the ability of routing information maintenance and repair are the main concern to design the routing protocol. How to choose the role of a node and the bridge node in Bluetooth Scattetnet is the key point for developing routing protocol. Section 2 will introduce three relative research papers about routing in Bluetooth Scatternet. Section 3 presents a routing protocol (BNRP) based on the DTCP. Section 4 presents the simulation and analysis of BRNP and MANET style routing protocols. Section 5 concludes this chapter and points out future work.

Relative Research

We will introduce three papers about Bluetooth Scatternet in this chapter.

IP Services over Bluetooth: Leading the Way to a New Mobility (Albrecht et al., 1999)

This paper was presented by University of Bonn and R&D Center of Nokia in Germany. They provide a concept for an extension of IP for mobility issue in Bluetooth networks called BLUEPAC IP, where BLUEPAC stands for "BLUEtooth Public Access." "Public access" means access to various kinds of information in public areas (i.e., airplane, train, hotel room, department store, museum). The Bluetooth Node gets a legal IP address by connecting the BLUEPAC from wireless to wire Internet backbone (GSM network, PSTN or Internet) and combining Mobile IP (Perkins, 2000) and Cellular IP. The network architecture of BLUEPAC shows in Figure 2.

Mobile node gets a local IP address by the DHCP mechanism in the local network, and connects to Internet by proxy server. When the mobile node roams in the BLUEPAC network, it gets a foreign IP address by the mobile IP mechanism. Combining the mobile IP and cellular IP mechanism can realize the handoff /roaming ability of Mobile Node.

Handoff Support for Mobility with IP over Bluetooth (Frank et al., 2000)

This paper was presented in 25th Local Computer Network Conference. This paper is based on the BLUPAC and supports the mobile IP and DHCP

Figure 2. The network architecture of BLUEPAC

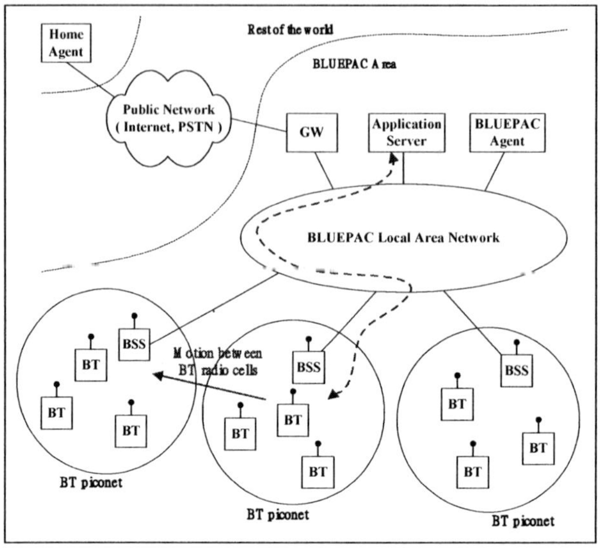

mechanisms for roaming ability on layer 2. The Bluetooth Piconet design is discussed and the IP adaptation layer is presented for the exchange of IP datagram between a mobile Bluetooth device and an access point. There are two fundamental approaches to the basic Piconet designed in a BLUEPAC network.

First, the Base Station acts as a Bluetooth slave and the other Bluetooth devices are the masters. The disadvantage of this Piconet scenario is that the Base Station has to take part simultaneously in several Piconets. The Base Station must to apply the Time-Division-Multiplexing scheme and degrade the performance.

In the second Piconet design approach, the Base Station acts as the master and the Bluetooth devices are slaves. The main disadvantage of this Piconet design is that BLUEPAC devices cost a substantial amount of time for waiting the master (Base Station) to initiate an inquiry and page procedure.

To prevent the disadvantages of designed Piconet, a combination of both approaches is suggested. An IP adaptation layer is inserted between IP and L2CAP to provide the data link and protocol transformation. The IP adaptation layer divides into three statues: discovery, configuration, and connected, shown in Figure 3 and Figure 4.

Figure 3. The IP adaptation layer for mobile node

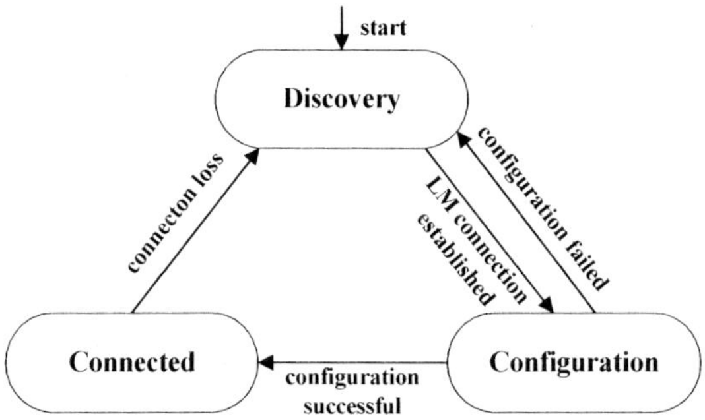

Figure 4. The IP adaptation layer state diagram for mobile node

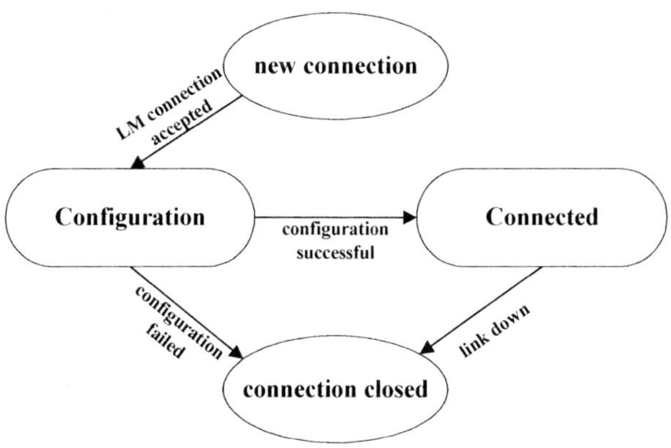

A Routing Vector Method (RVM) for Routing in Bluetooth Scatternets (Bhagwat & Segall, 1999)

This paper was presented by IBM and the department of Electrical Engineering, Technician in Mobile Multimedia Communication Conference 1999. This paper provides a routing method for Bluetooth Scatternet and supports the characteristic and flexibility of MANET routing protocol.

The main concept is adding the routing information in the Bluetooth packets payload of layer 2. The RVF field of the routing information records the order (LocID) and the master MAC address of those Piconets that packet has traveled. It divides into two routing architectures to record routing information in route SEARCH packets: Inter-Piconet and Intra-Poconet. Source Node can calculate the routing path from receiving the REPLY packets of the destination node.

The disadvantages of this paper are: First, the problems of maintaining and discovering the routing information when devices are shut down or out of the communication range; second, the Bluetooth device is acting as the master and the relay node simultaneously. The RVF records additional LocID and MACAddr and costs the routing delay, also degrades performance.

Effective Transmission Protocol in Bluetooth Scatternet

Distributed Topology Construction Protocol (DTCP) (Salonidis, Bhagwat, Tassiulas, & LaMaire, 2001)

The protocol consists of three phases: "coordinator election," "role determination," and "the actual connection establishment."

Phase I: Coordinator Election

During this phase, there is an asynchronous distributed election of a coordinator node. And then the coordinator will know the count, identities, and clocks of all the nodes in the network.

- Each node will have a variable called VOTE that set to 1 when the node powers on.
- Each node switches in the INQUIRY or the UNQUIRY mode.
- Any two nodes that discover each other will perform "one-to-one confrontation" and compare their VOTE values. The node becomes the winner of the confrontation if it has the larger VOTE value, and the other node is the loser. If two nodes have the equal value of VOTE, the winner is the node has larger Bluetooth MAC address.
- The winner node plus 1 to the value of VOTE for each confrontation and records the information of nodes that has been confronted. The loser node transfers frequency-hop synchronization (FHS) packets to the winner node

and disconnect the connection to winner, then it enters into PAGE SCAN mode.

- If there are N nodes in the Scatternet, there will be N-1 one-to-one confrontations. The winner of the N-1 confrontations will be the coordinator node and the rest of nodes will be in the PAGE SCAN state.

Phase II: Role Determination

- The coordinator that was elected during phase I and has the FHS packets of all nodes and hence knows the total number in the network.
- If the total number of nodes is less than eight, one Piconet is formed. The coordinator becomes the master and the rest of nodes are slaves. If the total number of nodes is greater than seven, more than one Piconet will be formed and intercommunicate to each other with bridge node.
- The number of master nodes can be calculated by the following relation

$$P = \left\lceil \frac{17 - \sqrt{289 - 8N}}{2} \right\rceil, \ 1 \leq \mathrm{N} \leq 36$$

- After calculating the value of P, the coordinator selects itself and other P-1 node to be the masters and the other $\frac{P(P-1)}{2}$ nodes to be the bridges of Scatternets. For each master x the coordinator has a connectivity list set (SLAVELIST(x), BRIDGELIST(x)) consisting of the master's assigned slaves and bridges, masters can page its slave and bridge nodes.
- Then the coordinator node connects the designated masters by paging. Thus, a temporary Piconet is formed instantly with the coordinator as the "master" and the designated masters as the "slave." The coordinator transfers the connectivity list set to each designated master to start phase III procedure and disconnects later.

Phase III: The Actual Connection Establishment

- Each designated master x pages and connects to the slaves and bridges according its list (SLAVELIST(x), BRIDGELIST(x)).
- If a node is notified to be a bridge, it waits to be paged by other masters. When the node receives the page from other masters, it sends a CONNECTED notification to both masters.

Figure 5. DTCP N=16 connection establishment

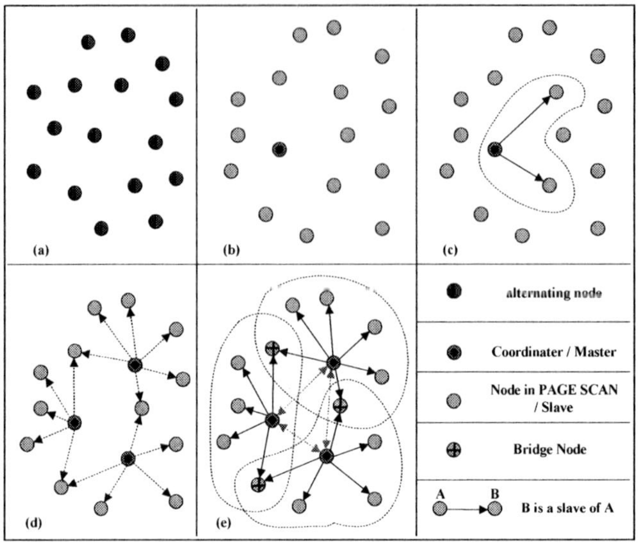

- When the master node receives the CONNECTED messages from all bridge nodes, a fully connected Scatternet is formed and the protocol terminates.

In Figure 5, (a) all nodes start to discovery the neighborhood nodes and switches between the UNQUIRY and INQUIRY modes. (b) At the end of phase I, the coordinator is elected and the value of P is calculated to be 3, the designated masters, bridge nodes and slaves are assigned. (c) The coordinator forms a temporary Piconet with the designated masters and transmits connectivity list to them. (d) Phase III: each master pages the nodes according to its connectivity list. (e) Finally, a Scatternet constructed by several Piconets.

Bridge Node Routing Protocol (BNRP)

Because of the characteristics of MANET and Bluetooth previously mentioned, we provide an on-demand routing protocol to query and get routing information without sending periodic query packets to waste bandwidth, and use the bridge nodes to maintain an effective routing protocol.

At the third phase of DTCP, we add an additional step that keeps the connections between the coordinator and the masters when the number of slaves connected to coordinator is less than seven. Using the BNRP will shorten the routing path from one master to another master that is in different Piconets. There is no need to go through the bridge nodes and hence reduces the delay time of routing. The BNRP divides into two parts: route discovery and route maintenance.

1. **Route discovery:** The addressing of the nodes in a Piconet are PID and NID. Because the maximum number of node in a Piconet is one master and seven slaves, the id of Piconet (PID) can be presented with the MAC address of the master in the Piconet, and the slaves get the node ID (NID) set by master can be presented by additional three bits.

   The "service discovery protocol" starts querying routing information. It's a kind of on-demand methods to denote the query process. Source node sends route request packets to the neighboring nodes, the master node broadcasts RREQ packets to its slaves and waits for responding messages from the slave nodes via route reply (RREP) packets. This information consists of the PID and NID. Route discovery procedure can be divided into two parts in detail: intra-Piconet mode and inter-Piconet mode.

   a. **Intra-Piconet mode:** It is called intra-Piconet mode if the destination node and the source node are in the same Piconet. In this situation, the RREQ packets will not be broadcasted to the other Piconet by the bridge node.

   b. **Inter-Piconet mode:** When the master gets RREP packets from it's slave nodes and the destination node is not in the same Piconet, it's called Inter-Piconet mode. The RREQ packets that sent by the source node will across the bridge node to the other Piconet, then the RREQ packets will broadcast to the destination node in other Piconets. The bridge node will record the routing information in the cache about the addresses of nodes in the Piconets connected to it, thus the query process will be rapid next time.

2. **Route maintenance:** When the routing path is established, two methods are used to maintain the routing information: route update and route repair.

   a. **Route update:** Master sends the update packets to the bridge node for updating the routing table when the Bluetooth devices transfer from active mode to sleep or parked mode. If one new node enters into this Piconet, the master node uses the update packets to notify the bridge node for updating routing table information.

   b. **Route repair:** If the node on the routing path cannot work or the node is interrupted by the influences, the master will obtain the acknowledgement messages, record the information of that node, and send route error messages to the bridge node. The bridge node will check if there is an existing record in the routing table according this route error messages. If yes, the routing path is broken, routing path should rebuild again; if no, restart the route discovery process.

We provide a bridge node routing protocol (BNRP) to improve delay and the throughput of the existing MANET style routing protocol without periodic routing query and extra broadcast routing information in the Bluetooth Scatternet environment. This protocol can provide the flexibility and the routing discovery with the characteristics of the Bluetooth environment like sleep mode or rapidly roaming architecture. The next section will use the OPNET to simulate this protocol and analyze it.

Simulation and Analysis

The Bluetooth Scatternet Environment

In this chapter, we will use the OPNET software to simulate the Bluetooth Scatternet environment and compare the MANET style routing protocol with our BNRP. Following are the simulation environments and the parameters as listed in Table 2.

According to the specification of Bluetooth, the packet format is fixed in the Figure 6, Figure 7 is the detail format of Access Code, and Figure 8 is the Header part of the packet.

Figure 9 shows the payload of layer 3 packet format of our BNRP. The means for each field are shown next.

Table 2. Simulation environment parameters

Number of MN	Two scenarios of 8 and 16
Spatial Distribution of MN	Random distribution in square length 500m
Node Movement Pattern	Pause-and-go movement
Traffic Pattern	Best-Effort, generated by conversations initiated by nodes
Data Rate	723.2Kb/sec

Figure 6. Specification of Bluetooth packet format

LSB 72	54	0 - 2745 MSB
ACCESS CODE	HEADER	PAYLOAD

Figure 7. Specification of Bluetooth packet format – access code

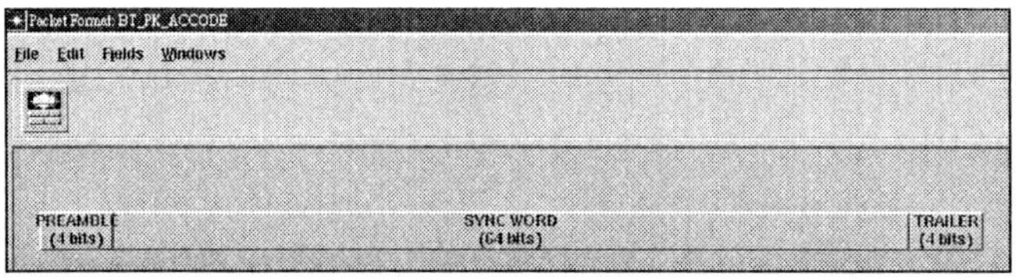

Figure 8. Specification of Bluetooth packet format – header

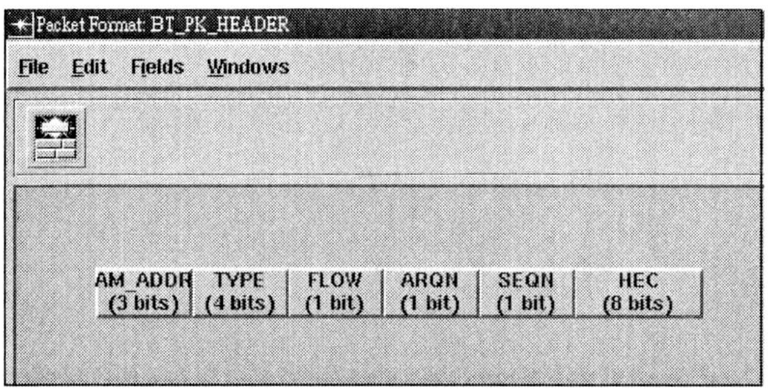

Figure 9. Specification of Bluetooth packet format – layer 2 (layer 3 Payload embedded)

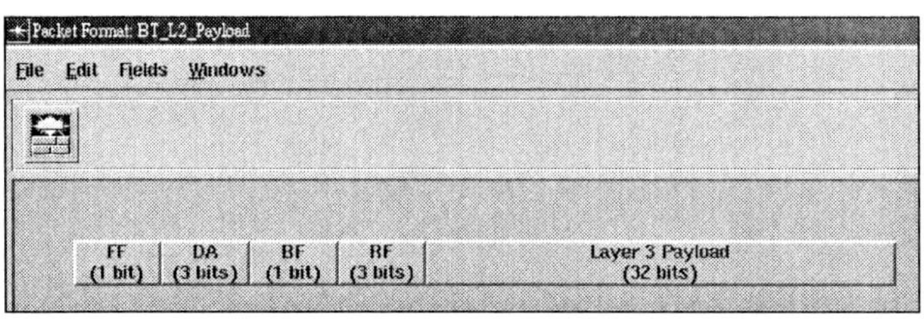

- **FF – Forwarding field:** The FF field represents the Intra-Piconet or Inter-Piconet mode. If the FF equals to 1, this packet will be relayed by bridge node to another Piconets
- **DA – Destination MACAddr:** The MAC address of destination node
- **BF – Broadcast field:** If the value of BF set to 0, this packet will be sent with unicast transmission, otherwise with broadcast transmission
- **RF – Routing field:** This field records the Piconet ID (PID) and the node ID (NID) according the routing path of RREQ packets

BNRP Finite Status Diagrams

The status transfer among ACK, error, and route reply, the packets come from upper layer and receive from MAC layer as shown in Figure 10.

Simulation of 8 Bluetooth Nodes

Figure 11 shows the network topology of 8 nodes. There are two Piconets connected each other with one bridge node. The bridge node relays packets and records routing information between two Piconets.

Running the simulation, the results of end-to-end delay and data throughput produced by MANET style routing protocol and BNRP are shown in Figure 12 and Figure 13.

Figure 10. The finite status of BRNP

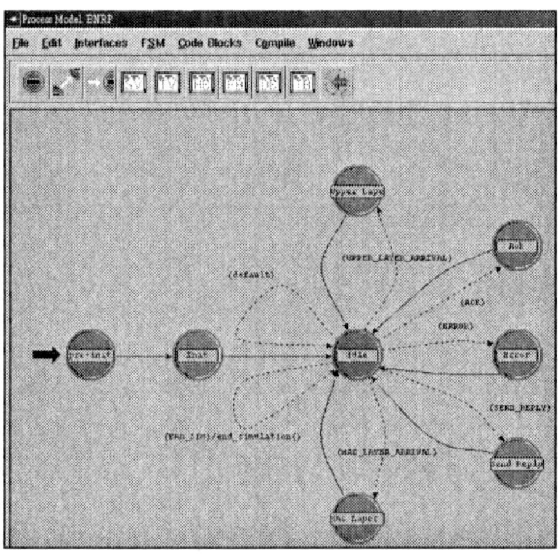

Figure 11. The scenario of 8 nodes

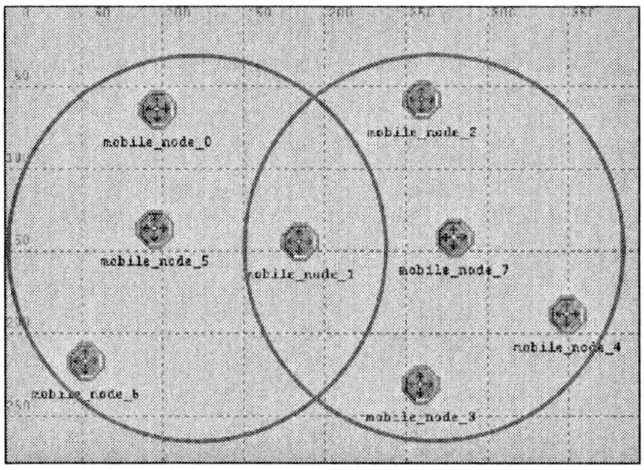

Figure 12. End-to-end delay

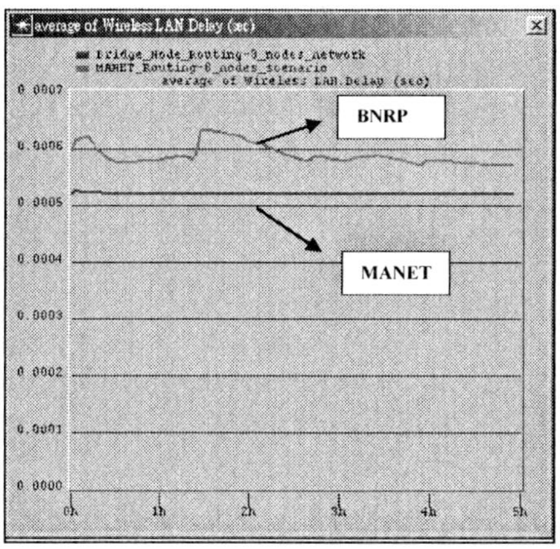

The result of figure 12 shows that the BNRP improves the end-to-end delay about 0.1 ms comparing with MANET style routing protocol. The performance improves about $\left(\frac{0.1}{0.6}\right) \times 100\% = 16.6\%$.

Due to MANET style, routing protocol sends a lot of ineffective routing request query packets to degrade the throughput of all data transmission. The BNRP gets the better performance of data transmission.

Figure 13. The throughput

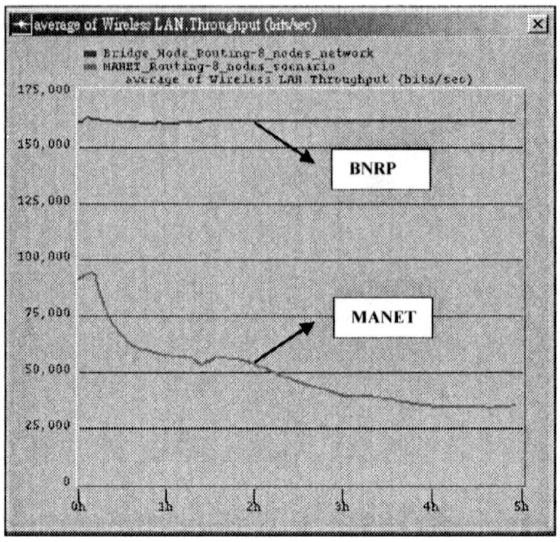

Simulation of 16 Bluetooth Nodes

Figure 14 shows the scenario of 16 nodes. There are four Piconets connected with three bridge nodes. When the number of total nodes increases to 16, the End-to-End Delay shown in Figure 15 is similar to Figure 12. For the overall throughput, the MANET style routing protocol degrades when the total nodes increase to 16. Ineffective update and repair the routing information cause the MANET style routing protocol degrades the overall throughput.

Figure 14. The scenario of 16 nodes

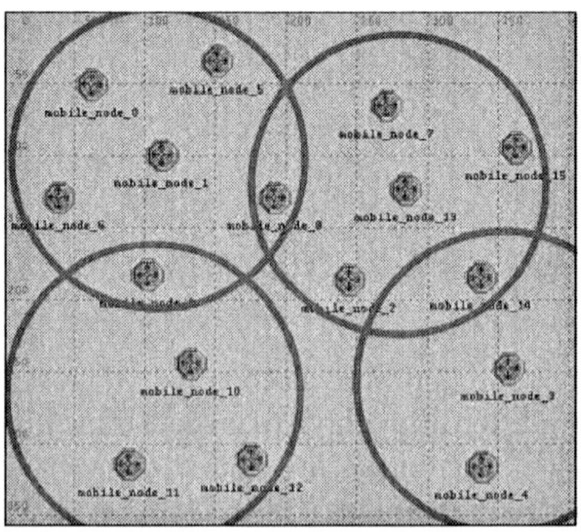

Figure 15. End-to-end delay

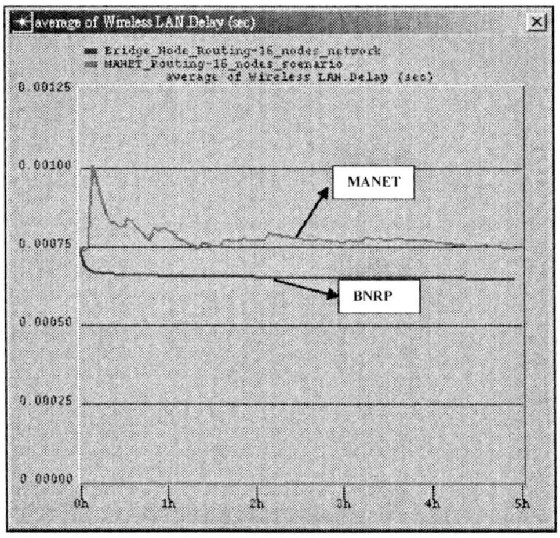

Figure 16. The throughput

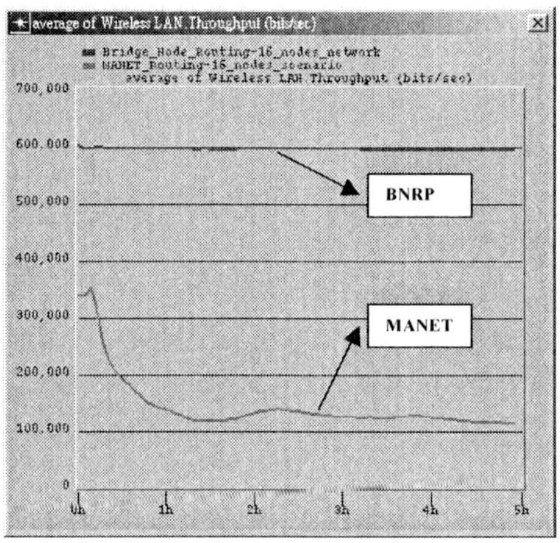

The results of end-to-end delay and throughput indicate that BNRP has better performance than MANET style routing protocol in the Bluetooth Scatternet environment.

Conclusion

To extend the usage of distance education, especially when students are out of classroom and are within a museum or a field investigation process, using ad hoc mechanism of MANET to access the real time brief or introduction can definitely improve their learning interests greatly. In this chapter, we propose a BNRP routing protocol in Bluetooth Scatternet in the special case of MANET. Base on the DTCP protocol to process three phases to elect coordinator, determinate the roles of each node and establish connection. Adding an additional step at phase III that keeps the connections between the coordinator and the masters when the number of slaves connected to coordinator is less than seven. Using the BNRP will shorten the routing path from one master to another master that is in different Piconets. This protocol can provide the flexibility and the routing discovery function with the characteristics of the Bluetooth environment like sleep mode or rapidly roaming architecture. It preserves effective transmissions and achieves better Bluetooth Scatternet performance than traditional MANET environment. Finally, it can apply for outdoor distance education environment and make teaching and learning anytime and everywhere.

Acknowledgment

This chapter is a partial result of project no NSC 90-2219-E-259-002- and NSC 91-2219-E-259-004 conducted by National Dong Hwa University under the sponsorship of the National Science Council, ROC.

Reference

Albrecht, M., Frank, M., Martini, P., Schetelig, M., Vilavaara, A., & Wenzel, A. (1999). IP services over Bluetooth: Leading the way to a new mobility. *IEEE LCN'99 Conference* (pp. 2-11).

Bhagwat, P., & Segall, A. (1999). A Routing Vector Method (RVM) for routing in Bluetooth Scatternets. *The 6th IEEE International Workshop on Mobile Multimedia Communications (MOMUC'99).*

Frank, M., Gopffarth, R., Kassatkine, D., Martini, P., Schetelig, M., & Vilavaara, A. (2000). Handoff support for mobility with IP over Bluetooth. *IEEE LCN 2000* (pp. 143-154).

IEEE 802.15. (n.d.). Working Group for WPANsTM. Retrieved from http://www.ieee802.org/15/

IETF MANET Working Group. (n.d.). Retrieved from http://www.ietf.org/html.charters/manet-charter.html

Instructional Technology Council. (n.d.). Retrieved from http://www.itcnetwork.org/

The Official Bluetooth SIG Web site (n.d.). Retrieved from http://www.bluetooth.com

Perkins, C. E. (2000). *Ad hoc networking*. Reading, MA: Addison-Wesley.

Perkins, C. E., & Johnson, D. B.(2000). *Route optimization in mobile IP*.

Salonidis, T., Bhagwat, P., Tassiulas, L., & LaMaire, R. (2001). Distributed topology construction of Bluetooth personal area networks. *IEEE INFOCOM 2001*.

Chapter V

A Ubiquitous Agent-Based Campus Information Providing System for Cellular Phones

Akio Koyama, Yamagata University, Japan

Leonard Barolli, Fukuoka Institute of Technology, Japan

Abstract

In this chapter, a campus information providing system (CIPS) for cellular phones is proposed. By using this system, the search time to find the necessary information in the campus is reduced. Users can access the system using the cellular phone terminal and by clicking the links or by inserting a keyword in the form they can get easily the campus information. The system has four agents, which deals with Web information required by users, Net News, the student's login state, campus navigation and the filtering of the received campus information for cellular phone terminal.

Therefore, the proposed system can provide different media information to a cellular phone. By using the proposed ubiquitous system, the users are able to get the information anywhere and anytime. The system performance was evaluated using a questionnaire. From the questionnaire results, we found that the system was able to show the required information.

Introduction

Presently, the number of cellular phone users is increasing at a very fast rate. They have Internet access from their phones and have access to many different kinds of information (ZDNet, 2001). By using the cellular phone, it is possible to get various services such as everyday life information, money exchange rates, databases, games, and music distribution. NTT DoCoMo has already started a service called IMT-2000, which is an international standard of the mobile communication systems and can be used all over the world (NTT DoCoMo, 2003). Therefore, a lot of information can be handled using the cellular phone.

Now, many universities have their own campus information on their homepages and the students by using homepage, e-mail, Net News, campus bulletin board can get a lot of information (Fujii & Sugiyama, 2000; Kubota, Maeda, & Kikuchi, 2001). However, the logging in a terminal, starting to work with a personal computer (PC), or going to see a bulletin board takes a lot of time. Also, getting information by starting a browser and typing a command such as "mnews" it will take time because two or more systems should be used. Therefore, getting the information by using only one system anywhere and anytime will decrease the number of operations and will save more time for users.

In order to solve these problems, we propose campus information providing system (CIPS). This system supports a user which acquires the campus information. By using the cellular phone, the user is able to get the information anywhere and anytime. The proposed system is implemented by the common gateway interface (CGI) and consists of four agents (Hattori, Sakama, & Morihara, 1998). The Web information agent (WIA) gets the information on Web databases, such as a timetable, examination schedule and syllabus information. The Net News agent (NNA) gets the information on Net News, such as newsgroups of the university. The Personal Information Agent (PIA) can search the information of a vacant terminal or the users who login. The navigation agent (NA) navigates a room in the campus. Using these agents, the proposed system can provide different media information for the cellular phone. When a user wants to get the information using the proposed system, the system gets the information and filters it in order to optimize the information for cellular phone.

In order to evaluate the performance of the proposed system, the system was used by ten cellular phone users, and by using a questionnaire we asked them some questions such as how was the information search by the proposed system compared with other information searching systems, how was the system operation, and what merits and demerits have the proposed system.

The chapter is organized as follows. First, we introduce the proposed system. Next, we discuss the performance evaluation. Finally, some conclusions are given.

Proposed System

System Outline

The proposed system has the following features.

- It is possible to check the campus information anytime and anywhere
- One system realizes various services (Web, news, students login state, vacant terminal information in the computer rooms and campus navigation)
- The information retrieval and the information filtering are done in the real time. If the information is updated, a new information can be retrieved automatically

The system is implemented by CGI using Perl language. The system structure is shown in Figure 1. When a user accesses the system, a menu screen appears as shown in Figure 2. The user selects the information by choosing a link in the menu. After that, the system agents are activated and they check for the required information in the WWW and news servers. They refer the commands output and analyze the order how the maps should be shown. Then, they filter this information in order to be appropriate to be shown in the mobile phone terminal.

WIA

The information of some universities is accessible via the university homepage. The students can get via the homepage the information such as timetable, examination schedule, and the syllabus information. However, when the information whereabouts are unknown, it is necessary to follow the links in order to

Figure 1. System

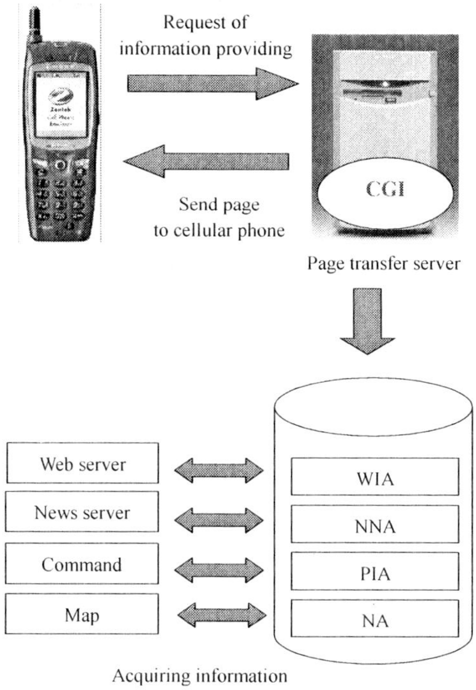

Figure 2. System interface

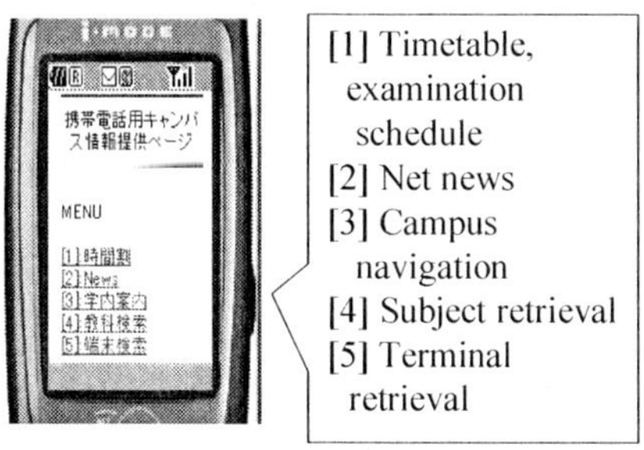

search inside the Web page. Even if the page structure is known, it may take time to get the required information. Furthermore, when someone wants to find some information, he needs to find a computer in order to access the homepage. Therefore, considering these cases, it will be better to use a mobile phone information system. By using WIA, the proposed system is able to support the information retrieval anywhere and anytime.

Flow of Web Information Retrieval

When a user wants to find Web information, a link related to the timetable, examination schedule, or subject retrieval is chosen from the menu screen. When, the timetable and examination schedule are chosen, a new screen by which can be selected the class and a day as shown in Figure 3 is displayed. When the subject retrieval is chosen, a new screen which depicts a form where

Figure 3. Operations required for timetable information

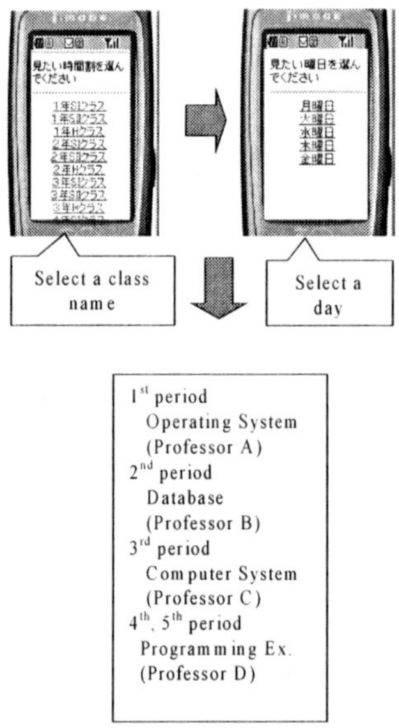

Figure 4. Operations required for subject retrieval

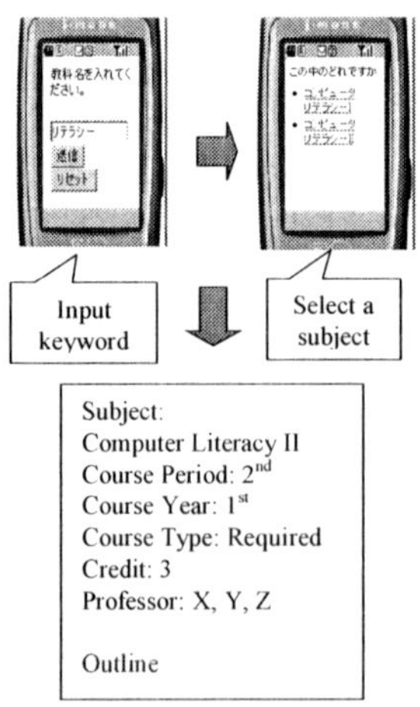

a keyword can be inserted as shown in Figure 4 is displayed. An agent accesses the WWW server and requires a corresponding page. From the retrieved page, the agent extracts the information related with the required subject information (subject name, professor name, the number of units, etc.) and deletes unnecessary character sequences such as the line tags. Then, the character sequence which processing is finished is used in the HTML sentence and is displayed in the cellular phone. The timetable shows the subject name, professor name, and classroom name from the first period to the fifth period. The examination schedule shows the examination subject name, class, and classroom name from the first period to the fifth period. The subject reference shows the subject name, course year, required/selection, the number of units, and the professor name. Furthermore, in the subject reference, if the link showing the outline of a subject is chosen, the outline and the purpose of the subject can be seen.

WIA Algorithm

1. When a user demands information providing, the agents accesses the WWW server and retrieve the related page information.
2. The source of the retrieved page is checked line by line. In the case of timetable or examination schedule, a line with the subject name is extracted. In the case of subject retrieval, the line containing the character sequence which the user inserted in the form is searched and the line which matches the information is extracted.
3. The tag is deleted from the extracted line.
4. In the case of a timetable or an examination schedule, the character sequence whose the unnecessary tag was deleted is stored in array based on the day information. In the subject retrieval case, the information is stored in the variables for every subject name or number of units, and the subject outline and purpose are stored in an array.
5. In the case of the timetable information or examination schedule, based on the user demands, a suitable information is chosen from the array. The information is adapted for the HTML format of the cellular phones.
6. In subject retrieval case, a variable is used for the HTML sentence of the cellular phones, and when a link related to the subject outline is chosen, the information stored in the array is displayed.

NNA

There is another way to get the campus information by using Net News. A student can get news by typing "mnews" command. By using Net News various information such as newsgroups, announcements, circle information, class information, part-time job, lost articles, can be found. However, the same as in WEB information, to get Net News information the user should have a computer connected to the campus network. In our system, by using NNA, the user is able to find the information anywhere and anytime.

Flow of Net News Information Retrieval

When a user wants to find some information using Net News, from the menu, the "News" link is selected. As shown in Figure 5, an agent accesses a news server and chooses a group to which the report is submitted from the newsgroup of the University of Aizu. Then, it makes a list and the prepared list is displayed. The user chooses a group from a newsgroups list. The agent selects from the chosen group 10 articles and prepares and displays the title list.

Then, the agent investigates whether in the selected articles there is any space in the head of line. Since the space is displayed as it is on a cellular phone, in the case when there is a space, it is deleted. The article which processing is finished is used in the HTML sentence and it is displayed on the cellular phone.

Figure 5. Operations required for net news information

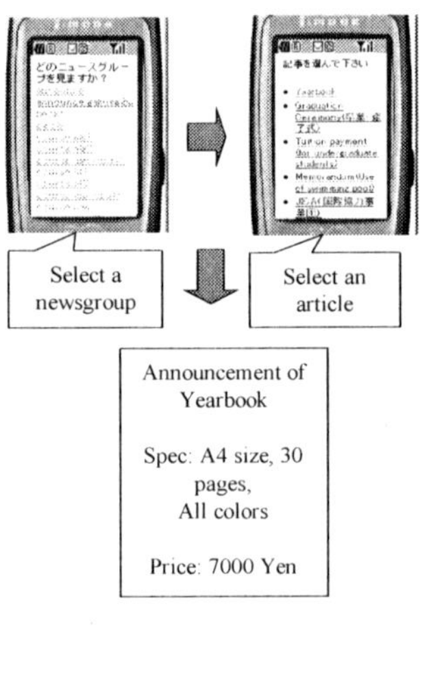

NNA Algorithm

1. When there is a demand for information providing from a user, a news server is accessed and the university newsgroups list is displayed.
2. Each newsgroup is investigated whether exist or not submitted articles. If there are groups which have not submitted articles, they are deleted from the newsgroups list.
3. The newsgroup which the user selected is accessed, and the titles for ten articles are retrieved and displayed.
4. The article which the user selected is retrieved and stored in an array.
5. The array information is filtered to be appropriate for displaying in the cellular phone.

PIA

The students of the University of Aizu receive the lectures and solve the exercises using UNIX workstations. To find who is using the terminal, a special command is used. However, for the sake of security, we will not give the command name in this paper. If the special command can be used for cellular phone, it will save a lot of time. By using the PIA, the student login state can be displayed on a cellular phone.

Figure 6. Personal information in cellular phone

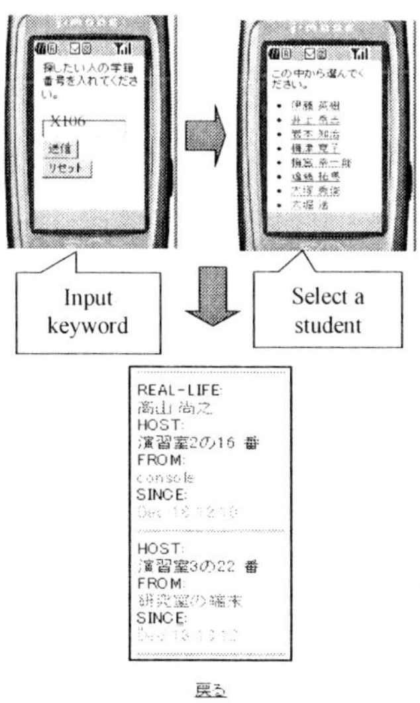

Flow of Personal Information Retrieval

In order to get the result from the special command, a link of terminal search is chosen from a menu screen. Next, as shown in Figure 6, a user inputs a keyword (student ID number or name or host name) into the form, and the form is transmitted. The results of the executed the special command are written in a file every five minutes using the "crontab" command. The PIA extracts the line which matches the keyword. When there are many people, the list of the individual name is created and displayed. The results of the executed the special command are ordered as login ID, name, host name, place, and login time. By using these data, the information of the person who matches the keyword is chosen from the name list and is displayed. But, for the sake of security, the login ID, host name and terminal names are not displayed. Instead, the terminal number and the room number are displayed. Moreover, when the same person has accessed two or more terminals using rlogin or telnet, the special command indicates the whole state of the user. In Figure 6, the user's name is shown after "REAL-LIFE," the terminal number and the room number are shown after "HOST." When many hosts are accessed by one person from the same place (this place is shown after "FROM"), only the host which the time is close to the present one is selected and shown after "HOST" and the login time is shown after "SINCE." This is done in order to ensure that the person shown in "FROM" is the same with the person logged here. Moreover, when the same person has accessed the system from the different places, both cases are displayed. The PIA can be used also for searching a vacant host, for getting how many terminals of each exercise room are vacant, or which terminal is vacant using the result of the special command.

NA

The campus map is placed everywhere in the University of Aizu. This is very convenient for the students who come for the first time to the university. However, if a place is far from another one, it is difficult to memorize the route. Also, if a student can not find the map, he can not get even the route. Recently, KDDI started a new service called "GPS keitai." The function called eznavigation provide the accurate location information (KDDI, 2001). However, the detailed navigation for inside a building does not exist. Based on NA, the proposed system is able to guide the students using the university map.

Figure 7. Navigation agent structure

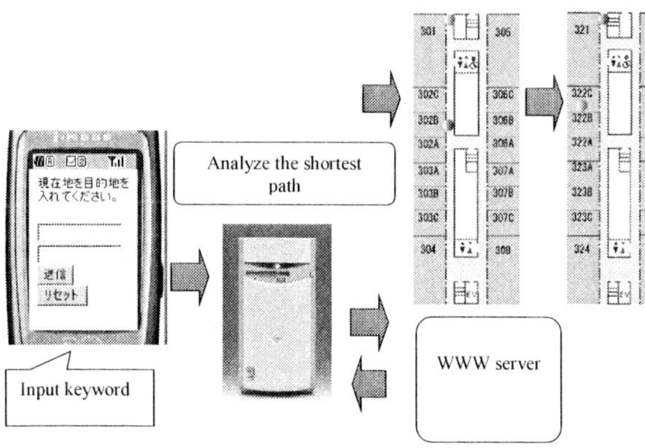

Flow of Navigation Information Retrieval

In the case when a user uses the NA for the university guidance, he inserts in the form its present location and destination as shown in Figure 7. The NA offers the map made beforehand by us. It may happen that a professor moves from a room to another one. In this case, if this information is updated in the university homepage, the map information can be also updated. On the map, a red circle shows a present location and a blue arrow shows the destination. A user moves from the present location to the destination. When a user arrives at the destination, as shown in Figure 8, the picture which shows the next destination from that place is displayed by choosing a link called "next." Thus, when a user arrives at a place shown in the map, the link which displays the next picture is chosen. When a user lose the way, a link showing the present location is selected. Then, the user inserts in a form as keywords the rooms of an institution, the number of stairs of a building, etc. By using these keywords, the present location is judged and the route from the present location to the destination is shown again.

Performance Evaluation

Experiment Outline

We evaluated the proposed system using a questionnaire. Ten cellular phone users used the system and the performance of the system was evaluated using three items: the system operation, viewability, and convenience.

Figure 8. Navigation operation

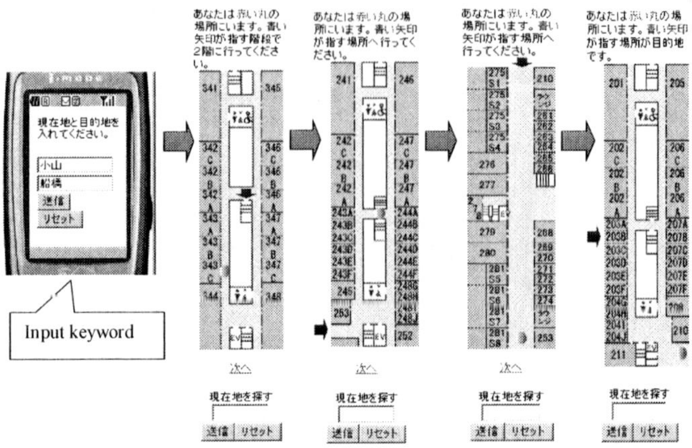

Table 1. Questionnaire results

Users	Operation	Viewability	Convenience
A	Good	Normal	Good
B	Normal	Good	Good
C	Normal	Good	Good
D	Good	Normal	Good
E	Normal	Normal	Good
F	Good	Normal	Good
G	Normal	Bad	Good
H	Normal	Normal	Good
I	Good	Normal	Good
J	Normal	Bad	Good

Questionnaire Results and Considerations

The questionnaire results are shown in Table 1. The name of users are shown as A, B, C, D, E, F, G, H, I, and J.

We received the following comments for the agents

1. WIA
   - For timetable and examination schedule it will be better to be able to select a day and a period.

2. NNA
   - In some articles, without reading the full text, the user could get the meaning. Therefore, if the text will be divided in some parts it will be better.
3. PIA
   - Sometime the special command can not be used. Therefore, in such a case if there is another procedure it will be better.
4. NA
   - The entrance of the room was not clear.

Based on the previously mentioned comments, we conclude that a cellular phone system provides good campus information. However, the system operation and its viewability should be improved.

Conclusion

In this chapter, a campus information providing system for cellular phones was proposed. A user can check the campus information easily using the cellular phone anywhere and anytime. In order to get the information, a user needs to insert only the keywords in a form and to click a link. After that, the system retrieves the information and filters it in order to be appropriate for a cellular phone. When information is updated, the retrieved information is updated automatically. The proposed system can provide different media information such as Web, News, login state, vacant terminal, and campus navigation to the cellular phone. The performance evaluation shows that a cellular phone system is convenient and provides good campus information. However, the system operation and its viewability should be improved.

References

Fujii, K., & Sugiyama, K. (2000). Route guide map generation system for mobile communication. *IPSJ Journal, 41*(9), 2394-2403.

Hattori, F., Sakama, Y., & Morihara, I. (1998). Intelligent agent communication, Ohmsha.

KDDI Corporation. (2001). Retrieved from http://www.kddi.com/release/2001/1129-1/

Kubota, K., Maeda F., & Kikuchi, Y. (2001). Proposal and evaluation of pedestrian navigation system. *IPSJ Journal*, *42*(7), 1858-1865.

NTT DoCoMo Home Page. (2003). Retrieved from http://www.nttdocomo.co.jp/

ZDNet JAPAN. (2001). Retrieved from http://www.zdnet.co.jp/mobile/0112/07/n_tca.html

Section III Intelligent Technologies

Chapter VI

An XML-Based Approach to Multimedia Engineering for Distance Learning

T. Arndt, Cleveland State University, USA

S. K. Chang, University of Pittsburgh, USA

A. Guercio, Kent State University, USA

P. Maresca, University of Naples Federico II, Italy

Abstract

Multimedia software engineering (MSE) is a new frontier for both software engineering (SE) and visual languages (VL). In fact, multimedia software engineering can be considered as the discipline for systematic specification, design, substitution, and verification of visual patterns. Visual languages contribute to MSE such concepts as: Visual notation for software specification, design, and verification flow charts, ER diagrams, Petri nets, UML visualization, visual programming languages, etc. Multimedia software engineering and software engineering are like two sides of the same coin.

On the one hand, we can apply software engineering principles to the design of multimedia systems. On the other hand, we can apply multimedia technologies to the software engineering practice. In this chapter, we concentrate on the first of these possibilities. One of the promising application areas for multimedia software engineering is distance learning. One aim of this chapter is to demonstrate how it is possible to design and to implement complex multimedia software systems for distance learning using a tele-action object transformer based on XML technology applying a component-based multimedia software engineering approach. The chapter shows a complete process of dataflow transformation that represents TAO in different ways (text, TAOML, etc.) and at different levels of abstraction. The transformation process is a reversible one. A component-based tool architecture is also discussed. We also show the first experiments conducted jointly using the TAOML_T tool. The use of an XML-based approach in the distance learning field has other advantages as well. It facilitates reuse of the teaching resources produced in preceding decades by universities, schools, research institutions, and companies by using metadata. The evolution of the technologies and methodologies underlying the Internet has provided the means to transport this material. On the other hand, standards for representing multimedia distance learning materials are currently evolving. Such standards are necessary in order to allow a representation which is independent of hardware and software platforms so that this material can be examined, for example, in a Web browser or so that it may be reused in whole or in part in other chapters of a book or sections of a course distinct from that for which it was originally developed. Initial experiments in reuse of distance learning carried out at the University of Naples, Kent State University, and Cleveland State University are described. The authors have also developed a collaboration environment through which the resources can be visualized and exchanged.

Introduction: Multimedia Software Engineering

For many years, the need to represent data in a portable format has grown in the industrial and in the academic community. In the past, data was kept in a format that couldn't be read by a different computer and the applications couldn't be run under different operating systems or on other hardware platforms. Today, with the spread of computer networks, it is necessary to support portability and interoperability so that data can flow through many networks in a way transparent to the user.

Once data is represented in a portable way, it is easy to transform it for specific uses. For example, during its' route from sender to receiver, data may be represented several times at different level of abstraction so that it can be easily handled by the software or hardware devices and transmitted across the network (Maresca & Guercio, 2000b). Often information or data are used as representations of other information in order to support reuse. This concept of information that describes some other information is known as *metadata*. Using metadata it is possible to take a structured document, parse it, and store the contents in a database or an application, local or remote. In this way, the document assumes an exchangeable structured form in which all parts of it may be reused. Metadata also supports resource discovery. This concept can be extended to all textual and multimedia applications. In this context, it's easy to understand why XML (Bray, Paoli, & Sperberg-McQueen, 1998) has become widely accepted as a new generation of languages that has promoted data and application portability with the possibility to use them on most browsers, offering moreover the possibility to handle information exchange in a better way for the Internet. It's natural to think that the advantages offered by software engineering and XML could be immediately tested in multimedia software engineering. It's worth remembering that multimedia software engineering is really a new frontier for software engineering as well as visual languages. In fact, multimedia software engineering can be regarded as the discipline for systematic specification, design, substitution, and verification of patterns that are often visual (Chang, 2000a). Visual languages give contribution to multimedia software engineering such as: visual notation for software specification, design, and verification flow charts, E-R diagrams, Petri nets, UML visualization, visual programming languages, etc. The good news is that we can apply software engineering principles to the design of multimedia systems (Chang, 2000a). At this point, we can start experimenting with multimedia methodologies, techniques, and languages. But first we must ask ourselves: "What is multimedia?"

In Maresca and Guercio, *multimedia* was defined as composition of two components: *multiple media* and *hypermedia.*

$$Multimedia = Multiple\ Media + Hypermedia$$

Multiple media means different media (audio, video, text, etc.) while *hypermedia* means objects + links. The definition contains the conceptual model for multimedia software engineering applications: the *multimedia language*.

A multimedia language is a language where the primitive objects can include media types and where the operators include spatial and temporal operators. We think that four fundamental aspects describe a multimedia language

- **Syntactic:** A multimedia application is constructed from a collection of multimedia objects. The primitive objects can include media. The complex multimedia objects are composed of these primitive objects and in general are of mixed media type. The syntax of a multimedia language describes how the complex multimedia objects are constructed from the other multimedia objects. Spatial and temporal composition rules must be taken into consideration
- **Semantic:** Multimedia applications nowadays are seldom passive. A static multimedia language can specify a passive multimedia application, but a dynamic multimedia application requires the system to take actions in response to user input and/or internal/external stimuli. The semantics of multimedia languages describes how the dynamic multimedia objects are derived from other multimedia objects when certain internal/external events occur. Since an important characteristic of multimedia is the ability to create links and associations, the semantics of multimedia languages must take that into consideration
- **Pragmatic:** Multimedia applications are heavily content-based and require a lot of hard manual work to put together. Tools are needed to assist the designer in building a multimedia application in a timely fashion. The pragmatics of multimedia languages can be based upon the patterns for various multimedia structures or sub-structures, such as navigation structures, content-based retrieval structures, etc. Once such structures and sub-structures are identified, they can be used as building blocks in putting together a multimedia application
- **Systems:** Last but not least, the systems aspects of multimedia applications must be considered. Multimedia applications require the support of operating systems, networks, and middleware. Increased support for multimedia in such systems will improve the performance of multimedia applications. Both QoS (quality of service) and QoP (quality of presentation) must be considered in systems design.

An example of a multimedia language used in distance learning among other application areas is TAO. TAO is based on the tele-action object paradigm (Chang, Chang, Hou, & Hsu, 1995a). The language has gone through evolutions improving the expressivity (Arndt, Guercio, & Chang, 1998; Arndt, Guercio, & Chang, 2000; Change, 1995b; Chang & Ho, 1989; Chang, Tortora, Yu, & Guercio, 1987) and ability to be transformed into other languages as HTML (Chang, 1996).

The authors believe that the combination of the expressive power of the TAO hypergraph and the interoperability offered by the XML language can be used to create a new multimedia software engineering paradigm: the TAOML language (Maresca, Arndt, & Guercio, 2001a; Marmo, 1999). This approach seems to be very promising, not least for its portability characteristics. For these reasons, many experiments have been developed in order to define an architecture for rapid prototyping tools able to design and to develop a multimedia software engineering application (see e.g., Maresca, & Guercio, 2000a). It is also true that this system design requires new software process models and paradigms, such as an object-oriented approach and the RUP-UML process (Booch, Jacobson, & Rumbaugh, 2000; Krutchen, 2001). But the authors believe that one of the software engineering techniques useful for multimedia software engineering is the component based software engineering (CBSE) paradigm since that paradigm is one of the fastest ways to implement reusable Multimedia components that follows the principals of object-oriented technology in multimedia software development. Component-based multimedia software engineering (CBMSE) (Agresti, 1986) enables the reuse of those components in other multimedia applications and makes it easier to maintain and to customize those components to produce new functions and features (Taylor, 1990). CBMSE should provide both a methodology and tools for developing components that work continuously, handle exceptional cases safely, and operate without corrupting other interrelated components. This approach employs a top-down design to subdivide a multimedia software system into modules and objects that can be easily implemented.

A valid application of CBSE approach in multimedia software engineering is represented by the complex transformations of tele-action objects based on the TAOML language.

The TAOML Multimedia Software Architecture

The TAOML multimedia software architecture is based on six basic entities that are represented in the following figure. In the next section we will show an instance of this architecture. It is worth pointing out that the architecture in Figure 1 shows a component-based architecture in which the different parts are integrated in order to obtain the main objective: transforming the multimedia flow into the TAOML language.

Now we will briefly describe each of the components of the architecture shown in Figure 1.

Figure 1. TAO_XML-based multimedia software architecture

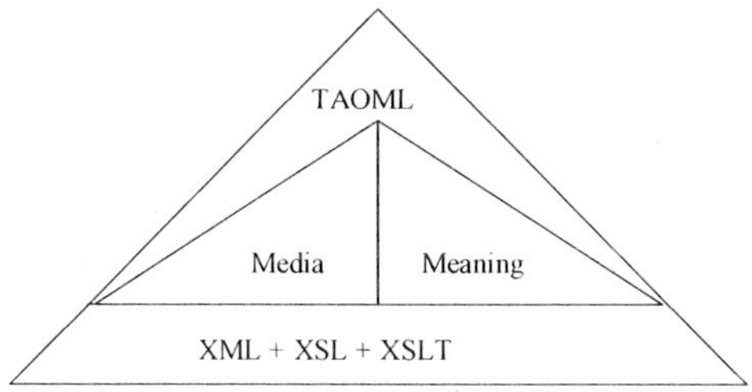

- The extensible markup language (XML) (Bosak & Bray, 1999), ratified by the World Wide Web Consortium (W3C) (Bray et al., 1998), is quickly becoming the standard way to identify and describe data and exchange machine-understandable information on the Web; XML describes a class of data objects called XML documents and provides a mechanism that maximizes the interoperability among different platforms.
- The extensible style sheet language (XSL) (Ahmed et al., 2001) Working Draft describes a vocabulary recognized by a rendering agent to render abstract format expressions into a particular presentation medium. An XML document can have more than one XSL style sheet applied, each style sheet producing a (usually) different result (e.g., txt/html/PDF format document or a generic format dependent on custom visualization).
- The XSL transformations (XSLT) 1.0 (Kay, 2000) recommendation describes a vocabulary recognized by an XSLT processor so that it can transform information from a source file structure into a different one suitable for continued downstream processing. The main goal of an XSLT processor is to transform an XML source document into an abstract hierarchical result. Furthermore the result is serialized into a desired standard format.
- Media that represents the form and technology used to represent and to communicate information. Multimedia presentations, for example, combine sound, pictures, and videos, all of which are different types of media
- Meaning that represents the concepts and the meaning of the information that will be transferred.
- TAOML represents the tele-action object paradigm (Chang, Chang, Hou, & Hsu, 1995a) realized using XML (Marmo, 1999) technology. It is fundamentally composed of two parts: a hypergraph which specifies the multimedia objects which constitute the TAOML and their relations, and a knowledge structure which describes the environment and the actions of the TAOML.

In this chapter, we will address the problem of the transformation of multimedia data using a CBSE approach. The chapter is structured as follows: section 2 introduces some of the problems associated with distance learning and introduces the growing book approach. Section 3 discusses related research. Section 4 considers dataflow transformations and finally section 5 states conclusions and contains discussion of future work.

Distance Learning

Interoperability of diverse hardware and software platforms is one of the most pressing needs in computing today. This problem is of particular relevance in academic environments where the software systems and materials used for teaching are extremely varied. Almost every university or school nowadays has a Web site and often course materials as well, developed by individual instructors. These may be regarded as "legacy" materials since, for the most part, they are unusable outside the context in which they were developed due to hardware and software dependencies.

We may add to this problem a strong trend in European universities towards a more modular set of course offerings in order to allow for a more realistic evaluation of course credits. This allows students to take advantage of course offerings from various universities (possibly from more than one country) but it also points out the obsolescence of the means of distributing course materials to students and of the software environments used for such a purpose.

The present trend favors the creation of synergistic relations between universities or the improvement of the means for exchange of documents among different university administrations, not necessarily of the same country. The situation is made more difficult since it is often the case that the exchanged documents must be reformatted, different databases must be queried and the results of the queries sent over the network in a format independent of that of the databases queried, among other local differences.

If we observe the present state of the art of distance learning in universities, we may observe that every university possesses a Web site and many online courses. This could cause us to conclude that we are seeing "distance learning" in action, but this would be a mistake. Distance learning is something more than this (Holmes, 1999) since there is a need for another level (one which is difficult to implement) that offers students a personalized and personalizable learning environment. In other words, the student needs to pass through three levels of learning environments (Chang & Ho, 1989; Harasim, 1999): the first, the internal environment, consists of the environment in which he works, his computer; the second, the external environment consists of the specific material that the university puts at his disposition for the specific course; the third, the global environment, consists of information that other universities put at his disposition to reach a specific objective. In this view, the instructor needs to be able to construct some virtual containers by composing resources that were not necessarily created by him but possibly by other colleagues and which are available on the network and reusable.

The distance learning activity is even more important than it seems at first glance. It is oriented towards distributed learning in which various areas intersect: learning resources; activities; enterprise (the infrastructure of the providers in which the learning activity is made available). It involves sectors including: financial software systems; digital libraries; information systems for students; courses of every type and level; authoring tools; etc. The market scenario involves everyone from 12-year-old students, through university age, and also involving corporate training extending also to the implications for the government and military sectors. The type of course which could support such a paradigm ranges from correspondence courses to HTML-based (both static and dynamic), from electronic performance support system (EPSS) (Stevens & Stevens, 1995), to legacy courses, from digital libraries to desktop simulations to the most sophisticated flight simulators. It is also interesting to examine the many forms of connectivity, which range from stand-alone to LAN. There are also various platforms (Windows, Lotus Domino, AS-400, Unix/Linux, Mainframe), diverse professional figures (instructor, administrator, content author, publicist, service provider) and varying technologies and teaching modes (constructionist, synchronous or asynchronous, skill-based, collaborative, simulative).

The use of Web browsers and the Internet only appears to have furnished interoperability for legacy didactic software systems since on the one hand the limited flexibility of the HTML language (and in particular its tags) doesn't allow for the creation of easily manipulated structured documents and on the other hand there still exist various hardware platforms and operating systems.

The student, for his part, often asks very simple questions of the type: "Who can offer me the most up-to-date C++ course?" or "Where can I find an exhaustive explanation of Laplace transforms?" or "Who has solutions for exercises on the subject of cinematography?" The answer to these questions often requires no more than a simple query of a database!

The need to exchange structured documents can be easily understood by thinking of any structured data that is normally used in the administration of a university such as a registrar's or admissions office.

There is a race to adopt Web technologies since there is a feeling that these technologies may be the wave of the future. Unfortunately, the need to use the data in a structured way so that the tools used to capture the information from the Web, and then organize it for presentation will not be excessively expensive is often ignored.

It is true that sophisticated techniques to identify keywords in Web documents have been developed for search engines, but none of these are able to satisfy our needs. For this reason a new generation of markup languages with a new generation of tags able to describe the contents of the document itself have been developed. The concept of information that describes some other information is known as *metadata*.

Using metadata it is possible to take a structured text document (if it is not structured then it can be given a structure), parse it, and store the results in a database, local or remote. In this way, the document assumes an exchangeable structured form in which all or parts of it may be reused. Naturally, this concept is relevant to other application domains besides the educational one we are interested in. Initiatives undertaken to develop innovative methodologies and learning techniques are scarce (IMS Global Learning Consortium, Inc., 2006; Graziano, Maresca, & Russo, 2000). The environments that exist are often heterogeneous or meant to support classical didactic techniques (e.g., WebCT, FirstClass, Cyberprof, Maestro, etc.). The fundamental problem has been the absence of a standard for didactic environments. Besides this, the only technology that seems to be currently exploited for distance learning is the Web with the use of streaming media. In the following section, we will suggest a methodology for distance learning based on the tele-action object.

The Growing Book

Many visionaries point at the desirability of combining the educational resources from a large number of academic institutions, thus creating a rich learning environment. Without losing sight of the individual student's needs, it is hoped that the coupling and coalition of academic institutions will constitute an ideal learning environment for the students. In some states and countries, the local government has taken the initiative to form a consortium of universities offering online courses from each institution (IVC, 1999). On the other hand, to provide an effective distributed learning environment through a consortium of institutions is not an easy task. Just to offer some courses on the Internet does not provide an effective distributed learning environment. The students can easily get confused and disoriented, if left alone on the Internet. Beneath the virtual university, there needs to be another layer, offering the students a personalized and personable learning environment.

It is for these reasons that we conceived the Growing Book project. A *growing book* is an electronic book co-developed by a group of teachers who are geographically dispersed throughout the world and collaborate in teaching and research. Since the learning materials are constantly evolving, the growing book must be frequently updated and expanded. The growing book is used by each teacher in both the local classroom and the distance learning environment. The various chapters of the growing book are owned by different teachers who may utilize and/or provide different tools for distance learning, self learning, and assessment. The growing book can be accessed in the distributed learning environment by people with different linguistic skills, cultural background and perceptual preferences for effective learning, and also can be used for teaching and research.

The objectives of developing the growing book are to: (1) share resources in developing learning materials, (2) share experiences through the teaching of a common online course on the Internet, (3) test and evaluate the distance learning and/or administration tools, and (4) discover problems and possible solutions in distance learning. The growing book is intended to support the multi-level, multi-lingual, and multi-modal usage of the shared learning materials.

a. **Multi-level usage:** The same learning materials can be organized in different ways to be used in a regular semester course, a short course, an introductory exposition, an advanced seminar and so on, and by people with different linguistic, cultural and perceptual preferences. Therefore, multi-level usage is at the heart of the growing book. To support multi-level usage of the growing book, we need a formal specification of the type of objects to be managed. We use tele-action objects to provide different level of abstractions for multi-level usage of the growing book, which will also facilitate multi-lingual and multi-modal usage of the growing book.

b. **Multi-lingual usage:** The same learning materials can be transformed into different languages so that the presentation of the growing book is multi-lingual. We associate *language translation functions* with the tele-action objects to transform the tele-action objects into different languages. We do not develop language translators in this project. Rather, commercially available language translators are used to test the concepts.

c. **Multi-modal usage:** The same learning materials can be used by physically challenged people or people with different perceptual preferences, so that the presentation of the growing book is multi-modal. We will apply *perceptual translation functions* to transform the tele-action objects into different media. Instead of attempting to handle all types of media, we concentrate on the visualization of tele-action objects and the development of gesture-oriented interface because it can be used by people with hearing disabilities and shared by people with different languages and cultures. Therefore, it only partially addresses the requirements of multi-lingual and multi modal usage. This is a necessary restriction on the scope of our research project so that the research can become more focussed in order to yield significant results.

The prototype growing book is intended as a textbook for an undergraduate course on *data structures and algorithms*. The prototype growing book has the following characteristics: (1) learning materials accessible with a browser or customized interface with common look-and-feel and common buttons, (2) common assessment tools with adjustable granularity, (3) individual tools downloadable as plug-ins, (4) common programming examples, (5) adaptive learning with embedded audio/video clips. The growing book thus facilitates collaboration in content and tools evaluation.

In the Growing Book project, *adaptability*, *scalability,* and *accessibility* are emphasized, which are driven by both the teacher and the student, so that the student feels to be actively driving her/his course like a helmsman in a motor boat, requesting explanations, special documents, homework corrections, etc. In this sense *interactivity* is a basic issue in the growing book model. We emphasize interactivity in managing all the different type of documents (images, text, video clips, audio, etc.), reflecting a teaching/learning communication model. The teacher may send multimedia documents and, without cumbersome delays, students may request explanations and other ad-hoc documents that may enrich the lecture/exercise on a real-time or semi-real-time basis. Students may utilize an interactive language, or a series of communication tools (triggered as events on specific and specified parts of the multimedia documents) that simplify their response with respect to novel concepts in a given course, retrieving extra documents from virtual libraries, or simply communicating with other students and/or other teachers. In this way there will be an enrichment with respect to the standard series of documents as when a new view is obtained with respect to the processing of a query in a given database management system.

In order to support multi-level, multi-lingual, and multi-modal usage of the growing book and to facilitate the exchange of information in a heterogeneous computing environment, a formal specification of objects and an open standard for information exchange are required.

TAOML

The formal specification of objects is based upon tele-action objects (TAOs). Each tele-action object is a dual representation (G, K) consisting of a hypergraph structure G and a knowledge structure K (Chang, 2000a). The hypergraph G is used to describe the connections and relations between the sub-TAOs, and the knowledge structure K the actions and how to synchronize the actions. A formal model called the *index cell* that combines the desirable features of finite state diagram and Petri net is used to specify the knowledge structure. The presentation of the multimedia document, the hypergraph component, and the knowledge component are specified using a tele-action object markup language (TAOML)(Chang, 1996). A multimedia development environment called MICE (multimedia IC developer's environment) supports the prototyping of multimedia applications using formal specification based upon TAOs. The front-end to this environment is a visual specification tool that allows the user to specify a TAO in a user-friendly way and that automatically converts the specification to TAOML.

TAOML has been defined as an XML application (Marmo, 1999). A DTD (*document type definition*) that contains the elements and the attributes necessary for the specification of a multimedia system described via TAOs.

We briefly review some aspects of the TAO and then we describe how they are described by the elements in TAOML. In general multimedia systems are composed of a set of elementary TAOs connected and interacting. Each TAO is obtained by constructing a hypergraph whose nodes are attached to the index cells that provide the knowledge necessary to the system to react to external events. The hypergraph contains base and composite nodes that are connected via links that describe the relations between the components nodes of the TAO. The types of available links are classified as *structural*, *temporal,* or *spatial*. Table 1 shows the correspondence between the link names and the link types.

The *attachment* link has not been inserted in the table because it is not necessary in TAOML since the attachment relation is implicitly described by the structure of the document. In other words a TAO, whose name is TAO1, which is obtained by connecting it to TAO2 and TAO3, is formally describe simply defining TAO2 and TAO3 as sub elements of TAO1. The whole multimedia system is composed of a single TAOML document, which offers a clear and efficient description of the graph structure of the TAO and of their composition in the system.

The whole system is defined via the MULTITAO element, the root element of the document, which contains the whole system. A multitao is composed of one or more TAOs, where the tag TAO defines the element that describes the real TAO. The elements called, respectively, NODEC and NODE, describe the composite nodes and the base nodes composing the TAO. To each of these

Table 1. Types of links in TAOML

Types of links in TAOML	Corresponding link names in TAO
spatial	*location*
temporal	*synchronization*
structural	*annotation* and *reference*

elements an attribute *name* of type ID has been attached. Such an attribute represents a unique identifier of the element and can be used to identify a specific TAO or a base node or a composite node by using XML xpointers, or simply the attributes of type IDREF.

The template of the TAO contains information about which nodes are involved and in which way such nodes are connected. The element TAO_TEMPLATE is used to define a template of a TAO. To be more precise, the tag: TAO_TEMPLATE defines how and which composite nodes or base nodes constitute the TAO NODEC_TEMPLATE defines how and which nodes, either composite or base node, constitute the composite node.

NODE_TEMPLATE defines which file types in the system are attached to the base node. When a TAO is built, the base nodes, which represent the different media types available in the systems such as *image, text, audio, motion_picture, video*, should be associated with a corresponding file or stream. A file with .txt or .rtf extension can be attached to a text type base node, while a .gif or .jpeg file can be attached to the image type base node. A .wav or a .ra file is attached to a sound type base node while an .avi file can be attached to a video or a movie type base node. Those file are considered non XML and can be introduced inside an XML document (FAQ) by defining an XML link of type *simple*, and instantiating the relative attributes *xlink:title*, *xlink:role*, *xlink:href*, *xlink:show* and *xlink:actuate*. In particular, the NODE_TEMPLATE element has the attribute *xlink:type* instantiated with the value *simple,* while the attribute *xlink:role* is instantiated to the type of the file (i.e., text, image, audio, video, movie) which is attached to the base node. The attributes *xlink:show* e *xlink:actuate* are used to indicate that the media type attached to the base node (i.e., image or sound) will be automatically included in the visualization as soon as the document is loaded, without the user's intervention in the same way as the IMG tag in HTML. The type of media is indicated only for the base nodes since the composite nodes of the TAO are just a combination of the several media types of the component nodes.

The element LINK describes the links of the TAO as well as the links between TAOs composing a multimedia system. In particular

- The attribute *name* defines the name of the relation between the nodes of the TAO as well as between the TAOs composing a multimedia system. This attribute specifies whether a spatial or a temporal relation exists between the nodes. For structural links, the attribute distinguishes between *annotation* and *reference* links. The *attachment* link does not require an attribute for its description because it is implicitly described by the structure of the TAOML document.

- The attribute *type* is an enumerative type and indicates the link type (structural, spatial, temporal).
- The attribute *obj* is of type IDREF and indicates the name of the TAO (composite or base node) which the links points to.
- The attribute *start* is of type IDREF and indicates the name of the TAO (composite or base node) from which the links is starting.

After the description of the nodes and the links, we still need to describe the index cells, the sensitivity and the database associated with the TAO. For such a purpose, the elements TAO_IC, TAO_SENSI and TAO_DATA have been introduced. For index cells, in particular, the following attributes have been added

- The attribute *flag*, which can be set to *old* or *new* to describe whether the cell is an existing one or if it is newly created
- The attribute *ic_type*, which specifies the index cell type
- The attribute *ic_id_list*, which contains the names of the index cells which the message is sent to
- The attributes *message_type* and *message_content*, which contain procedure calls with parameters
- The attribute *cgi_pgm*, which contains the name of the program, usually, a CGI program, to be executed when the cell is activated

For the element TAO_SENSI, the attribute *type* is designated to specify whether the object is *location_sensitive*, *time_sensitive*, *content_sensitive* or *non sensitive*. This type can be specified by the user according to the specific needs of the multimedia application.

Finally, the element TAO_DATA describes the database that can be accessed by the TAO.

To facilitate formal specification, we introduce a number of special XML tags, called the match-abstract-weave-customize (MAWC) tags (Chang, 2001). The structure is kept by the order in which the strings appear in the file, in a top-down manner. So the structure and sequence of the presentation is preserved. The same pattern will be used for the multimedia strings as well. The BNF and DTD for the TAOML language are given in Maresca, Guercio, Arndt, and Donadio (2001b).

Operations for Multi-Level Tele-Action Objects

Students, teachers and authors all need an interactive language built upon some basic operations (triggered as events on specific and specified parts of the multimedia documents) that simplify their response with respect to novel concepts in a given course, retrieving extra documents from virtual libraries, or simply communicating with other students and/or other teachers. In this way there may be an enrichment with respect to a standard series of documents as when a new view is obtained with respect to the processing of a query in a given database management system.

The basic operations are divided into several groups.

a. **Operations for multi-level, multimedia customization:** The first group of operations support the matching, abstraction, weaving, and customization of multimedia documents. These are called MAWC operations.

b. **Operations for increasing/updating awareness:** The user can specify an awareness vector, so that he/she can be informed about certain events. The awareness vector is a binary vector where each entry indicates the absence/presence of an awareness attribute. For example, the awareness vector can be (1,0,1,1,0), indicating the user wants to be aware of any changes in fellow students (1st entry), domain experts (2nd entry), centers of excellence (3rd entry), references (4th entry) and tools (5th entry). A user can also set privacy, so that he or she is not included in any awareness information.

c. **Operations for communication:** Communication operations are for sending messages to authors, teachers, and fellow students. A user may not know their exact names and/or e-mail addresses, but he or she still can send messages to the group of people he or she wants to communicate with.

d. **Operations for watermarking:** Watermarks can be added or displayed for a multimedia document, including text document.

e. **Operations for managing the growing book:** There are many operations for gathering statistics and managing the growing book.

The previously described operations can be implemented as commands for the customized IC manager (Chang, 1996) of the growing book. When the user submits a command to the growing book, the customized IC manager processes this command. The command consists of a name and its parameters. The command name is treated as a message type by the IC manager to be passed on, together with the parameters, to the appropriate IC for processing. The growing book operations are implemented as "actions" (C programs) of the ICs managed by the IC manager.

Related Research on Multimedia for Distance Learning

Many researchers have begun investigating how multimedia can be used to help improve the distance learning experience. Schär and Krueger (2001) list multimedia didactic among the five major aspects to be considered when developing computer-aided learning tools since it allows knowledge to be represented in different ways according to different criteria — media characteristics, cognitive models, or according to classifications of the learning content. This observation points out the importance of XML since separation of content from presentation is one of its key features. Multimedia can also support interactive and collaborative learning in a distance-learning environment. Constantini and Toinard (2001) present a distributed building site metaphor that provides distribution services for sharing a virtual world and enables different collaboration styles. An instructor can introduce a virtual scene that represents the learning subject. Users interact with each other by modifying, annotating, and sharing the virtual scene. Unlike this approach, our approach supports a number of different learning metaphors. Both El Saddik, Fischer, and Steinmetz, (2001) and Megzari and colleagues make use of metadata to support their work on multimedia for distance learning. Megzari extends IEEE learning object metadata in order to realize a component-based architecture for reusability. Dynamic metadata to support interactive visualizations were added to IEEE-LOM. In an experimental lesson visualizing the Ethernet protocol five components representing the Ethernet were implemented as Java Beans. The lesson was composed of the five components enhanced with the dynamic metadata. Mezdari adopts a new metadata model based on actors and their roles (learners, authors, or service providers), actions for metadata and metadata structures. The metadata structures are based on IEEE-LOM with an extension for digital media. After the metadata has been generated it is stored in a courseware database server. Media objects are stored in a multimedia content database. A document architecture for multimedia documents is described as is a run-time environment for choosing and presenting multimedia courseware based on the needs of the students. Our approach shares the component-based philosophy of El Saddik et al. (2001) along with the use of metadata to describe the distance learning materials. If it differs from El Saddik et al. (2001) in supporting reactivity to user and external events due to the Active Index component of the TAOs (see next section). It also differs from these approaches in explicitly supporting various presentation styles via TAOML transformations. An example of how distance learning materials can be transformed is given by Day, Liu, and Hsu (2001). They present an automated authoring method based on a formal specification for dynamically generating ISO DSSSL document styles. Whereas our approach uses XML to store distance learning content, they use SGML. XML is an extended subset of SGML. DSSSL resembles the XSLT and XSL we use in our work. They concentrate on transforming existing storage-based product documents into large-scale presentation-based product training manuals. Arcelli and De Santo (2002) describe a multimedia distributed learning system developed using Java in an Intranet environment. An innovative aspect of this research is the use of intelligent software agents able to adapt to changing network conditions and to meet the users' communication needs. The work concentrates more on the communication aspects than on semantic aspects of multimedia applications, which is the reverse of our focus. Another work concentrating on communication concerns for multimedia distance learning is by Fernández et al. (2000) experimented with a variety of multimedia distance learning applications running over an IPv6/ATM-based broadband network. A number of applications were adapted to work over IPv6 and to allow users to control the QoS. Deshpande and Hwang (2001) developed a set of tools to allow recording of live classroom sessions and the automatic creation of a synchronized multimedia integration language (SMIL) presentation for later viewing. Since SMIL is an XML-based language, it can easily be translated into TAOML using the transformation techniques presented later in this chapter. This would allow such a set of tools to be used as a front end for our system.

TAOML Dataflow Transformation Process

In section 1, we described the TAOML environment architecture. In this section, we will describe a scenario in which it will be possible to use such an architecture. Specifically, among the entire possible scenarios, two have been identified corresponding to the usage mode of the dataflow transformation: stand-alone or distributed. In the stand-alone scenario, the main dataflow transformation process is local. The stand-alone PC or workstation loads the TAOML/XSLT engine and delivers a combination of the style sheet and the source information to be transformed on the same platform. The results are various media formatted as requested by the user (e.g., PDA format, video format, audio format, etc.).

In the distributed scenario, the dataflow transformation main process is distributed: the server can distribute the TAOML/XSLT engine and provides a transformation process to the clients that require it.

The client forwards the TAOML document to the TAO_XSLT server or an equivalent generic dataflow; furthermore it also requests data transformation and specifies the desired output data format. The server loads the TAO_XSLT processor and delivers a combination of the style sheet and the source data to be transformed to the recipient's platform. In the distributed scenario it is possible to use of style sheet document and TAO_XSLT transformation not only for receiving a desired media format, but also possibly to receive a data flow properly formatted for some other distributed system such as a wireless application protocol terminal, personal digital assistant terminal, and so forth. The following figure describes the TAOML dataflow transformation process in a distributed scenario.

The TAOML dataflow transformation process is composed of two main subprocesses, described in the following figure.

The first sub-process called "Generic stream to XML-TAOML transformer" implements the extraction of the semantic contents and outputs a TAOML document. The following functional blocks compose it

Figure 2. TAOML-based dataflow transformation process: Distributed scenario

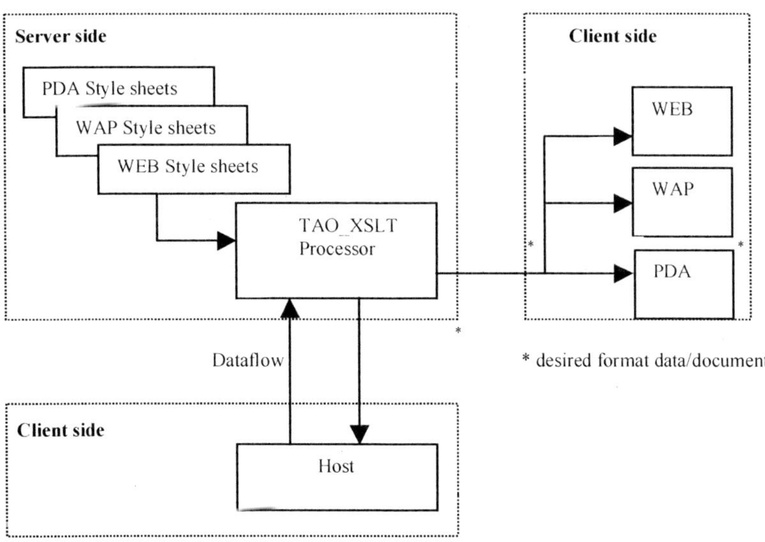

Figure 3. TAOML-based dataflow transformation process: Architecture

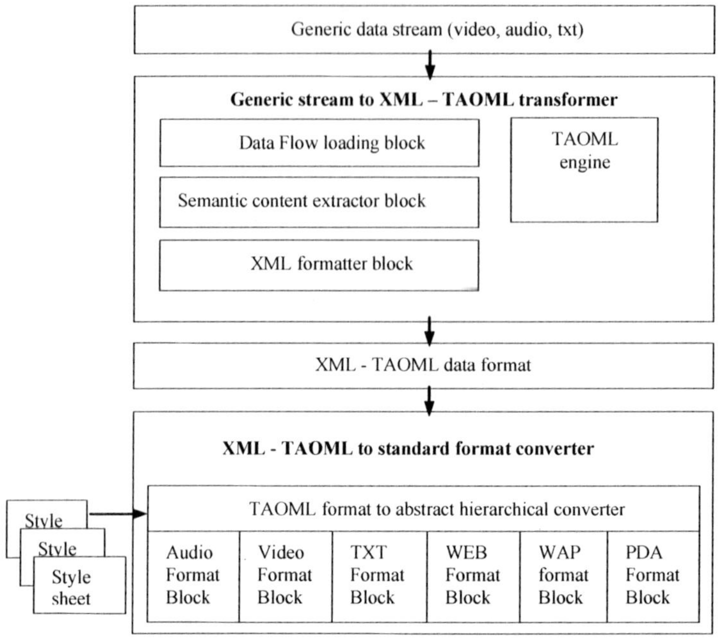

- **Data flow loading block:** Loads the generic data stream from a generic source
- **Semantic content extractor block:** Parses the generic data source and extracts from it the valid semantic content
- **XML formatter block:** Loads the semantic content retrieved in the previous step and writes it in a well-formed TAOML format
- **TAOML engine:** Provides the document manipulation that satisfies the requirements described in the TAO standard

The following functional blocks compose the second sub-process, called "XML-TAOML to standard format converter":

- TAOML format to abstract hierarchical converter, which transforms the document from the XML format to an application-independent representation of it
- Several functional blocks that depend on the data format desired in output

Growing Book Customization by Dataflow Transformation

The growing book is intended to support multi-level, multi-lingual, and multi-modal usage of shared learning material. This goal is fully supported by the decision to use XML to represent the TAOs comprising the growing book since the XML approach separates content from presentation (Bray et al., 1998; Bosak & Bray, 1999). We propose to customize the growing book using a tele-action object transformer based on XML technology by applying a component-based multimedia software engineering approach (Agresti, 1986). We propose a complete process of dataflow transformation that presents the growing book in different ways and at different levels of abstraction. The tele-action objects comprising the growing book can also be transformed to conform to summary and awareness information collected during a distance learning session. The tele-action object transformer is implemented using the XSLT transformation language, XSL style sheets, and the SAX API Java parser. In the context of this research, the output of the tele-action object transformer will be a sentient map. The main idea of the sentient map (Chang, 2000b) is to present all kind of objects visually in a virtual map that can sense the user's input gestures and react by retrieving and presenting the appropriate information. We use the term "map" here in the general sense. Geographical maps, directory pages, list of 3D models, Web pages, documents, slides, images, video clips, etc. are all considered maps, as they all may serve as indexes and lead the user to more information. In practice, a sentient map is a gesture-enhanced interface for an information system. In advanced distance learning applications, students and instructors can use the sentient map environment in a virtual course-room. When the user, or the user's surrogate (the user's avatar), points at the sentient map on the wall, more information becomes available and is also visible to all the participants in the virtual course-room.

Two scenarios have been identified corresponding to the usage mode of the dataflow transformation: stand-alone or distributed. In the stand-alone scenario, the main dataflow transformation process is local. The stand-alone PC or workstation loads the tele-action object transformer and delivers a combination of the style sheet and the growing book information to be transformed on the same platform. The results are various media formatted as requested by the user (e.g., video format, audio format, text format, etc.) and transformed in accordance with the collected summary and awareness information. In the distributed scenario, the dataflow transformation main process is distributed: the server can distribute the tele-action object transformer and provides a transformation process to the clients that require it.

The client forwards the TAOML document to the tele-action object transformer or an equivalent generic dataflow; furthermore it also requests data transformation and specifies the desired output data format. The server loads the tele-action object transformer and delivers a combination of the style sheet and the source data to be transformed to the recipient's platform. In the distributed scenario it is possible to use of style sheet document and tele-action object transformer transformation not only for receiving a desired presentation format, but also possibly to receive a data flow properly formatted for some other distributed system such as a wireless application protocol terminal, personal digital assistant terminal, and so on

The dataflow transformation process is shown in the Figure 4. Note that the main components of the tele-action object transformer are shown inside of the transformer itself. Another advantage of the use of XML is also illustrated in the figure — we have adopted the IEEE LOM (learning object metadata) (IEEE, 1998) which is an evolving standard for metadata for learning objects as the

Figure 4. Dataflow transformation for the growing book

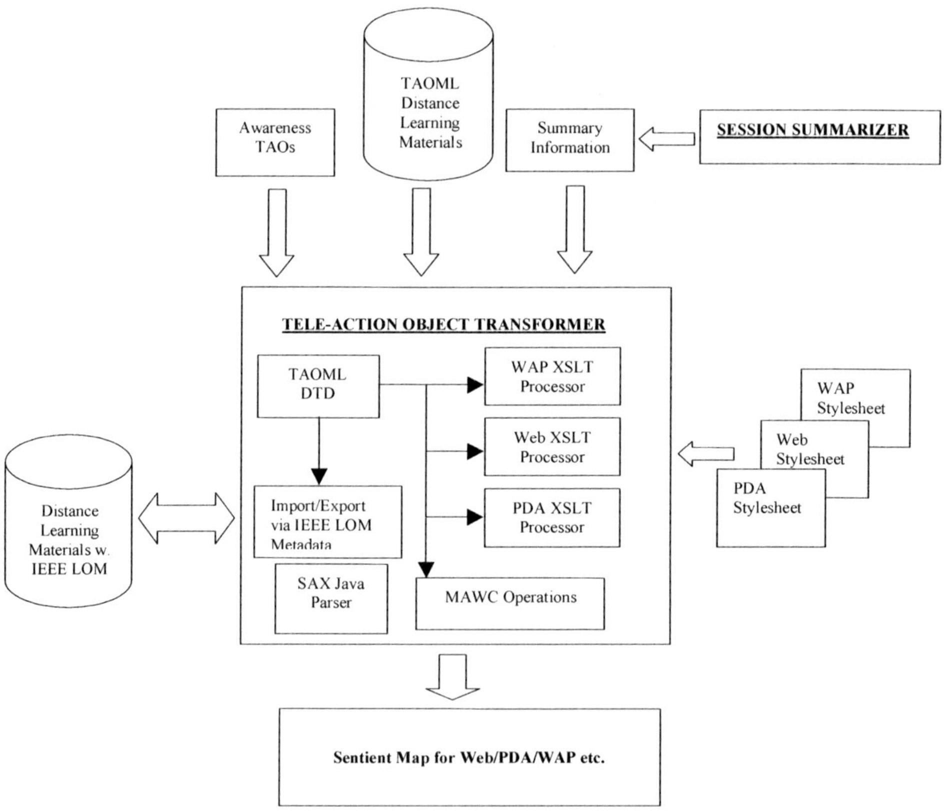

metadata format for TAOs. This makes our approach interoperable with other distance learning systems and allows us to reuse learning resources produced in preceding decades by universities, schools, research institutions, and companies.

A Prototype System for Dataflow Transformation

In this section, we will illustrate first a complete process for dataflow transformation in component-based multimedia software engineering, and second our experience gained in implementing and experimenting with a complete Java-based prototype called TAOML_T.

The process for generic TAOML-based data stream manipulation is principally composed of two main transformations

- Transformation from a generic data format (not necessarily hierarchically organized) to a well-formed XML/TAOML format
- Transformation from XML/TAOML format to a document format (e.g., text, Microsoft Word, PDF, html, etc.) or a media format (e.g., audio, video)

The prototype developed reflects this organization. The modular approach adopted allows us to obtain a standard document format in a modular prototype that can be reused or extended in a very easy way in other similar Java-based applications.

The main driver of "Transformation from generic data format to well-formed XML/TAOML format" is the SAX API validating Java parser (Mordani, 2001). It parses an input data stream and prints it out in XML format; moreover, it generates events that correspond to different features found in the parsed XML document. In this context, the SAX API Java parser is superior to the DOM API Java parser (Mordani, 2001) in many aspects of runtime performance. The SAX API parser used in this prototype is the Java-based open-source tool called Xerces produced by the open-source Apache XML project team (Apache).

The main driver of "Transformation from XML/TAOML format to document or media format" is the XSLT processor. The XSLT processor reads in both the XML document and the XSLT style sheet. The XSLT style sheet describes a set of patterns to match within the XML document and the transformations to apply when a match is found. Pattern matches are described in terms of the tags and attributes for elements found within an XML document. Transformations extract information from the XML document and format it into a desired format. Each match-transformation pair is called an XSLT template.

The XSLT transformation process works in a way very analogous to the way scripting languages such as Python or Perl operate — applying regular expressions to an input stream and then transforming the elements that were found to an output stream. In that sense XSLT could really be called a scripting language, especially since it contains control flow elements similar to a scripting language.

The XSLT processor used in this prototype is an excellent Java-based, open-source tool called Xalan, a product of the Apache XML project previously cited (Apache).

The following figure explains the entire component-based structure of the dataflow transformer prototype. Two main layers compose the TAOML_T prototype architecture

- The graphic user interface (GUI) layer that represents the human-machine interface of the prototype.

Figure 5. Dataflow transformation process: Prototype architecture

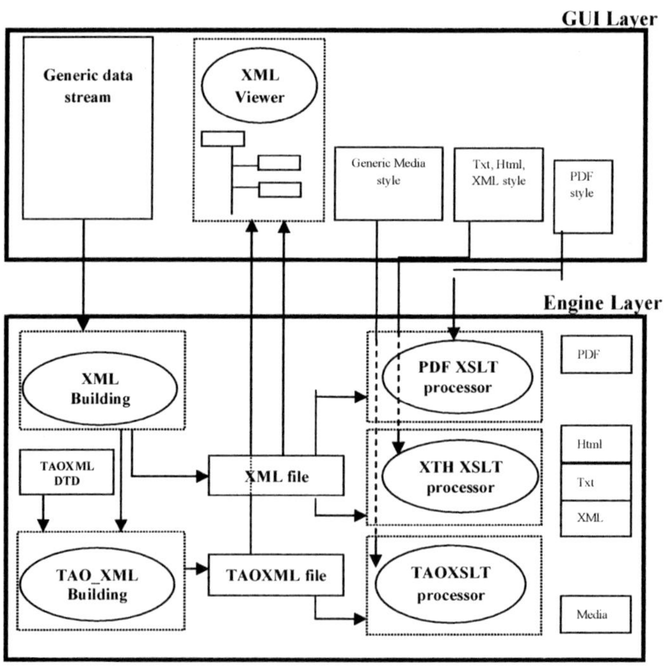

- The engine layer that represents the core of the prototype.
- The first component, called "XML building" implements the "Generic stream to XML transformer," described in the "Dataflow transformation process" section. This mechanism builds an XML file (well formed) from a generic data flow. This mechanism is based on the Xerces SAX API Java parser.
- The second component, called "TAOML building" implements part of the "TAOML engine," described in the "Dataflow transformation process" section above. This mechanism builds a TAOML file (well formed) from the corresponding TAO DTD file and the XML file produced in the preceding step.
- The third component, defined at the GUI level, is called "XML viewer." It implements an XML display that shows the hierarchic objects of an XML file. It uses a DOM Parser that analyses XML tags and converts the file into a hierarchic tree representation.
- The fourth component, called "PDF XSLT processor," implements a part of "XML format to abstract hierarchical converter" and the "PDF format Block" described in the "Dataflow transformation process" section above. It implements the sub layer strictly dependent on the PDF format desired.

Figure 6. An example of output obtained with the TAOML CBSE based prototype

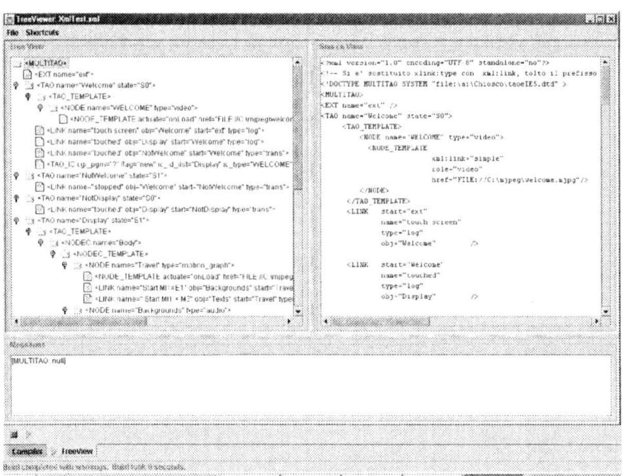

It uses an independent XSLT processor that transforms XML format into PDF format in two steps

- The first step transforms XML format into intermediate format object (FO) representation
- The second step, transforms the FO representation into PDF format.

The implementation of this component is based on the FOP routine, a print formatter driven by XSL formatted objects. It is a Java application that reads a formatting object tree and then turns it into a PDF document. The formatted object tree can be in the form of an XML document (the output of the XSLT Xalan engine) or can be passed in memory as a DOM document or Sax events. FOP is a part of the Apache project.

- The fifth component, called "THX XSLT" processor implements a part of the "XML format to Abstract hierarchical converter," and the Html, Txt, XML format blocks described in the "Dataflow transformation process" section above. It provides a common API sub layer, independent from document formats and a specific sub layer strictly dependent on the format of the desired document. It uses the XSL style sheets previously defined and an XSLT engine. The implementation of this component is based on XML Parser and XSL Processor provided by EZ/X routines. EZ/X is a collection of fast, highly conformant, and easy to use XML foundation technologies.
- The sixth component called "TAOXSLT processor" implements part of the TAOML engine described in the "Dataflow transformation process" section above. It realizes a sub layer strictly dependent on the media format desired in output and uses the XSL style sheet previously defined. The TAOXSLT processor works in conjunction with the desired media style sheet and loads and synchronizes the desired media across the XSL script commands.

The prototype, completely developed in the Java language, is under experimentation and is an example of how is possible to transform a generic multimedia data flow into an XML format. The XML_TAO format can be considered a specific case of this transformation. Moreover using the TAOXSLT processor it is possible to define a desired media output as a generic XSLT.

Conclusion and Future Research

In this chapter, we have shown the design and the implementation of complex multimedia software systems, like dataflow transformation mechanisms, with a component-based software engineering approach. We have also introduced our methodology for distance learning based on TAOs and the growing book. TAOs support multimedia courseware and can be integrated with distance learning courseware developed under other paradigms through the metadata capabilities provided by XML. The growing book supports multi-lingual, multi-modal, and multi-level learning. These methodologies are currently being used on an experimental basis by the University of Naples, Cleveland State University, and Kent State University. The approach followed in producing the multimedia courseware is component-based multimedia software engineering. Following this approach, existing components have been reused and/or adapted to produce the multimedia courseware in diverse contexts, aided by the metadata which has been added to the legacy media objects and courseware where necessary. The fact that the students are using a metadata enhanced TAO system is completely transparent, since they see only the final product in the form of HTML. Since the final product is HTML, the students gain much flexibility in their choice of hardware/software platform.

The goals of the authors were to emphasize the following main aspects

- Interoperability of a standard process based on a standard language for metadata: TAOML, defined using the XML language and a DTD
- Reusability of the entire system due to the CBSE approach
- Reuse of the XML paradigms in the TAOML environment
- Dataflow transformation for the growing book

The authors have also implemented a Java-based prototype named TAOML_T that demonstrates the main functions of the data flow transformer implemented in terms of TAOML basic functions. The prototype is currently under experimentation.

The authors are planning a future development to extend the component-based multimedia software engineering approach to the CORBA environment. In particular, we'll be transforming the TAO multimedia application into metadata in order to have a more portable platform in which to represent multimedia educational material so that it can be transferred on a CORBA channel in a completely secure client-server application. This activity can enable us to reuse a lot of material coming from different universities and with different formats.

We are currently working on converting distance learning courseware developed under other paradigms into the TAOML framework as well as the reverse process. This work is supported by the continuing development of XSLT (Kay, 2000), which effectively supports the manipulation, and transformation of XML data.

Acknowledgments

This work has been developed with funds provided by MURST as part of the "Progetti Cluster," Cluster 16: Multimedialità.

References

Agresti, W. W. (1986). *New paradigms for software development.* Washington, DC: IEEE Computer Society Press.

Ahmed, K., Ancha, S., Cioroianu, A., Cousins, J., Crosbie, J., Davies, J., et al. (2001). *Professional Java XML.* Birmingham, UK: Wrox Press.

Apache Project Web site. (n.d.). Retrieved from http://www.apache.org

Arcelli, F., & De Santo, M. (2002). Multimedia distributed learning environments: Evolution towards intelligent communications. *Multimedia Tools and Applications, 16*(3), 187-206.

Arndt, T., Guercio, A., & Chang, S. K. (1998). Visual tools for a Multimedia IC Development Environment (MICE). *Proceedings 1998 IEEE Symposium on Visual Languages.*

Arndt, T., Guercio, A., & Chang, S. K. (1999, June 17-19). Formal specification and prototyping of multimedia applications. *Proceedings of SEKE '99*, Germany.

Arndt, T., Guercio, A., & Chang, S. K. (2000). Formal specification and prototyping of multimedia applications. *International Journal of Software Engineering and Knowledge Engineering, 10*(4), 377-409.

Booch, G., Jacobson, I., & Rumbaugh (2000). *Rational unified process with UML.* Reading, MA: Addison Wesley.

Bosak, J., & Bray, T. (1999, May). XML and the second-generation Web. *Scientific American, 280*(5), 89-93.

Bray, T., Paoli, J., & Sperberg-McQueen, C. M. (1998, February 10). *Extensible markup language (XML) 1.0*. W3C Recommendation 10. Retrieved from http://www.w3.org/TR/1998/REC-xml-19980210

Chang, H., Chang, S. K., Hou, T., & Hsu, A. (1995a). The management and applications of tele-action objects. *ACM Journal of Multimedia Systems, 3*(5-6), 204-216.

Chang, S. K. (1995b). Towards a theory of active index. *Journal of Visual Languages and Computing, 6*(1), 101-118.

Chang, S. K. (1996). Extending visual languages for multimedia. *IEEE Multimedia, 3*(3), 18-26.

Chang, S. K. (2000a, October). Multimedia software engineering. The *24th IEEE Computer Software and Application Conference (Compsac 2000)*.

Chang, S. K. (2000b, August). The sentient map. *Journal of Visual Languages and Computing, 11*(4), 455-474.

Chang, S. K. (2001). MAWC operations for the growing book. In M. Tucci (Ed.), *Proceedings of the 2nd Workshop on Multimedia Databases and Image Communication (MDIC 2001)* (LNCS 2184, pp. 3-15). Berlin; Heidelberg, Germany: Springer-Verlag.

Chang, S. K., & Ho, C. S. (1989, February). Knowledge tables as a unified knowledge representation for office information system design. *IEEE TC on Office Automation Newsletter, 3*(1), 12-25.

Chang, S. K., Tortora, G., Yu, B., & Guercio, A. (1987). Icon purity—toward a formal theory of icons. *International Journal of Pattern Recognition and Artificial Intelligence, 1*(3&4), 377-392.

Constantini, F., & Toinard, C. (2001, July-September). Collaborative learning with the distributed building site metaphor. *IEEE Multimedia, 8*(3), 21-29.

Day, Y. F., Liu, P., & Hsu, L. H. (2001, July-September). Transforming large-scale product documentation into multimedia training manuals. *IEEE Multimedia, 8*(3), 39-45.

Deshpande, S. G., & Hwang, J. N. (2001, December). A real-time interactive virtual classroom multimedia distance learning system. *IEEE Transactions on Multimedia, 3*(4), 432-444.

El Saddik, A., Fischer, S., & Steinmetz, R. (2001, July-September). Reusable multimedia content in Web-based learning systems. *IEEE Multimedia, 3*(4), 30-38.

Fernández, D., García, A. B., Larrabeiti, D., Azcorra, A., Pacyna, P., & Papir, Z. (2000, July-September). Multimedia services for distant work and education in an IP/ATM environment. *IEEE Multimedia,* 68-77.

Ferrandez, T. (1998). *Development and testing of a standardized format for distributed learning assessment and evaluation using XML*. MS thesis, Department of Electrical and Computer Engineering, University of Central Florida.

Graziano, A., Maresca, P., & Russo, S. (2000, September 5-7). Experience with the GESTALT online learning support system. *Proceedings of the 26th EUROMICRO Conference,* Maastricht, The Netherlands (pp. 86-93).

Harasim, L. (1999, September). A framework for online learning: The virtual–U. *Computer*, *9*(32), 44-49.

Holmes, W. N. (1999, September). The myth of the educational computer. *Computer*, *9*(32), 36-42.

IEEE LTSC Draft Document. (1998, December 14). *Learning object metadata* (Vol. 2.5).

Illinois Virtual Campus. (1999). Retrieved from http://www.ivc.illinois.edu

IMS Global Learning Consortium, Inc. (2006). Retrieved from http://www.imsproject.org/background.html

Kay, M. (2000). *XSLT: Programmer's reference*. Birmingham, UK: Wrox Press.

Kouzes, R. T., Myers, J. D., & Wulf, W. A. (1996, August). Collaboratories: Doing science on the Internet. *Computer*, *29*(8), 40-46.

Krutchen, P. (2001). *Rational unified process*. Reading, MA: Addison Wesley.

MACROU. (n.d.). *Macro University*. Retrieved from http://www.cs.pitt.edu/~chang/cpdis/macro-u.html

Maresca, P. (2000, May 4-6). Collaboration environment: le nuove tecnologie multimediali per la didattica. *Atti del Congresso Didamatica 2000,* Cesena (pp. 258-266).

Maresca, P., Arndt, T., & Guercio, A. (2001a). Unifying distance-learning resources: The metadata approach. *Journal of Computers*, *13*(2), 60-76.

Maresca, P., & Guercio, M. (2000a, September 14). Multimedia software engineering collaboratory. *Workshop on Multimedia Computing on the World Wide Web in IEEE Conference on Visual Languages*, Seattle, WA.

Maresca, P., & Guercio, A. (2000b, July 23-26). Logical approach for the construction of tools for multimedia representation and simplification. *World Multiconference on Systemic, Cybernetics and Informatics,* Orlando, FL (pp. 701-706).

Maresca, P., Guercio, A., Arndt, T., & Donadio, P. (2001b). Transformation dataflow in multimedia software engineering using TAO_XML: A component-based approach. In M. Tucci (Ed.), *Multimedia databases and image communication* (LNCS 2184, pp. 77-89). Berlin; Heidelberg, Germany: Springer.

Marmo, C. (1999). *Un linguaggio XML-based per i tele-action object: Progettazione e Realizzazione di un Ambiente TAOXML.* Laurea degree thesis, Università degli studi di Napoli and Università degli studi di Salerno.

Megzari, O., Yuan, L., & Karmouch, A. (2002). Meta-data and media management in a multimedia interactive telelearning system. *Multimedia Tools and Applications, 16*(1), 137-160.

Mordani, R. (2001). *Java API for XML Processing.* Sun Microsystems.

Numaker, F. (1999). Collaborative computing: The next millennium. *Computer, 32*(9), 66-71.

Schär, S. G., & Krueger, H. (2001, July-September). Using new learning technologies with multimedia. *IEEE Multimedia, 8*(3), 40-51.

Stevens, G. H., & Stevens E. F. (1995). *Designing electronic performance support tools.* Englewood Cliffs, NJ: Educational Technology Publications.

Taylor, D. A. (1990). *Object oriented technology: A manager's guide.* Reading, MA: Addison-Wesley.

Chapter VII

Open Multi-Agent Systems for Collaborative Web-Based Learning

Hongen Lu, La Trobe University, Australia

Abstract

Web-based learning plays an important role in modern teaching environment. Many Web based tools are becoming available on this huge marketplace. Agent technology contributes substantially to this achievement. One of the fundamental problems facing both students and education services providers is how to locate and integrate these valuable services in such a dynamic environment. In this chapter, I present mediator-based architecture to build open multi-agent applications for e-learning. An agent services description language is presented to enable services advertising and collaboration. The language exploits ontology of service domain, and provides the flexibility for developers to plug in any suitable constraint languages. Multiple matchmaking strategies based on agent service ontology are given to help agents finding appropriate service providers. The series of strategies consider various features of service providers, the nature of requirements, and more importantly the relationships among services.

Introduction

The World Wide Web has the largest collection of knowledge ever in man kind history. It is one of the most important resources in modern education. With the success of search engines, such as Google, and the vast acceptance of online learning systems, such as WebCT, students and teachers can search text and images efficiently. These tools are changing our learning process in schools and universities all over the world everyday. However, the Web has not reached its full potential. At its early stage, the Web is solely a huge collection of digital information. Nowadays, it is evolving into a huge growing marketplace for information providers and consumers. Agent technology makes a substantial contribution to this achievement.

However, how to find information providers and how to integrate information agents in such an open environment are new challenges. Information agents, such as Ahoy (Shakes, Langheinrich, & Etzioni, 1997), ShopBot (Doorenbos, Etzioni, & Weld, 1997), and SportsFinder (Lu, Sterling, & Wyatt, 1999) are programs that assist people to find specific information from the Web. They are information service providers, which have the capabilities to find information for users, for example locating a person's homepage, finding the cheapest available prices for music CDs, or finding sports results of a team or a player. For a novice user, a challenge is how to find these services; for an information agent, the challenges are how to locate the service providers, and how to communicate with them to solve its tasks cooperatively. This is one of the basic problems facing designers of open, multi-agent systems for the Internet is the connection problem — finding the other agents who might have the information or other capabilities that you need (Decker, Sycara, & Williamson, 1996).

In Genesereth and Ketchpel (1994), two basic approaches to this connection problem are distinguished: direct communication, in which agents handle their own coordination and assisted coordination, in which agents rely on special system programs to achieve coordination. However, in the Web application domain, where new agents might come into existence or existing agents might disappear at any time, only the latter approach promises the adaptability required to cope with the dynamic changes in the environment.

Related Works

Ontology

Ontologies are content theories about objects, their properties, and relationships among them that are possible in a specific domain of knowledge (Chandrasekaran, Josephson, & Benjamins, 1999). In a given domain, its ontology clarifies the structure of knowledge in the domain. It forms the heart of any system of knowledge representation for that domain. Without ontology, or the formal conceptualisations, there cannot be any vocabulary for representing knowledge, let alone automatic knowledge reasoning and inference. Ontology gives the terms used in a certain domain, as well as their relationships, so that we can use these terms provided to assert specific propositions about a situation. For example, in computer science education domain, we can represent a fact about a specific unit: unit SCC303, Software Engineering, is a third year undergraduate unit, where SCC303 is an instance of the concept unit. Once we have the basis for representing propositions, we can also represent more advanced knowledge, such as hypothesise, believe, expect, etc. Thus, we can construct domain ontology step by step to describe the world.

Web Service Description Languages

Web services are Web accessible programs and devices that not only provide information to a user, but to enable a user to effect change in the world. Web services are among the most important resources on the Web, and they are garnering a great deal of interest from industry. Many emerging standards are being developed for low-level descriptions of Web services.

- **WSDL:** Web service description language provides a communication level description of the messages and protocols used by a Web service. WSDL is an XML format for describing network services as a set of endpoints operating on messages containing either document-oriented or procedure-oriented information. The operations and messages are described in abstract, and then bound to a concrete network protocol and message format to define an endpoint. Related concrete endpoints are combined into abstract endpoints (services). WSDL is extensible to allow description of endpoints and their messages regardless of what message formats or network protocols are used to communicate

- **Semantic Web:** The huge collection of information on the Web is fare beyond a person's ability to search and index. So machine-understandable data is a high priority to automatic processing online information. Semantic Web is a step to define and link data on the Web in a way that it can be used by machines not just for display purposes, but for automation, integration and reuse of data across various applications

WebCT

WebCT is one of the leading online education tools. It provides teachers a powerful and convenient way to build up Web sites dedicated to publishing teaching materials for their subjects; meanwhile it is also a place for students to feedback their progress. No wonder WebCT is widely accepted in various levels of education institutes, especially for long distance learning. However, WebCT is a closed system. It can only let the teachers and students in the same university or in the same class to communicate each other. In this point of view, WebCT has not taken the full advantage of the World Wide Web, which now is a fast growing collection of services. WebCT is still based on the conventional client-server architecture. While the Web offers more flexible options, for example everyone on the Web could be an information provider and consumer at the same time. Peer-to-peer communication is becoming the mainstream of online publishing and marketing. I believe this is the future trend for online education, because in such architecture teachers and students can easily swap their roles and learn from each other. In addition, this architecture is open for everyone to join in.

Mediator-Based Architecture

I present a mediator-based middle agent architecture for agent services advertising and requesting. The architecture is given in Figure 1. A possible solution is a software mediator. A mediator is a software module that exploits encoded knowledge about some sets or subsets of data to create information for a higher layer of applications (Wiederhold, 1992). In Dao and Perry (1996), a mediator is an information producing or serving entity in a large-scale networked environment.

A mediator is a special kind of information agent acting as middle man to take as input, a request to find an agent that provides a service, and returns as output, a list of such agents and their cooperation relationships. A mediator also stores

Figure 1. Mediator-based architecture

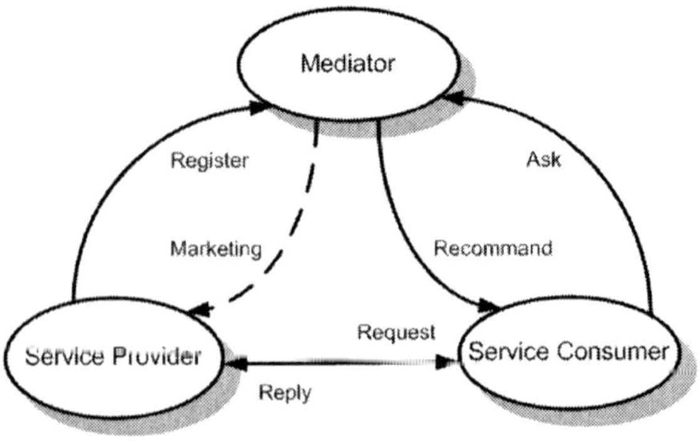

the services offered by different agents in the existing environment, and when a new agent is introduced into the environment it can register its capability to the mediator, using an agent service description language, if this agent wants its service to be used by others. Information agents also can unregister their services to the mediator when they want to quit the cooperation or exit. Also when an information agent receives a query or a subtask within a query that can not be solved by itself, it can request the mediator to find out other agents that have the capability or a set of agents who can work cooperatively to provide that service.

Agent Services Ontology

Since information agents are developed geographically and dispersed over the Web, their capabilities are different from each other. SportsFinder (Lu, Sterling, & Wyatt, 1999) can find the sports results of golf, cycling, football, and basketball etc. for users; while Ahoy (Shakes, Langheinrich, & Etzioni, 1997) is good at locating people's homepages. However considering in an application domain, such as computer science subjects, there exist a hierarchical relationships among these information agents. For example, information agent A can answer students' queries about software engineering, while agent B is only capable of consulting on Risk Analysis, which is a part of the subject of software engineering; in this case the service agent B can provide is a subset of agent A.

Following are the relationships among services

- **Identical service:** This means the two services can provide the same function in spite of the fact that they may have different service names. As we know, information agents are being built over the Web using different programming languages and architecture. It is no surprised to have two agents running on different hosts that can offer the same service. Obviously, two identical services can substitute each other.
- **Subservice:** This relationship characterises two services offered by agents, in which one service's function is only a part of another. For instance, an expert on C/C++ programming is good at tutoring lab project on object oriented design in software engineering unit; but he/she may not capable at formal methods in the same unit. In this point of view, the service offered by a tutor on C/C++, is only a part of a lecturer on the whole subject.
- **Substitute service:** From the previous description, we know that identical service and subservice are two special cases of substitute service relationship. But the difference is that identical services can substitute each other, while the subservice can only be alternated by its "parent" service, not vice versa.
- **Partial substitute service:** This relationship describes two services that have some common subservices. In some circumstances, partial substitute services can be alternated with each other, such as where the service agent is offering, just by chance, the common subservice with its partial substitute service, that is, the agent is not offering its full service to others at the moment.
- **Reciprocal service:** If two services are reciprocal, that means they have no subservices in common, but they can work together to offer a "bigger" service. From this definition, we know that in case there is no current agent available to provide the "bigger" service, these two reciprocal services can cooperate as a single agent for this task. This gives us a message that by combining the current agents in a different manner, we can tailor the system to meet new requirements.

Agent service ontology gives a formal method to describe the relationships among agent services. Agent service ontology contains all the services of information agents as well as their relationships. Basically, a directed cyclic graph (DCG) is able to present the relations between agent services. The nodes in the graph present the services, and the edges are labelled with the service relationships. In Figure 2, a fragment of the ontology on computer science subjects is given, in sense of the content of the topic and their relationships.

Figure 2. Fragment of computer science subjects ontology

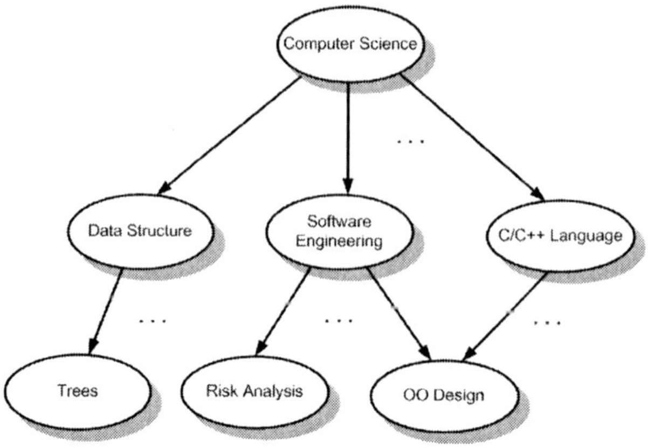

Mediating Agent Services on the Web

Mediating is a process that utilises the knowledge on service domain to introduce service providers and consumers. Mediating is a high-level services matching and brokerage, in terms of level of knowledge applied, and directions of information flow.

First of all, why do we need to mediate agent services on the Web? Let us look at the vast diversity of services that can be provided by agents all over the Web. Services are different in many aspects; I just name a few in the following

- **Function:** It is obvious to note that different services have different functions. A sports agent has a totally different function to a shopping agent.
- **Constraints:** Even agents with the same function may impose different constraints on their input, output and input-output. For example, two lecturers both can be tutors on the subject, data structure and algorithms, but one can only answer C questions, while the other is good at Java. In spite that they are able to consult on the same assignment question, but they require it in their capable language.
- **Quality and privacy:** Quality and privacy are also varied from agent to agent, since they are run on different machines. Even when agents have the

same function, due to the different implementations of the function, the qualities of their services may vary.

- **Names:** Agents may have different names despite the fact that they can provide the same service and have the same constraints and quality and privacy values.

The reasons that cause so many differences among agent services are mainly because of the open feature of the environment. Agents are developed over the Internet with heterogeneous architecture, and their functions vary from one to another.

Due to diversity of agents, the requests of services are also various. In most cases, we can not expect that for a service request there is at least one agent to exactly provide that service, even through we suppose the service advertisement and request can fully express what the services are. In fact, a single agent can not have a global view of the whole system, it is not practical to do that, its request of service is also limited by the agent's "partial" knowledge of the environment.

Multiple Strategies for Services Matching

Type Matching

This is the simplest strategy that only matches the types in the input and output fields of service advertisements against the correspondent field in requirements. It makes sure that a provider can take the inputs of requester, and its outputs are compatible with the requester's.

Constraint Matching

Constraint matching considers the constraint parts in agent service descriptions. Since all the constraints are given in constraint-language, the details of substitution depend on the constraint-language. For the above two strategies, it is straightforward to design algorithms to check all the relevant variables and constraints.

Partial Matching

Partial match is a combination of type match and constraint match, but both loose a little bit. This strategy aims at services that are not completely matched, but have some functions in common. Partial matching means for two capability descriptions, if some of their input, output variables have subtype relations, and there are constraint clauses in their input and output constraint specifications that can be substituted, these two services are partial matched. Semantically, in some circumstances (i.e., the unmatched variables and constraints are irrelevant) the partial matched service is applicable.

Privacy Matching

Due to a service provider agent's privacy restriction, the matching result actually is sent to the service provider instead to the service requester. In other words, the provider agent wants to control the communication with consumers, it does not want to expose itself before knowing who are requesting its service.

Cooperative Matching

This strategy requires an arbitrary amount of deduction and knowledge to match any given service and request. It exploits service ontology, knowledge on the application domain, to discover the hidden relationships among currently available services. It returns the agents contact information and their relationships. Briefly speaking, cooperative matching infers the available services to find a set of available information agents that can cooperate in some way to provide the requested service.

TutorFinder: An Open Online Learning Tool

One great advantage of Web based learning is its openness. Everyone on the Internet can participate the learning and education process at any time they like. Traditional computer aided instruction (CAI) systems based on client-server architecture cannot cope with this requirement. In order to take the full advantages offered by the Web, a new trend of online learning is open systems architecture, which introduces middleware to solve the connection problem.

Figure 3. Tutor mediator

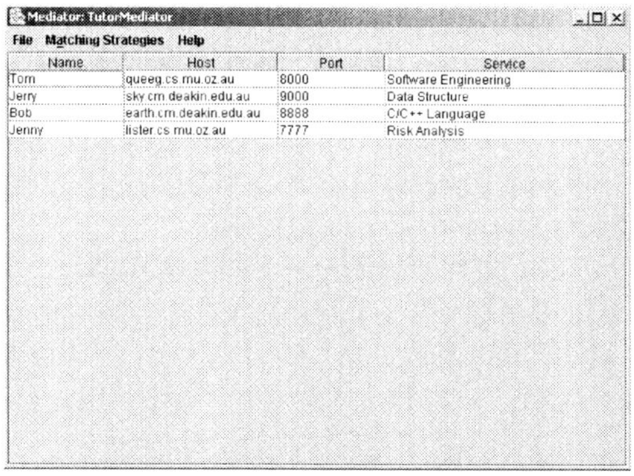

Based on the previous mediator architecture and strategies, TutorFinder, an online tool for students and lecturers to locate suitable tutors, is presented in this section. TutorFinder is a mediator based open system. Any new available agent, who is able to offer services related to a specific eLearning subject, can register or advertise its ability to the TutorMediator, shown in Figure 3, who acts a middle man to mediate services requests and advertisements. This paradigm is open to any educators who wish to make their tools public over the Internet; in addition it is also open to any learners who are seeking some kind of helps. Service requests and advertisements are written in the proposed agent services description language, which can be easily plugged into any agent communication language. TutorMediator applies the multiple matching strategies to find out a or a team of service providers to inform to a consumer. The matching process can be reversed as a marketing campaign, in case the service provider would like to remain unknown until it knows who are seeking its services, and then the provider will target its marketing to the potential consumers. This procedure is depicted in Figure 1 as the dash line labelled with "Marketing."

Services Description and Matching in Tutorfinder

The presented agent services description language based on ontology provides a meaningful tool for service providers to express their capabilities. This is critical in a Web based learning environment, considering the open nature of e-learning. Using this language, online learning service providers can prescribe what kind of services they can offer to the community. For example, a Web service dedicated to answer students' queries on subject SCC303 Software Engineering can register its service to the previous TutorMediator in the following format

```
( service
   :service-id SCC303Tutor
  :constraint-language fopl
   :input ( (SCC303Question ?question) )
   :output ( (Answer ?answer) )
   :input-constraints (
     (elt ?question Question)
    (SubjectIn ?question SoftwareEngineering) )
   :io-constraints (
     (Correct ?question ?answer) )
  :service-ontology ComputerScience )
```

In this description, we know that the service SCC303Tutor takes questions in subject SCC303, software engineering, as input, and gives the correspondent answers. It requires an input to be a valid question defined in computer science subjects ontology, and the question should be in the topics of software engineering; on these conditions, SCC303Tutor is able to give a correct answer. Please note that the constraints in this example are written in first order predicate logic (FOPL), which is specified in constraint-language field. Actually, developers can choose any formal languages independent from ASDL to write constraints, and simply specify it in this field.

The ontology of computer science subjects is not only exploited in service advertising, in which it defines all the terms and their relationships used in the description, but also in service matching. Here I present a scenario in Figure 3.

In this scenario, there are four information agents available, and they can provide tutoring services on subjects of software engineering, data structure, C/C++ language, and risk analysis to students. These four agents can be located at different universities and institutes. When a student or an agent requests services on computer science, TutorMediator can recommend a provider, or a list of service providers working as a team in case that the requested service can not be accomplished by any single agents. Considering a student who is doing a programming project on object oriented design and analysis, at the current situation, there is no single agents has the capability on OO design and analysis programming; but this requested service can be achieved by two agents Tom and

Bob, who have the expertise on software engineering and C/C++ language respectively, working cooperatively as a team. So by exploiting service ontology and cooperative matching strategy, TutorMediator can reply the student's query with Tom and Bob's contact information, as well as their relationship in forming the team. Without ontology and various matching strategies, this can not be achieved. Powered with knowledge on the domain and a series of matching strategies, TutorMediator in our architecture is not a conventional middle agent, but an intelligent mediator who can reason and refer service providers' relationships, and guide them into cooperation.

Conclusion

The proposed agent service description language gives a flexible method for developers to plug in a suitable independent constraint language; it is more expressive for service quality and the privacy of service providers. The mediator, TutorMediator, in the presented open multi-agent architecture serves as middle agent that not only solves the connection problem, but also infers the cooperation relationships among information agents, this will direct service providers to forge a cooperation to answer a user's query. In such a way, tutoring agents can improve their capabilities, and online learning system becomes open and more scalable. This architecture with the service description language and matching strategies provides a solution to build open online learning system step by step. It also enables developers to integrate new tutoring services with legacy eLearning systems, since the architecture and language are open. This is critical for the success of online education, because both the educator and learner can take the full advantage of the World Wide Web, which gives people the freedom to pursue education from anywhere at anytime.

References

Arisha, K., Kraus S., Subrahmanian, V. S., et al. (1999). IMPACT: Interactive Maryland platform for agents collaborating together. *IEEE Intelligent Systems*, *14*(2), 64-72.

Chandrasekaran, B., Josephson J. R., & Benjamins, V. R. (1999). What are ontologies, and why do we need them? *IEEE Intelligent Systems*, *14*(1), 20-26.

Dao, S., & Perry, B. (1996). Information mediation in cyberspace: Scalable methods for declarative information networks. *Journal of Intelligent Information Systems*, *6*(2/3), 131-150.

Decker, K., Sycara, K., & Williamson, M. (1996). Matchmaking and brokering. *Proceedings of the 2nd International Conference on Multi-Agent Systems (ICMAS-96)*.

Decker, K., Sycara, K., & Williamson, M. (1997). Middle-agents for the Internet. *Proceedings of 15th International Joint Conference on Artificial Intelligence (IJCAI-97)* Nagoya, Japan (pp. 578-583).

Doorenbos, R. B., Etzioni, O., & Weld, D. S. (1997). A scalable comparison-shopping agent for the World Wide Web. *Proceedings of the 1st International Conference on Autonomous Agents*.

Genesereth, M. R., & Ketchpel, S. P. (1994). Software agents. *Communications of the ACM*, *37*(7), 48-53.

Lu, H., & Sterling, L. (2000). Sports agents: A mediator-based multi-agent system for cooperative information gathering from the World Wide Web. *Proceedings of the 5th International Conference on the Practical Application of Intelligent Agents and Multi-Agent Technology (PAAM 2000),* Manchester, UK (pp. 331-334).

Lu, H., Sterling L., & Wyatt, A. (1999). Knowledge discovery in sportsfinder: An agent to extract sports results from the Web. In N. Zhong & L. Zhou (Eds.), *Methodologies for knowledge discovery and data mining. Third Pacific-Asia Conference (PAKDD-99) Proceedings,* Beijing, China (LNAI 1574, pp. 469-473).

Shakes, J., Langheinrich, M., & Etzioni, O. (1997). Dynamic reference sifting: A case study in the homepage domain. *Proceedings of the 6th International World Wide Web Conference* (pp. 189-200).

Wickler, G. J. (1999). *Using expressive and flexible action representations to reason about capabilities for intelligent agent cooperation.* PhD thesis, University of Edinburgh, Scotland.

Wiederhold, G. (1992). Mediators in the architecture of future information systems. *IEEE Computer*, *25*(3).

Chapter VIII

Concept Effect Model: An Effective Approach to Developing Adaptive Hypermedia Systems

Gwo-Jen Hwang, National University of Tainan, Taiwan

Abstract

With the recent rapid progress of network technology, researchers have attempted to adopt artificial intelligence and use computer networks to develop adaptive hypermedia systems. The idea of adaptive hypermedia is to adapt the course content for a particular learner based on the profile or records of the learner. Meanwhile, researchers have also attempted to develop more effective programs to evaluate the student learning problems, so that the adaptive hypermedia systems can adapt displayed information and dynamically support navigation accordingly. Conventional testing systems simply give students a score, and do not give them the opportunity to learn how to improve their learning performance. Students would benefit more if the test results could be analyzed and hence advice could be provided accordingly. Concept effect model *is an effective approach to coping with this problem. In this Chapter, the model and its relevant work are introduced.*

Advance of Hypermedia Systems

With accelerated growth of computer and communication technologies, researchers have attempted to adopt computer network technology for research on education. Snow and Farr (1987) suggested that sound learning theories are incomplete or unrealistic if they do not include a whole person view, integrating both cognitive and affective aspects, which implies that no educational program can be successful without due attention to the personal learning needs of individual students. Brusilovsky (1998) suggested using adaptive hypermedia to support individual learning. The idea of adaptive hypermedia is to adapt the course content for a particular learner based on the profile or records of the learner (Hwang, 1998).

Most of the adaptive hypermedia systems can adapt displayed information and dynamically support navigation through hypermedia material. For example, Vasandani and Govindaraj (1989, 1991, 1995) proposed an intelligent tutoring system that can assist operators in organizing their system knowledge and operational information to enhance operation performance; Gonzalez and Ingraham (1994) developed an intelligent tutoring system, which is capable of determining exercise progression and remediation automatically during a training session according to the students' past performance. Moreover, Harp, Samad, and Villano (1995) employed the technique of neural networks to model the behavior of students in the context of an intelligent tutoring system. They used self-organizing feature maps to capture the possible states of student knowledge from an existing test database. Later, Ozdemir and Alpaslan (2000) presented an intelligent agent to guide students throughout the course material on the Internet. The agent can assist the students in learning concepts by allocating navigational support based on their knowledge levels. Clearly, the development of adaptive hypermedia systems has become an important issue in both computer science and education (Pugliesi & Rezende, 1999; Rosic, Slavomir, & Glavinic, 2000, Wong, Quek, & Looi, 1998; Yoshikawa, Shintani, & Ohba, 2000).

Paolucci (1998) addressed the importance of individualization in hypermedia that any strategy should be adaptive and personalized. To insure personalization, adaptive hypermedia systems should be capable of diagnosing and identifying each student's misconceptions. Therefore, it becomes an important issue to identify student learning problems such that the adaptive hypermedia systems can assist the students in improving their learning performance accordingly.

In the meanwhile, the development of online testing systems has also attracted the attention of researchers. Taking GRE (graduate record examinations) as an example, students have taken this test on computers since 1992, and the paper-and-pencil form had almost been abandoned in 1999. Lots of companies and educational institutes have been working on developing computerized testing systems, and systems which replace traditional paper-and-pencil testing systems with online testing are proliferating rapidly.

In New Zealand, three researchers developed a "knowledge based computer assisted instruction system" which can change the numerical part of test items while the test is in progress to prevent students from memorizing the answers (Fan, Mak, & Shue, 1997). Another branch of relevant research is computerized adaptive testing, which applies prediction methodologies to reduce the length of the test without sacrificing accuracy (Wainer, 1990).

Nevertheless, such conventional testing systems represent the learning status of a student by assigning that student with a score or grade. This approach makes the student aware of his or her learning status through the score or grade, but the student might be unable to improve his or her learning status without further guidance. The teacher can give students additional suggestions to improve their learning performance after the test. However, it is time-consuming for a teacher to give personalized suggestions to each student, particularly when the number of the students in the class exceeds twenty. Therefore, intelligent testing system could be very helpful to teachers and students for identifying learning problems.

Concept effect model is an effective approach to cope with these problems (Hwang, 2003). The relationships between subject concepts and test items are determined by analyzing the subject materials and the item bank, and the learning problems of each student are then identified based on these relationships. A testing and diagnostic system based on this approach has been presented by Hwang (2003), in which different test items are given even if an identical subject unit is tested repeatedly. This system can provide objective assessments and personalized suggestions for each student by analyzing student answers and the relationships among the subject concepts and the test items.

Concept Effect Model

During tutoring, students learn new concepts and new relationships among previously learned concepts, and this knowledge can be represented as a conceptual map (McAleese, 1994, 1998). Salisbury indicated that learning information, including facts, names, labels, or paired associations, is often a prerequisite to efficiently performing a more complex, higher-level skill (Salisbury, 1998). For example, the names and abbreviations of chemical elements and their atomic weights must be thoroughly learned to comprehend scientific writings or chemical formulae. That is, relationships exist that indicate the effect of learning one concept on the learning of other concepts. Such relationships are called "concept effect relationships," and the following discussion presents such conceptual maps diagrammatically as "concept effect graphs" (Hwang, 2003).

Structure of Subject Materials and the Conceptual Map Model

Subject materials can be viewed as a tree diagram comprising chapters, sections, sub-sections and key concepts to be learned (see Figure 1). This approach offers an overall cognition of the subject contents, but additional information is required to diagnose student learning status. For example, if a student fails to learn the concept "common divisor," this may be because he or she did not learn the concept "factors" well. In this case, the student will be advised to study "factors" more thoroughly before attempting "common divisor." That is, when the relationships among those concepts are identified, it is possible to determine the learning problems of individual students and provide suggestions.

To model these learning effect relationships among concepts, a conceptual map-based notation is proposed, namely *concept effect relationships*. Consider two concepts, C_i and C_j, if C_i is prerequisite to efficiently performing the more complex and higher level concept C_j, then a concept effect relationship $C_i \rightarrow C_j$ exists. A single concept may have multiple prerequisite concepts, and can also be a prerequisite concept of multiple concepts.

For example, the concept "addition" must be learned before "multiplication." Likewise, "multiplication" and "subtraction" must be learned before learning the concept "division." Figure 2 presents the concept effect relationships for the subject unit "numbers."

Figure 1. Tree structure for "numbers"

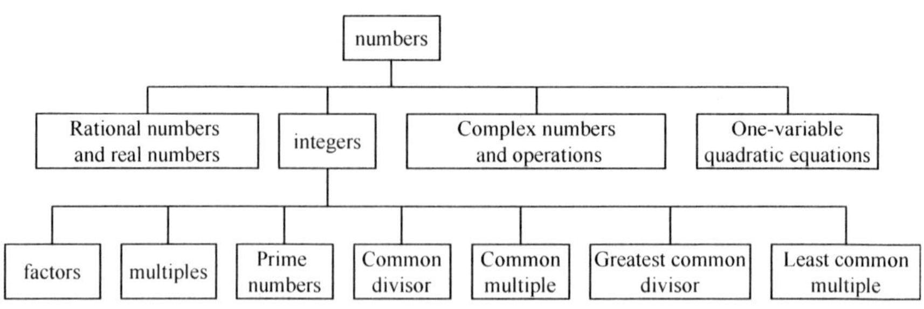

Figure 2. Concept effect graph for the subject unit "numbers"

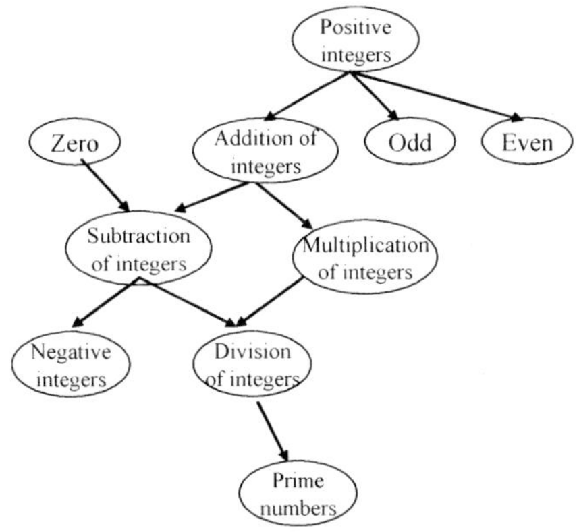

Constructing the Concept Effect Graph

To construct the concept effect graph, the relationships among the concepts to be learned are represented by a two-dimensional table, namely, the *concept effect table (CET)*. Consider the example presented in Table 1. C_i represents the possible prerequisite concept of C_j, while NP_j represents the number of prerequisite concepts of C_j. If $CET(C_i, C_j)=1$, it is said that "C_i is one of the prerequisites of C_j." One possible reason for a student failing to learn C_j is that he or she did not learn C_i well.

Learning Diagnosis Procedure

Table 2 displays a *test item relationship table* (TIRT) for a test sheet containing 10 test items ($Q_1, Q_2, Q_3, \ldots, Q_{10}$) on a learning unit for a subject involving the concepts illustrated in Figure 3. Each value of $TIRT(Q_i, C_j)$, ranging from 0 to 5, represents the relationship between test item Q_i and the concept C_j. 0 indicates no relationship; 1,2, ..5 represent the intensity of the relationship; $SUM(C_j)$ denotes the total strength of concept C_j in the test sheet; $ERROR(C_j)$ is the total strength of the incorrect answers which are related to C_j; and $ER(C_j) = ERROR(C_j)/ SUM(C_j)$ represents the ratio of incorrect answers to the total strength of concept C_j.

Table 1. Illustrative example of a CET

Prerequisite		C_j									
		C_1	C_2	C_3	C_4	C_5	C_6	C_7	C_8	C_9	C_{10}
		Zero	Positive integers	Addition	Odd	Even	Subtraction	Multiplication	Negative integers	Division	Prime numbers
C_i	C_1	0	0	0	0	0	1	0	0	0	0
	C_2	0	0	1	1	1	0	0	0	0	0
	C_3	0	0	0	0	0	1	1	0	0	0
	C_4	0	0	0	0	0	0	0	0	0	0
	C_5	0	0	0	0	0	0	0	0	0	0
	C_6	0	0	0	0	0	0	0	1	1	0
	C_7	0	0	0	0	0	0	0	0	1	0
	C_8	0	0	0	0	0	0	0	0	0	0
	C_9	0	0	0	0	0	0	0	0	0	1
	C_{10}	0	0	0	0	0	0	0	0	0	0
	NP_j	0	0	1	1	1	2	1	1	2	1

Table 2. Illustrative example of a TIRT

		C_j									
Q_i		C_1	C_2	C_3	C_4	C_5	C_6	C_7	C_8	C_9	C_{10}
	Q_1	5	1	0	0	0	0	0	0	0	0
	Q_2	0	4	2	0	0	0	0	0	0	0
	Q_3	0	0	3	1	2	0	0	2	0	0
	Q_4	0	0	0	5	0	0	0	0	0	0
	Q_5	0	0	0	0	5	0	0	0	0	0
	Q_6	1	0	0	0	0	4	0	2	0	0
	Q_7	0	0	0	0	0	0	5	0	0	0
	Q_8	0	0	0	0	0	0	0	0	1	0
	Q_9	0	0	0	0	0	0	0	0	4	5
	Q_{10}	0	0	0	0	0	2	0	1	0	0
	SUM	6	5	5	6	7	6	6	5	5	5
	ERROR	1	0	3	1	2	4	6	4	4	5
	$ER(C_j)$	0.16	0	0.6	0.16	0.28	0.66	0.63	0.8	0.8	1.0

Assuming that the student fails to answer Q_3, Q_6, Q_7 and Q_9, as indicated in Table 2, then $ER(C_1)=1/6=0.16$, $ER(C_2)=0/5=0$, $ER(C_3)=3/5=0.6$, etc., indicating that the student failed to answer 16% of the test items related to C_1, 0% of the test items related to C_2, 60% of the test items related to C_3, and so on. The ER values are then assigned to each concept in the conceptual effect graph, as displayed in Figure 3.

Figure 3. Illustrative example of a concept effect graph with ER values

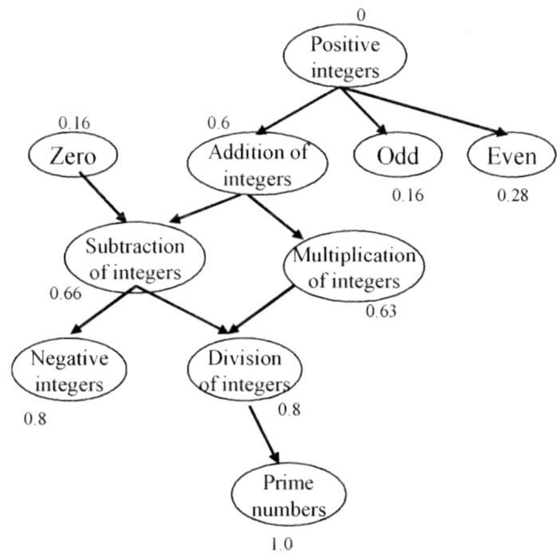

A threshold, θ, is used to indicate the acceptable error rate. When $ER(C_j)<\theta$, the student is said to have learned concept C_j; otherwise, the student is said to have failed to learn concept C_j and thus the concept is added to the *to-Be-enhanced learning path*. The value of can be determined by the following steps

1. Calculate the lower bound of the error ratios for each concept. The lower bound for C_j, called $LB(C_j)$, is determined by calculating the average error ratio of C_j for the students who get the bottom 50% of test scores.
2. The system calculates the difference in the student error ratio for concepts C_j and $LB(C_j)$. Assume that the lower bounds of the concepts are $LB(C_1)=0.33$, $LB(C_3)=0.5$, $LB(C_4)=0.4$, $LB(C_5)=0.33$, $LB(C_6)=0.45$, $LB(C_7)=0.5$, $LB(C_8)= 0.66$, $LB(C_9)=0.5$ and $LB(C_{10})=0.66$, thus

   $DIFF(C_1) = 0.16 - 0.33 = -0.17$

   $DIFF(C_3) = 0.6 - 0.5 = 0.1$

   $DIFF(C_4) = 0.16 - 0.4 = -0.24$

   $DIFF(C_5) = 0.28 - 0.33 = -0.05$

   $DIFF(C_6) = 0.66 - 0.45 = 0.21$

   $DIFF(C_7) = 0.63 - 0.5 = 0.13$

$DIFF(C_8) = 0.8 - 0.66 = 0.14$

$DIFF(C_9) = 0.8 - 0.5 = 0.3$

$DIFF(C_{10}) = 1.0 - 0.66 = 0.34$

3. The error ratios of C_1, C_4 and C_5 are lower than the corresponding lower bounds because their DIFF values are negative; therefore, the system suggests a value for è by determining the minimum error ratio among C_3, C_6, C_7, C_8, C_9 and C_{10}, i.e., $\theta = MIN\ (ER(C_j)) = 0.6$.

Consider the example given in Figure 4. Providing that θ is 0.6, the To-Be-Enhanced learning paths are as illustrated in Figure 4.

Among the to-be-enhanced learning paths, those with the maximum weight are defined as the critical learning paths, i.e. PATH2 and PATH3.

Clearly, the major problems in learning the subject unit originated from the misunderstanding of concepts C_3, C_6 C_7, C_8, C_9, and C_{10}. Furthermore, C_3 (addition of integers) is the root concept for the critical paths PATH2 and PATH3, and consequently students are asked to study C_3 in more detail before learning other concepts.

Fuzzy Output for Learning Guidance

To make the learning guidance more understandable to the student, Hwang (2003) defines some fuzzy sets on $ER(C_j)$, assuming that student understanding of a concept is determined by the ratio of incorrect answers they provide to test items related to that concept. Accordingly, Figure 5 illustrates a fuzzy membership function related to learning status of concepts and $ER(C_j)$.

Figure 4.

PATH1 : Addition → Subtraction → Negative integers

Weight=Max($ER(C_3)$, $ER(C_6)$, $ER(C_8)$)=0.8

PATH2 : Addition → Subtraction → Division → Prime numbers

Weight=Max($ER(C_3)$, $ER(C_6)$, $ER(C_9)$, $ER(C_{10})$)=1.0

PATH3 : Addition → Multiplication → Division → Prime numbers

Weight=Max($ER(C_3)$, $ER(C_7)$, $ER(C_9)$, $ER(C_{10})$)=1.0

Figure 5. Membership functions for learning status of concepts

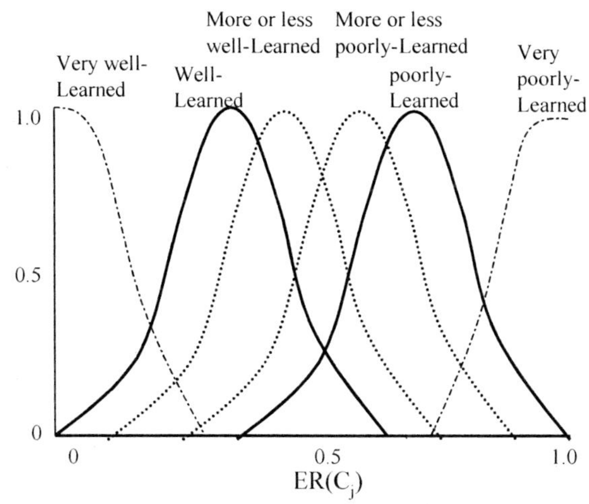

Assuming that the ratio of incorrect answers provided by a student to test items related to concept C_1 is $ER(C_1) = 0.16$, then from Figure 5, that student's learning status of concept C_1 is as follows

Very well-learned → 0.3

Well-learned → 0.55

More or less well-learned → 0.2

Therefore, we can conclude that the learning status of the student for concept C_1 is "well-learned." Table 3 displays an illustrative example for the learning guidance depicted to the student.

Algorithms for Deriving Concept Effect Relationships

While the concept effect model appears useful, it is time-consuming for teachers to apply it unaided. For most teachers who are unfamiliar with computer programming, a computer system with a friendly user interface and intelligent analytic functions would be a more convenient source of aid (Hwang, Hsiao, & Tseng, 2003). To cope with this problem, several algorithms have been proposed

Table 3. Illustrative example of a learning guidance

	Concept	Learning status of the concept
C_1	Zero	You have learned the concept well.
C_2	Positive integers	You have learned the concept very well.
C_3	Addition	It seems that you more or less misunderstood this concept.
C_4	Odd	You have learned the concept well.
C_5	Even	You have learned the concept well.
C_6	Subtraction	It seems that you misunderstood this concept.
C_7	Multiplication	It seems that you more or less misunderstood this concept.
C_8	Negative integers	It seems that you seriously misunderstood this concept.
C_9	Division	It seems that you seriously misunderstood this concept.
C_{10}	Prime numbers	It seems that you seriously misunderstood this concept.

To-Be-Enhanced learning paths:

PATH1: Addition →Subtraction →Negative integers (0.8)
PATH2: Addition →Subtraction → Division →Prime numbers (1.0)
PATH3: Addition → Multiplication → Division → Prime numbers (1.0)

Critical learning path:

PATH2: Addition →Subtraction → Division →Prime numbers (1.0)
PATH3: Addition → Multiplication → Division → Prime numbers (1.0)

Comments for the student:

1. According to the diagnosis from the system, we found that you have misunderstood concepts "Subtraction," "Negative integers," "Division," "Multiplication" and "Prime numbers," which perhaps results from the misunderstanding of "Addition." In other words, the major learning problem of yours is the misunderstanding of concept "Addition," which affects the learning of other concepts.
2. Suggestion: enhance the study in "Addition →Subtraction → Division →Prime numbers" and "Addition → Multiplication → Division → Prime numbers" sequences.

to obtain the initial concept effect relationships, and the teachers are then asked to revise the relationships via graphical user interfaces. The revised concept effect relationships are then used by the adaptive hypermedia systems to evaluate the learning status of individual student.

An answer sheet summary table (ASST) and a relationship ratio table (RRT) must be produced before applying the concept effect relationship-generating algorithms. An ASST is a collection of each student's answers for a test, and Table 4 presents an illustrative example. In the table, Si denotes the identity of an individual student and Q_i represents the test item number. If student Si correctly answered test item Q_i, ASST[Q_i,S_j] = 1; otherwise, ASST[Q_i,S_j] = 0. Entry Err_Count[Q_i] denotes the number of students who failed to correctly answer test item Qi.

A *relationship ratio table* (RRT) indicates the degree of association between concept Cj and test item Qi. Each RRT entry records the ratio of the concept in

Table 4. An illustrative example of an ASST

	Q_1	Q_2	Q_3	Q_4	Q_5	Q_6	Q_7	Q_8	Q_9	Q_{10}	Q_{11}	Q_{12}
S_1	1		1	1		1	1				1	
S_2						1		1			1	
S_3								1				
S_4	1		1	1		1	1				1	
S_5		1			1			1				1
S_6				1			1					
S_7			1									1
S_8					1		1			1		
S_9	1			1		1	1				1	
S_{10}	1		1			1	1					
S_{11}												
S_{12}		1					1				1	
S_{13}	1		1	1								
S_{14}												
S_{15}					1		1					
S_{16}	1		1	1						1		
S_{17}						1		1				
S_{18}												
S_{19}				1								
S_{20}		1					1					
Err_Count(Q_i)	6	3	6	7	3	6	8	4	0	2	5	2

Table 5. Illustrative example of an RRT

	Q_1	Q_2	Q_3	Q_4	Q_5	Q_6	Q_7	Q_8	Q_9	Q_{10}	Q_{11}	Q_{12}
C_1	1	0.3	-	-	-	-	-	-	0.2	-	-	-
C_2	-	0.7	-	-	1	0.8	-	-	-	-	-	-
C_3	-	-	-	0.7	-	-	-	1	0.8	-	-	-
C_4	-	-	-	0.3	-	0.2	-	-	-	1	-	-
C_5	-	-	-	-	-	-	-	-	-	-	-	1
C_6	-	-	1	-	-	-	1	-	-	-	1	-

the total ratings against the test item. For example, ΣITRT[Q_1, C_j] = 3+0+1+0=4; thus, RRT[Q_1,C_1]=3/4=0.75 and RRT[Q_1,C_3] = 1/4 =0.25, as listed in Table 5. An RPT[Q_i, C_j] value represents the possibility of a student failing to learn C_j if he or she answers Q_i incorrectly.

Statistical Prediction Algorithm

Hwang et al. (2003) proposed a statistical prediction algorithm to generate concept effect relationships from student test results. The algorithm first finds the test item that most students failed to answer correctly, then finds the other test items that were incorrectly answered by those students, and finally uses this information to determine the relationships among the test items. The relationships among concepts can thus be determined based on the relationships among test items, and between test items and concepts.

Symbols and Notations

The following symbols and notations are used in the concept effect relationship-constructing algorithm throughout this chapter.

- ***NS*** **:** Number of students tested
- E_{max} **:** Set of test items that most students failed to answer
- N_{max} **:** Number of students who failed to answer the test items in E_{max}
- Q_i **:** i-th test item
- C_j **:** j-th concept to be learned
- N_{Qi} **:** Number of students who failed to answer Qi
- $RC_{Qi}=\{C_1,C_2,C_3...C_k\}$: Set of concepts that are related to Q_i
- $FAIL_{Qi}=\{Q_1,Q_2,Q_3...Q\}$: Set of students who fail to answer Q_i
- $ES_{Qi}=\{Q_1,Q_2,Q_3...Q\}$: Set of test items that the students in $FAIL_{Qi}$ failed to answer
- $RRT[Q_i, C_j]$: The ratio of concept C_j in the total ratings to test item Q_i
- **n1 :** Number of accumulated test items
- **n2 :** Number of new test items
- $R(C_i,C_j)$ **:** Degree of certainty for $C_i \rightarrow C_j$ (if C_i is true then C_j is true). The value of $R(C_i,C_j)$ ranges from 0 to 1, indicating the relative degree to which "the learning status of C_i" influences "the learning status of C_j."
- $R(C_i,C_j)_{new}$ **:** New degree of certainty for $C_i \rightarrow C_j$
- **Support:** A threshold representing the proportion of students who failed to answer test item Q_i. For $N_{Qi}/N >=$ support, a sufficient number of students is assumed to have failed to answer Q_i such that Q_i is likely to be important in identifying concept effect relationships. For $N_{Qi}/N <$ support, since few students failed to answer Q_i, it may be difficult to find concept effect relationships using Q_i.
- **Belief:** A threshold representing the lowest acceptable connection level for two concepts that students failed to correctly answer based upon the conditional probability. Assume that x% students who failed to correctly

answer problems involving Concept X also failed to answer problems involving Concept Y. If the defined *belief* is b% and x%≥b%, then the implication relationship "If one failed to answer X, then he/she might fail to answer Y" is accepted and recorded for future use.

Statistical Prediction Algorithm

$step1$¡R$E_{\max} = \{Q_{e1}, Q_{e2}, \ldots Q_{em}\}$

$step2$¡R$N_{\max} = N_{Qei}$ for $Q_{ei} \in E_{\max}$

$step3$¡R$while(N_{\max} / N \geq \text{support})$

{

$for(i = 1; i \leq m; i++)$

{

Find RCQei //* Set of concepts that are related to Qei *//

Find FAILQei //* Set of students who fail to answer Qei *//

Find ESQei //* Set of test items which the ones in FAILQei fail to answer *//

$while(ES_{Qei} \neq \Phi)$

{

$\exists Q_j \in ES_{Qei}$

Find RC_{Qj} //* Set of concepts that are related to Qj *//

$\forall C_k \in RC_{Qei}$

$\forall C_l \in RC_{Qj}$

$$R(C_l, C_k)_{new} = \frac{N_{Qj} * RRT(C_l, Q_j) * RRT(C_k, Q_{ei})}{RRT(C_l, Q_j) * N_{\max}}$$

if ($R(C_l, C_k)_{new} >$ belief) $then$

$$R(C_l, C_k) = \frac{n_1 * R(C_l, C_k) + n_2 * R(C_l, C_k)_{new}}{n_1 + n_2}$$

$ES_{Qei} = ES_{Qei} - \{Q_j\}$

}

}

Remove the test records related to Qei

Find a new Emax set

}

In Step 1, E_{max}, the set of test items that most students failed to answer correctly, is constructed. In Step 2, for each test item in E_{max}, the number of students who failed to correctly answer that test item, say Q_{ei}, is counted. In Step 3, if the ratio of the number of students failing to correctly answer Q_{ei} equals or exceeds the support value, then the set of concepts related to Q_{ei} (i.e., RC_{Qei}), the set of students who failed to correctly answer Q_{ei} (i.e., $FAIL_{Qei}$) and the set of test items that the students in $FAIL_{Qei}$ failed to correctly answer are recorded for future use. The relationships among the concepts are then constructed based on the definition of $R(C_i,C_j)$.

Data Mining Algorithm

In 2005, Hwang (2005) employed a data mining approach to assisting teachers in constructing concept effect relationships in the following

Consider the RRT in Table 5, the relationships can be represented as Q_i $((C_1,X_1),(C_2,X_2),\ldots(C_j,X_j))$, where X_j is the relationship between C_j and Q_i. For example $Q_1((C_1,1.0))$, $Q_2((C_1,0.3),(C_2,0.7))$, $Q_3((C_6,1.0))$, $Q_3((C_3,0.7),(C_4,0.3))$, ...etc.

One of the most important data mining issues is the mining of association rules. Association rules represent the relationships among items in a given database such that the presence of some items in a transaction will imply the presence of other items in the same transaction. A set of items is called an itemset. First, one needs to identify all itemsets that are contained in a sufficient number of transactions above the minimum (support) requirement. These itemsets are referred to as frequent itemsets. Second, once all frequent itemsets are obtained, the desired association rules can be generated in a straightforward manner.

The data mining algorithm for obtaining concept effect relationships is based on the Apriori algorithm proposed by Agrawal and Srikant (1994). This algorithm first constructs a candidate set of frequent 2-itemsets, and then discovers the subset that indeed contains frequent 2-itemsets. Once the frequent 2-itemsets are determined, a set of concept effect relationships can be generated accordingly.

- N : Number of students who received the test
- Q_i : i-th test item in the test sheet
- C_j : j-th concept to be learned

- ***Dk*** **:** Candidate k-itemsets
- ***Lk*** **:** Frequent k-itemsets
- $\boldsymbol{\sim Q_i}$ **:** A test item that students fail to answer
- ***N~Qi*** **:** Number of students who fail to answer Qi
- ***MS*** **:** Minimum support
- ***MC*** **:** Minimum confidence
- ***IRC*** **:** Threshold of implication confidence between concepts
- ***DB*** **:** Database which keeps the test results
- $\mathbf{Support_{(Qi)} = N_{\sim Qi}/N}$

$L_2 = \{d \in D_2 \mid d.count / N \geq MS\}$

for all itemsets $d \in L_2$ *do begin*

$$d.confidence_{item_i \to item_j} = \frac{p(item_i \cap item_j)}{p(item_i)} \quad //item_i = \sim Q_i, item_j = \sim Q_j$$

$if\,(d.confidence_{item_i \to item_j} < MC)\, then$

$remove\ d$

else

for all $item_i.C_A \neq item_j.C_B$ *do begin*

$confidence(C_A \to C_B) = d.confidence_{(item_i \to item_j)} \times X_A \times X_B$

$if\ confidence(C_A \to C_B) < IRC$

$remove\ C_A \to C_B$

end

end

Consider the example given in Tables 4 and 5, there are 12 test items and 6 concepts in the RRT, and 20 students have received the test. Assume that MS = 0.4 and MC = 0.6, the test items with Err_Count (Q_i) $\geq 0.4 \times 20 = 5$ will be selected as the elements of the frequent itemsets. Therefore, the following conceptual relationship mining procedure can be obtained:

1. Generate D_1:

$\{(\sim Q_1,6), (\sim Q_2,3), (\sim Q_3,6), (\sim Q_4,7), (\sim Q_5,3), (\sim Q_6,6), (\sim Q_7,8), (\sim Q_8,4), (\sim Q_9,0), (\sim Q_{10},2), (\sim Q_{11},5), (\sim Q_{12},2)\}$

2. Determine L_1:

$\{(\sim Q_1,6), (\sim Q_3,6), (\sim Q_4,7), (\sim Q_6,6), (\sim Q_7,8), (\sim Q_{11},5)\}$

3. Generate D_2:

$\{(\sim Q_1 \sim Q_3,5), (\sim Q_1 \sim Q_4,5), (\sim Q_1 \sim Q_6,4), (\sim Q_1 \sim Q_7,3), (\sim Q_1 \sim Q_{11},3), (\sim Q_3 \sim Q_4,2), (\sim Q_3 \sim Q_6,3), (\sim Q_3 \sim Q_7,3), (\sim Q_3 \sim Q_{11},1), (\sim Q_4 \sim Q_6,3), (\sim Q_4 \sim Q_7,4), (\sim Q_4 \sim Q_{11},3), (\sim Q_6 \sim Q_7,4), (\sim Q_6 \sim Q_{11},3), (\sim Q_7 \sim Q_{11},3)\}$

4. Determine L_2:

$\{(\sim Q_1 \sim Q_3,5), (\sim Q_1 \sim Q_4,5)\}$

5. Calculate confidence values of $Q_i \rightarrow Q_j$, and determining the concept effect relationships between corresponding concepts according to the RRT in Table 5:

$Confidence_{(\sim Q1 \rightarrow \sim Q3)} = 5/6=0.83$, which implies $C_1 \rightarrow C_6=0.83\times1\times1=0.83$.
$Confidence_{(\sim Q3 \rightarrow \sim Q1)}=5/6=0.83$, which implies $C_6 \rightarrow C_1=0.83\times1\times1=0.83$.
$Confidence_{(\sim Q1 \rightarrow \sim Q4)}=5/6=0.83$, which implies $C_3 \rightarrow C_1=0.83\times0.7\times1=0.581$ and $C_4 \rightarrow C_1=0.83'0.3'1=0.249$.
$Confidence_{(\sim Q4 \rightarrow \sim Q1)} = 5 / 7 = 0.71$, which implies $C_1 \rightarrow C_3 = 0.71\times1\times0.7 = 0.497$ and $C_1 \rightarrow C_4 = 0.71\times1\times0.3 = 0.213$.

Experiments and Evaluation

To evaluate the efficacy of the concept effect model, several experiments have been conducted by researchers during the past decade. For example, an experiment was conducted from September 2001 to December 2001 on the natural science course taught at an elementary school (Hwang et al., 2003). Sixty K-6 students from two classes taught by the same teacher participated in the experiment, and were separated into two groups, A (control group) and B (experimental group), each containing 30 students. The students in *Group-A* (V1) received regular online tutoring and testing without learning guidance, while

Table 6. T-test of the pre-test results

Variable CLASSES	N	Lower Mean	Mean	Upper Mean	Lower Std Dev	Std Dev	Upper Std Dev	Std Err
Group A	30	80.775	83.067	85.358	4.8868	6.136	8.2487	1.1203
Group B	30	76.392	79.067	81.741	5.7045	7.1628	9.6291	1.307
GRADE Diff (1-2)		0.5531	4	7.4469	5.6457	6.6692	8.1494	1.722

t-testsα=0.05 tα(29)=1.699

Variable	Method	Variances	DF	t Value
GRADE	Pooled	Equal	58	2.32
GRADE	Satterthwaite	Unequal	56.7	2.32

Equality of Variances					
Variable	Method	Num DF	Den DF	F Value	Pr > F
GRADE	Folded F	29	29	1.36	0.4097

those in *Group-B* (V2) received the same online tutoring and testing, but with learning suggestions and relevant homework being supplied after each test. All 60 students were given three tests over the space of one semester (including a pre-test and two post-tests). The statistical results from applying SAS to analyze the tests are presented below.

- Pre-test

Table 6 lists the t-test values for the pre-test results. The mean scores for the pre-test reveal that Group A performed better than Group B. Since the "Pr>F" value is 0.4079, the t value of "Equal" variances is adopted. That is, $|t|$=2.32> $t\alpha$(29)−1.699, which implies that the performance of groups A and B in the pre-test differs significantly. Therefore, Group A performed significantly better than Group B in the pre-test, conducted before performing the experiment.

- Post-test

Table 7 lists the t-test values for the post-test results. From the mean value of the post-test, Group B performed better than Group A. Since the "Pr>F" value is 0.0782 (not significant), the t value of "Equal" variances is adopted, namely $|t|$=2.47 > $t\alpha$(29)=1.699, which implies a significant difference between the

Table 7. T-test of the post-test results

Variable CLASSES	N	Lower Mean	Mean	Upper Mean	Lower Std Dev	Std Dev	Upper Std Dev	Std Err
Group A	30	73.38	78.333	83.286	10.564	13.264	17.831	2.4217
Group B	30	82.149	85.7	89.251	7.5732	9.5092	12.783	1.7361
GRADE Diff (1-2)		-13.33	-7.367	-1.402	9.7693	11.54	14.102	2.9797

t-testsα=0.05 tα(29)=1.699

Variable	Method	Variances	DF	t Value
GRADE	Pooled	Equal	58	-2.47
GRADE	Satterthwaite	Unequal	52.6	-2.47

Equality of Variances					
Variable	Method	Num DF	Den DF	F Value	Pr > F
GRADE	Folded F	29	29	1.95	0.0782

performance of groups B and A in the post-test. Therefore, Group B has achieved a significant improvement compared to Group A after receiving learning guidance via the novel tutoring system developed here.

Summary

This chapter introduces the concept effect model and its relevant work. So far, several adaptive hypermedia systems have been developed based on this model to identify poorly-learned and well-learned concepts for individual students and to provide appropriate individual learning guidance to enhance their learning performance. Moreover, this model has been proved to be effective via conducting experiments on various courses of elementary schools and junior high schools. Consequently, it can be seen that the approach is worth further studying.

Although several experiments have achieved positive results by applying the concept effect model to science courses, it would be interesting to know whether the same approach would work, and how well, for various other kinds of courses, such as language courses, mathematics courses, science courses, engineering courses, and social science courses. Consequently, further investigations have been planned to apply the novel approach to online tutoring for different courses.

References

Brusilovsky, P. (1998). Methods and techniques of adaptive hypermedia. In A. Kobsa & J. Vassileva (Eds.), *Adaptive hypermedia and hypermedia* (pp. 1-43). London: Kluwer Academic Publishers.

Fan, J. P., Mak, T. K., & Shue, L. (1997). A knowledge-based computer instruction system. *Australian Journal of Educational Technology, 13*(2), 98-114.

Giarratano, J. R., & Riley, G. (1989). *Expert systems: Principles and programming*. Boston: PWS-KENT Publishing.

Gonzalez, A. J., & Ingraham, L. R. (1994). Automated exercise progression in simulation-based training. *IEEE Transactions on Systems, Man and Cybernetics, 24*(6), 863-874.

Harp, S. A., Samad, T., & Villano, M.(1995). Modeling student knowledge with self-organizing feature maps. *IEEE Transactions on Systems, Man and Cybernetics, 25*(5), 727-737.

Hwang, G. J. (1998). A tutoring strategy supporting system for distance learning on computer networks. *IEEE Transactions on Education, 41*(4), 1-19.

Hwang, G. J. (2003). A concept map model for developing intelligent tutoring systems. *Computers & Education, 40*(3), 217-235.

Hwang, G. J. (2005). A data mining algorithm for diagnosing student learning problems in science courses. *International Journal of Distance Education Technologies, 3*(4), 35-50.

Hwang, G. J., Hsiao, J. L., & Tseng, J. C. R. (2003). A computer-assisted approach for diagnosing student learning problems in science courses. *Journal of Information Science and Engineering, 19*(2), 229-248.

McAleese, R. (1994). A theoretical view on concept mapping. *ALT-J, 2*(1), 38-48.

McAleese, R. (1998). The knowledge arena as an extension to the concept map: Reflections in action. *Interactive Learning Environments, 6*(3), 1-22.

Ozdemir, B., & Alpaslan, F. N (2000). An intelligent tutoring system for student guidance in Web-based courses. *The 4th International Conference on Knowledge-Based Intelligent Engineering Systems and Allied Technologies* (Vol. 2, pp. 835-839).

Paolucci, R. (1998, June). Hypermedia and learning: The relationship of cognitive style and knowledge structure. *Proceedings of ED-MEDIA/ED-TELECOM 1998*, Freiburg, Germany.

Pugliesi, J. B., & Rezende, S. O. (1999). Intelligent hybrid system for a training and teaching environment. The *3rd International Conference on Computational Intelligence and Multimedia Applications* (pp. 148-152).

Rosic, M., Slavomir, S., & Glavinic, V. (2000). Intelligent tutoring systems for asynchronous distance education. *10th Mediterranean Electrotechnical Conference* (pp. 111-114).

Salisbury, D. F. (1998). Effect drill and practice strategies. In D. H. Jonassen (Ed.), *Instructional designs for microcomputer courseware* (pp. 103-124). Hillsdale, NJ: Lawrence Erlbaum Associates.

Snow, R., & Farr, M. (1987). Cognitive-conative-affective processes in aptitude, learning, and instruction: An introduction. In R. Snow & M. Farr (Eds.), *Conative and affective process analysis* (Vol. 3, pp. 1-10). Hillsdale, NJ: Erlbaum Associates.

Vasandani, V., & Govindaraj, T. (1991, October 13-16). Intelligent diagnostic problem solving tutor: An experimental evaluation. *IEEE International Conference on Systems, Man and Cybernetics*, Charlottesville, VA (pp. 1739-1744).

Vasandani, V., & Govindaraj, T. (1995). Knowledge organization in intelligent tutoring systems for diagnostic problem solving in complex dynamic domains. *IEEE Transactions on Systems, Man and Cybernetics, 25*(7), 1076-1096.

Vasandani, V., Govindaraj, T., & Mitchell, C. M. (1989, November 14-17). An intelligent tutor for diagnostic problem solving in complex dynamic systems. *IEEE International Conference on Systems, Man and Cybernetics,* Cambridge, MA (pp. 772-777).

Wainer, H. (1990). *Computerized adaptive testing: A primer*. Hillsdale, NJ: Lawrence Erlbaum.

Wong, L. H., Quek, C., & Looi, C. K. (1998). TAP: A software architecture for an inquiry dialogue-based tutoring system. *IEEE Transactions on Systems, Man and Cybernetics, Part A, 28*(3), 315-325.

Yoshikawa, A., Shintani, M., & Ohba, Y. (2000). Intelligent tutoring system for electric circuit exercising. *IEEE Transactions on Education, 35*(3), 222-225.

Chapter IX

A Virtual Laboratory for Digital Signal Processing

Chyi-Ren Dow, Feng Chia University, Taiwan

Yi-Hsung Li, Feng Chia University, Taiwan

Jin-Yu Bai, Feng Chia University, Taiwan

Abstract

This work designs and implements a virtual digital signal processing laboratory, VDSPL. VDSPL consists of four parts: mobile agent execution environments, mobile agents, DSP development software, and DSP experimental platforms. The network capability of VDSPL is created by using mobile agent and wrapper techniques without modifying the source code of the original programs. VDSPL provides human-human and human-computer interaction for students and teachers, and it can also lighten the loading of teachers, increase the learning result of students, and improve the usage of network bandwidth. A prototype of VDSPL has been implemented by using the IBM Aglet system and Java Native Interface for DSP experimental platforms. Also, experimental results demonstrate that our system has received many positive feedbacks from both students and teachers.

Introduction

Digital signal processing (DSP) (Mousavinezhad & Abdel-Qader, 2001; Texas Instruments, 2005) is one of the most powerful technologies in the twenty-first century and is a growing subject area in electrical, computer science, and other engineering/science disciplines. DSP is closely linked to our life and is widely applied in many fields such as: telecommunications, robotics, consumer electronics, medicine, military, instrumentation, aerospace industry, and automobile. Each of these areas has developed a deep DSP technology, with its own algorithms, mathematics, and specialized techniques.

Although DSP is the trend of current technology development, the learning of DSP is not an easy task for novices. Not only the DSP hardware architecture, but also the flexible and powerful instruction sets of DSP chips are difficult for students. Thus, fast and convenient CAI tools for the DSP learning are necessary. However, most DSP learning tools are stand-alone. This kind of learning approach has only human-computer interaction and lacks of human-human interaction (Dey, 2000; Dow, Lin, Shen, Lin, & Chen, 2002) such as teacher to student and student to student. In order to add human-human interactions, it is necessary to create network capability for DSP-learning tools. A network enabled DSP learning environment can support multiple users and allow them to interact with each other to increase their interests in learning DSP in any place and at any time via the Internet.

In addition to the network capability, a DSP virtual laboratory should support the features of multimedia and multi-level usage. The multi-level usage means that the same learning materials can be organized in different ways to be used in a regular semester course, a short course, an introductory exposition, an advanced seminar and so on, and by people with different linguistic, cultural, and perceptual preferences (Arndt, Chang, Guercio, & Maresca, 2002). Through multimedia demonstrations, students can easily understand various DSP theories. We can use the multimedia technology to enhance an experimental environment for students. Furthermore, a DSP course material should be organized in multiple levels so students can select DSP studying materials according to their ability to reduce the frustrations when learning and deepen their impressions about DSP.

This work designs, develops, and implements a virtual DSP laboratory, VDSPL using mobile agent and wrapper techniques. The autonomous feature of mobile agents can be used in the virtual laboratory to substitute for a teacher's behaviors and actions in a practical laboratory. Mobile agents could guide several groups of students in different places simultaneously. When a student needs to interact with the teacher, the virtual laboratory can dispatch a mobile agent to perform this function. For a student, the mobile agent can play a learning guide and arrange the learning activities, to improve the learning efficiency in a virtual laboratory.

The rest of this chapter is organized as follows. First of all, we discuss the background materials and related work. Next, the system architecture of our work is described. The system implementation and prototype are presented, as well as our experimental results.

Related Work

There are many research areas related to our work, including virtual laboratory, digital signal processing, mobile agent techniques, and wrapper concept. These topics are described in this section.

Distance education can be done in a wide variety of styles via different learning models. The virtual laboratory is one of the important components for macro university architecture (Arndt, Chang, Guercio, & Maresca, 2002; Dow, Lin, Shen, Lin, & Chen, 2002). Students are required to learn some courses through online experiments and simulations, and the virtual laboratory is provided for the students to conduct course related experiments and simulations via networks. Based on the equipment and user access in each experiment, laboratories can be classified into four types (Dow, Lin, Shen, Lin, & Chen, 2002). The first type of laboratory is the practical lab. This is a traditional laboratory. The second type of laboratory is the remote lab. This kind of laboratory uses physical experimental equipment and allows users to remotely access the equipment and instruments. The third type is the micro lab which provides some virtual equipment and allows only local access. Traditional computer-assisted instruction (CAI) tools belong to this type. The fourth type is the macro lab which consists of one or more micro labs and allows remote access through the Internet. Some Web-based learning environments (Chang, Wu, Chiu, & Yu, 2003) belong to this type. The virtual laboratory proposed in this work is a hybrid of the remote lab and the macro lab.

The theorems of DSP use the mathematics and the algorithms to manipulate the signals (Gan, Chong, Gong, & Tan, 2000; Wu, Hsiao, Chen, Su, Su, & Jiang, 2001) after they have been converted into a digital form. Currently, there are some DSP electronics manufactures (such as TI, Motorola, NEC, and Analog Device) to develop their own series of DSP chips. For instances, TI developed a series of high performance DSP chip called TMS320™ DSPs. In the past few years, it is a challenge for students to learn the DSP concepts, theorems, and algorithms without any auxiliary simulating/ emulating tools in a lecture class. With the rapid technological changing, there are several powerful simulation software tools (e.g., MATLAB and MATHCAD (Causen, Spanias, Xavier, & Tampi, 1998)) for students to learn DSP. Through these tools, students cannot practice DSP experiments with DSP hardware; they can only simulate digital signal processing by the simulation tools.

The mobile agent (Concepcion, Ruan, & Samson, 2002; Dorca, Lopes, & Fernandes, 2003; Dow, Lin, & Hsu, 2002; Lange & Oshima, 1998; Pham & Karmouch, 1998; Silva, Silva, & Delgado, 1998) is an emerging technology that can be applied in many fields, including electronic commerce, personal assistance, secure brokering, distributed information retrieval, telecommunication networks services, workflow applications and groupware, monitoring and notification, information dissemination and parallel processing, etc. The use of mobile agents can bring several advantages (Lange & Oshima, 1998; Silva, Silva, & Delgado, 1998), including the reduction of the network traffic and latency in client/server network computing paradigm, protocol encapsulation, dynamic adaptation, heterogeneity, robust, and fault tolerance. In the past few years, there are several contemporary mobile agent systems (Lange & Oshima, 1998; Silva, Soares, Martins, Batista, & Santos, 1999; IBM's Java Aglet, 2005) developed, and two main categories of mobile agent systems can be identified: systems based on the Java language (e.g., Mole (Pham & Karmouch, 1998), Aglets (Lange & Oshima, 1998; IBM's Java Aglet, 2005), Odyssey, Concordia, and Voyager (Pham & Karmouch, 1998) and systems based on scripting languages (e.g., Agent Tcl (Pham & Karmouch, 1998), Ara Tcl-based Ara, and TACOMA).

One important problem we face when building a virtual laboratory is where to place an extra function for a stand-alone learning tool without knowing its source code. To be included in a virtual laboratory and used via networks, these stand-alone learning tools have to be modified. In our approach, we use the wrapper concept to implement our virtual laboratory. Wrapper (Dow, Lin, Shen, Lin, & Chen, 2002; Sudmann & Johansen, 2001) is a technique that provides a convenient way to expand upon existing functions of an application program, without modifying its source code. Wrappers intercept function calls, method invocations, and messages to the application software that they wrap, redirecting or doing pre- and/or post-processing of input/output. Wrappers provide a way to compose applications from different parts. The fact that a mobile agent is wrapped should be transparent to other mobile agents in the system, and potentially to the agent itself.

System Architecture

The system architecture of our virtual laboratory and the functions of each component of the system are described in this section.

System Overview

In our proposed framework, we use the mobile agent techniques to construct the VDSPL. There are four major components in our virtual laboratory. These components are the mobile agent execution environments, mobile agents, DSP development software, and DSP experimental platforms, as shown in 0. 0 also shows the mobility of agents between teacher and student sides via agent execution environments. Various mobile agents are designed to assist a teacher. The mobile agents in the teacher side can be dispatched to the student side to represent the actual teacher and interact directly with the students. The development tools are stand-alone programs on the teacher and student sides. Furthermore, some middlewares are designed and wrapped into our agents to provide interactive functions and rules for mobile agents and the development tool.

Figure 1. System architecture

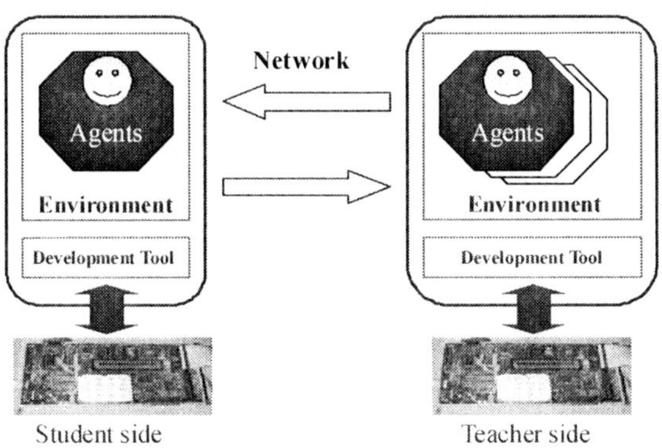

Figure 2. Overview of the virtual digital signal processing laboratory

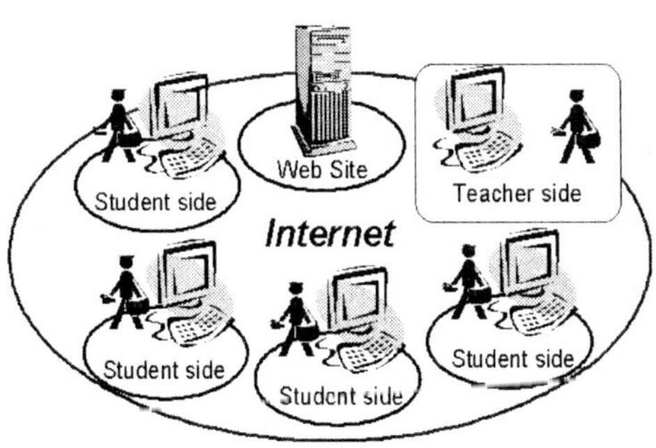

Figure 2 shows an overview of our virtual digital signal processing laboratory. There are students, teachers, and learning Web sites in the virtual laboratory. The teacher can dispatch teacher agents to the student sides, and the teacher agents will assist students and collect the information about the students' learning status. In our virtual laboratory, we also have a DSP Web site that provides the various DSP learning materials for students.

System Modules

The system modules are shown in Figure 3, and the details are described in this section.

Mobile Agent Execution Environment

A mobile agent requires an execution environment called the mobile agent execution environment (MAEE) (Lange & Oshima, 1998). This environment must be installed on the student and teacher sides to provide a necessary runtime environment for agents to execute. The environment's basic facilities include mobility, communications, naming and location, and security. All mobile agents are received and executed in the environment and we also regard it as an entry point or operating system for mobile agents. Furthermore, four important roles

Figure 3. System modules

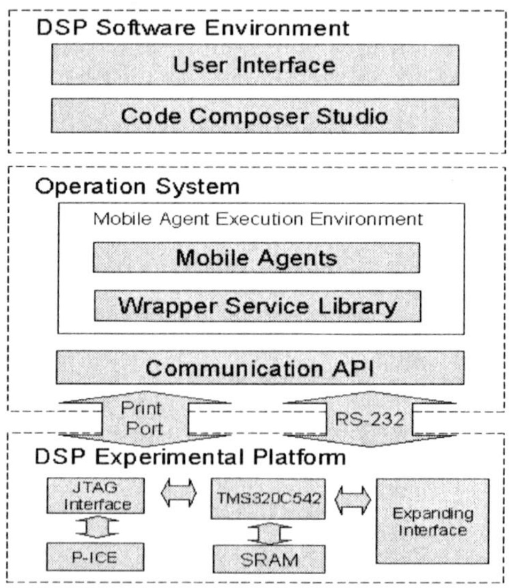

exist in MAEE, including the engine, resources, location, and principal. The engine serves as a workhorse or virtual machine for MAEE and mobile agents. The resources include networks, database, processors, memory and other hardware, and software services. The location can be typically written as an Internet protocol (IP) address and a port of the engine with a MAEE name attribute. Principals like agents that have the responsibility for the operation of MAEE. The MAEE is implemented by using the Java language. Therefore, MAEE is a Java application that runs on the Java virtual machine (JVM) and has the following good properties: platform independence, secure execution, dynamic class loading, multithread programming, object serialization, and reflection.

Mobile Agent

The mobile agent is a principal role in the virtual laboratory. Different mobile agents such as the guide agent, demo agent, learning agent, monitor agent, homework agent, and assessment agent can be designed for our learning environment. A teacher can use various mobile agents to assist students to learn. A guide agent can be used to provide an interactive interface between the teacher and the student. On the teacher side, the guide agent provides various assisting functions for the teacher. On the student side, the learning agent has some predefined FAQ rules and it will reply appropriate answers from a knowledge base when the students ask some common questions or the user's behavior matches certain rules. The monitoring agent could act as the teacher to monitor the student's actions and learning status. The homework agent could act as the teacher to dispatch homework to the student and record the student's homework execution status. The assessment agent could give an assessment to check the student's learning results and provide different levels of assessment materials. The demo agent helps the teacher to demonstrate the steps of the experiment and let the student have an overview of the experiment.

Wrapper

A wrapper is the key component that provides the communication function in our framework for the VDSPL. The wrapper provides system function calls and gathers learning platform actions and information. When the wrapper is running, the mobile agent can interact with the experiment platform via the interface provided by the wrapper agent. The wrapper agent includes a service library and can be regarded as a fixed agent. The union of a mobile agent and a wrapper looks just like a stationary agent. This union can be wrapped, creating an onion-like structure with a core agent in the center, and one or more wrappers around

Figure 4. Wrapping concept from a user's perspective

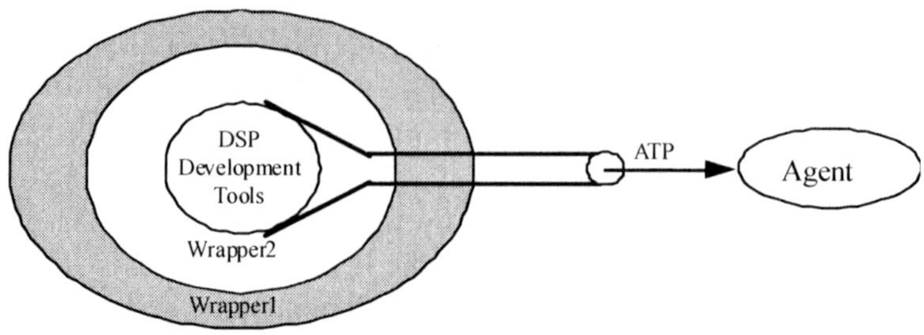

Figure 5. Wrapping concept from a system's perspective

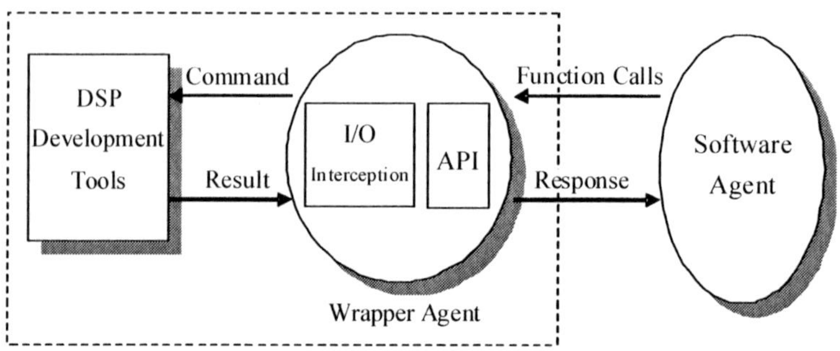

it. From a user's perspective, the wrappers are hidden. A wrapped DSP development tool looks like any other software application, as shown in Figure 4, where ATP denotes Agent Transfer Protocol.

However, from a system's perspective, wrapper is the agent itself. As shown in Figure 5, a wrapper agent consists of two parts, including I/O interception and application programming interface (API). I/O interception is in charge of exposing the functions of a DSP development tool as a set of methods by intercepting its I/O and commands.

DSP Experimental Environment

The DSP experimental environment contains two parts: hardware environment and software environment. In the DSP software environment part, the software is the DSP program development tool which is an existing application software without network capability and provides a powerful integrated environment and several necessary analysis tools to develop DSP programs. The software makes it easier and faster to implement DSP programs using C as opposed to the assembly language. The software also includes the debugging and real-time analysis capabilities. Currently, there are many DSP software environments such as Code Composer, Matlab, Altera, etc.

In the hardware part, the DSP experiment platform adopts the digital signal processor from the DSP chip manufacturer. The hardware platform consists of a DSP emulator and debuggers. They can support the user in debugging the DSP program code through a standard parallel port or PCI slot. Through the integration of the software and hardware environments, we can develop, debug, modify, and execute our DSP programs.

Implementation

This section describes our system implementation. The mobile agent and learning platforms are presented first. Expanding the network capability for the virtual laboratory system is described next. Then, agent models and the on-line learning implementation are presented.

Platforms

Our virtual laboratory system consists of two platforms. The first is the mobile agent platform and the second is the DSP experimental platform. These two platforms are installed on the teacher and student sides. The mobile agent platform is Aglets, which was developed by the IBM Research Laboratory in Japan. The Aglets Software Developer Kit (ASDK) requires the JDK 1.1 or higher to be installed and is the first Internet agent systems based on the Java classes. The ASDK provides a modular structure and an easy-to-use API for the programming of Aglets. The Aglets are Java objects and can travel from a host to another host via networks. The migration of Aglets is based on a proprietary agent transfer protocol. An Aglet that executes on a host can suddenly halt execution, be dispatch to a remote host, and resume execution. When the Aglet moves, it takes along its program code as well as the states of all of the objects that it is carrying. The security mechanism of Java virtual machine and Aglet makes a host safe when receiving the Aglets data.

The DSP experimental platform is composed of TI's integrated development tool CCStudio, Dmatek PRO-OPEN TMS320C542 DSP Controller, and PICE-DSP ICE 320C542 (DMATEK Co. Ltd, 2005). CCStudio software is a fully integrated development environment and supports TI's leading DSP platforms. It integrates all hosts and target tools in a unified environment, including TI's DSP/BIOS™ kernel, code-generation tools, debugger, and real-time data exchange (RTDX) technology to simplify DSP system configuration and application design. CCStudio also has an open architecture that allows TI and third parties to extend the IDEs functionality by seamlessly plugging-in additional specialized tools. Through the CCStudio, the students can learn DSP from multimedia presentation of real-world signals and system theories. Dmatek DSP Controller is an experimental board based on TI's TMS320C542 DSP chip and designed for users to realize the function of DSP chip and its peripheral device. PICE-DSP ICE 320C542 is an in-circuit emulator for DSPs.

Network Capability

The network-enabled VDSPL capability is implemented by using Aglet design patterns and the wrapper concept. Design patterns are reusable components and have been proven to be very useful in the object-oriented field to achieve good application designs. The wrapper concept is used to expand new capabilities for an existing tool without modifying the original source code. The implementation of wrapper concept uses Aglet design patterns and the Java native interface (JNI). The Aglets design patterns include traveling patterns, task patterns, and interaction patterns. We add the network capability for the virtual laboratory by inheriting the traveling patterns. These patterns can deal with various aspects of managing the movements of mobile agents, such as routing and quality of service and they also allow us to enforce encapsulation of mobility management that enhances reuse and simplifies aglet design. Furthermore, the traveling patterns include three traveling models, including itinerary pattern, forwarding pattern, and ticket pattern. In our approach, we use the itinerary pattern and forwarding pattern.

Agent Models

In order to remotely control VDSPL, we use the JNI to connect the Win32 API in the initialize interface. The Java native interface and Visual C++ are used to bind the Win32 API such as the "jni2c.dll" dynamic link library (DLL). An interface is initialized between other mobile agents and VDSPL for the wrapper agent. Moreover, the wrapper agent can execute a doCommand function that can be called by other mobile agents to control and monitor VDSPL. The wrapper agent can also respond to the results based on a wrapper script. Figure 6 shows the trigger of Windows API using JNI.

Figure 6. Trigger of Windows API using JNI

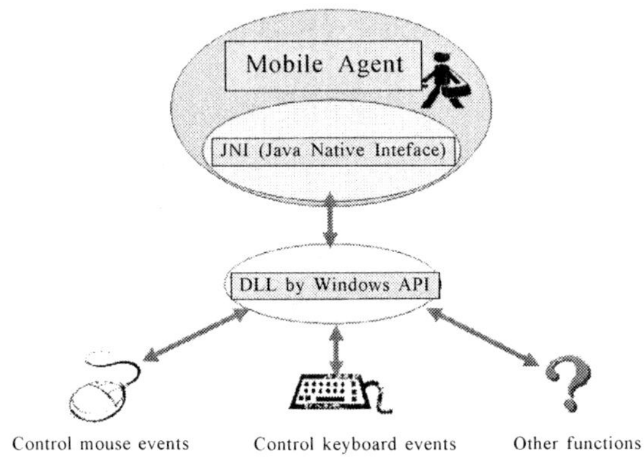

In our system, there are six mobile agents implemented, including guide agent, monitor agent, demo agent, assessment agent, homework agent, and learning agent. These agents are designed for the platform on the teacher side and the student side, and each mobile agent has different capability. The guide agent, assessment agent, demo agent, and homework agent work in the foreground. Above agents have user interface to allow the user to interact directly with the system. Other agents without the awareness of their existence by the user work in the background.

There are three basic patterns for an agent, the aglet class object, wrapper class object, and guide class object. The aglet class allows the mobile agent to execute in the aglet agent execution environment. This object class provides VDSPL the network capability. The wrapper class object provides mobile agent a way to interact with the wrapper agent. The guide class allows agents to communicate and interact with the user. This class provides function calls for the wrapper script. Each type of mobile agent uses different teaching and learning knowledge-based rules. If the predicate of each rule is satisfied, the mobile agent will take predefined actions.

System Prototype

A prototype of VDSPL is presented in this section. As shown in Figure 7, when the mobile agent platform starts running, it will first initiate an experimental platform and provide an agent list for the teacher. If the teacher needs an agent

Figure 7. Guide agent

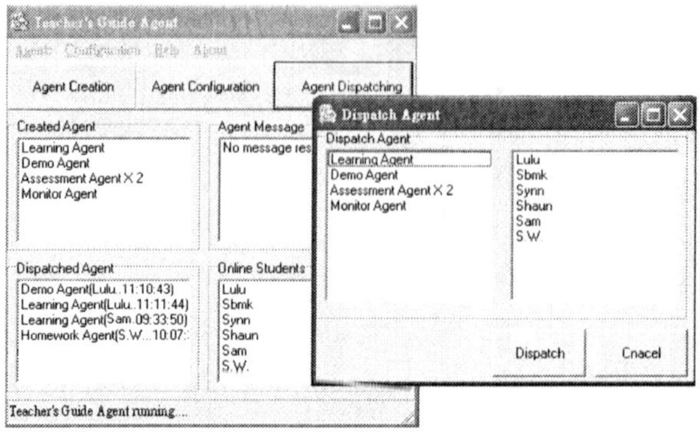

Figure 8. Learning agent

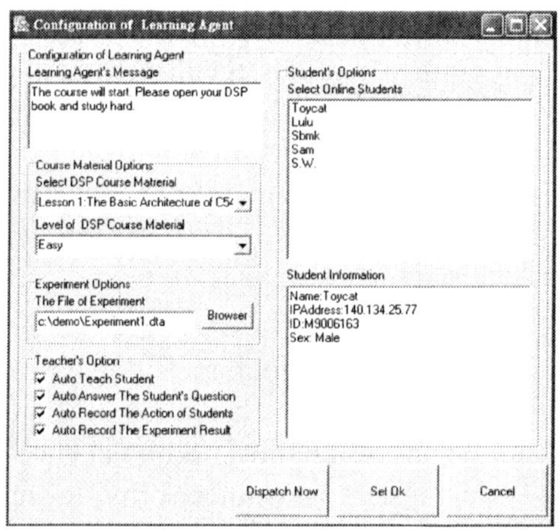

service or wants to communicate with students, the guide agent can be used to do so. Figure 8 shows a learning agent which supports different materials and topics. After the guide agent clones a learning agent for students, the learning agent will carry the learning materials, which are determined by the teacher. When the learning agent starts, the students will receive a message informing them and the learning program will start and then load the DSP learning materials. Sometimes, the teacher wants to provide a demonstration of the experiment for students in an experimental course. The learning agent can employ the guide agent to collect the student actions and experimental results, and dispatch a demo agent to students. After the guide agent clones a demo agent

Figure 9. A snapshot of the system when the demo agent starts

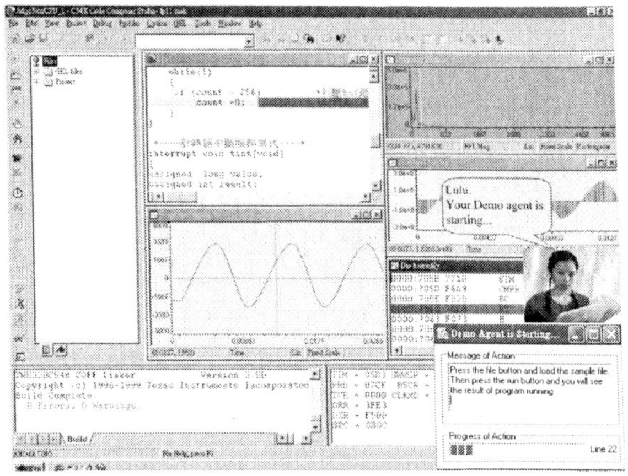

Figure 10. Assessment dispatching

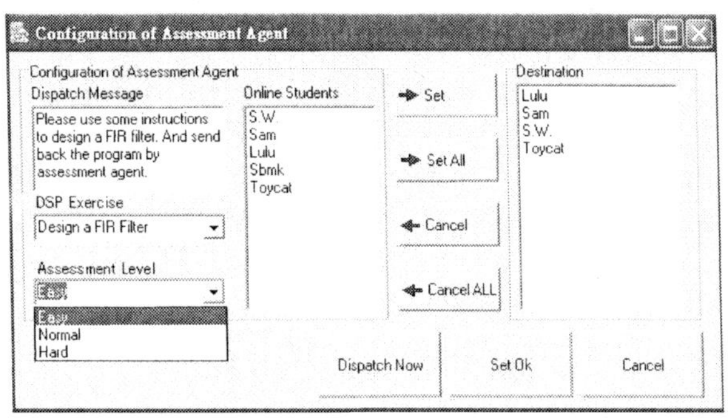

for students, the demo agent will carry a predefined script. If the students have problems, then the learning agent will notify the teacher's guide agent. The teacher will then interact with the student through the guide agent.

Figure 9 is a snapshot of the prototype when the demo agent starts, and the demonstration example will be presented step by step according to the demo script. In VDSPL, we have also created a Web site that provides news, DSP introduction, DSP material zone, on-line learning, download, discussion board, and related links.

According to each student's status, the teacher can assign an assessment to the students. The assessment agent supports different assessment levels and exercises as shown in Figure 10. The students will be informed and the assessment program will start and then an assessment is loaded. The agent will automatically record the scores or carries the assessment results and send to the teacher's guide agent when they finish their work.

Experimental Results

Experiments were conducted and surveys were taken to evaluate the user satisfaction of our system. Graduate students and teachers in our department were recruited to conduct these experiments. A total fifteen graduate students and five teachers are inquired in our experiments. We investigated the user satisfaction of our system from the point of view of both students and teachers for the following system metrics, including demonstration, interaction, monitoring, assessment, and network capability. The demonstration function could demonstrate the steps of the experiment and let students have an overview of the experiment; this function is provided by the demo agent. The interaction function could provide an interface between a teacher and a student to interactive with each other; this function is provided by the guide agent. The monitoring function could act as the teacher to monitor the actions and learning statuses of students; this function is provided by the monitor agent. The assessment function could give an assessment to check a student's learning results and provide different levels of assessment materials; this function is provided by the assessment agent.

Figure 11. VDSP metrics from the point of view of students

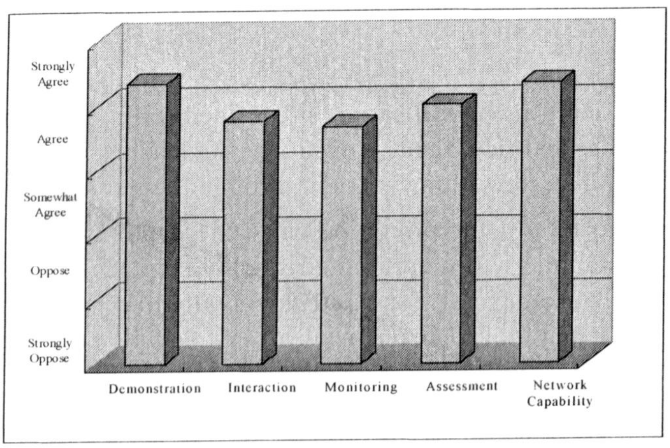

Figure 12. VDSP metrics from the point of view of teachers

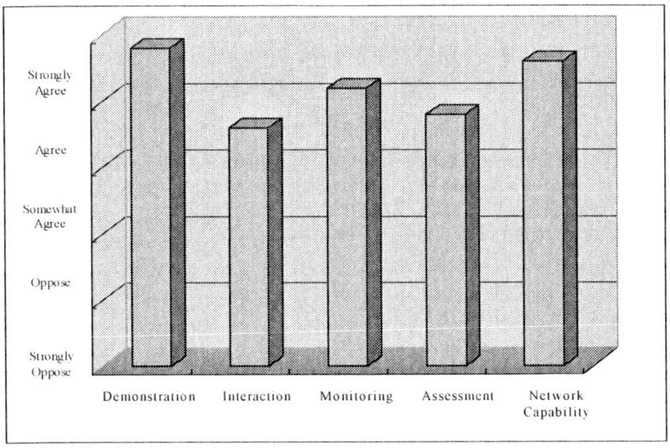

The network capability is provided by using the wrapper and agent techniques to enable the network function of stand-alone DSP development tools. The feedbacks of students and teachers for the five system metrics are shown in Figures 11 and 12, respectively. We can observe that both students and teachers have positive feedbacks for our system, especially for the functions of demonstration and network capability.

In addition to evaluating the user satisfaction of our system, experiments were also conducted to evaluate the importance of these five functions for a virtual laboratory of DSP experiments. From the point of the view of students, the importance of these functions from high to low is demonstration, network capability, interaction, assessment, and monitoring. From the point of the view of teachers, the importance of these functions from high to low is demonstration, monitoring, assessment, network capability, and interaction. We can observe that demonstration is the most importance function for a virtual laboratory from the point of view of both students and teachers. The reason is because demonstrating the steps of an experiment is very important for conducting a laboratory. From the point of view of teachers, the function of monitoring is also very important. However, it is less important from the point of view of students. This is because a teacher may want to know the learning statuses and behaviors of their students. However, most of the students prefer a more carefree learning environment without the teacher to tie them down. As shown in Figures 11 and 12, it is also very interesting that the monitoring function provided by our system is enough from the point of view of students but it could be improved from the point of view of teachers.

Conclusion

In this chapter, we present VDSPL, a mobile agent-based virtual digital signal processing laboratory. Our system incorporates agent techniques with DSP development tools to provide teachers and students with various instructions and interactions. The mobile agent and wrapper techniques are used to enable the network capability of stand-alone DSP development tools and improve the teacher to student interaction for distance DSP learning. Furthermore, the students can get guidance and learn in the personalized environment through mobile agents. In addition, the mobile agent and design patterns are also used to perform software re-engineering and provide a virtual laboratory.

References

Arndt, T., Chang, S. K., Guercio, A., & Maresca, P. (2002). An XML-based approach to multimedia software engineering for distance learning. *Proceedings of the 14th International Conference on Software Engineering and Knowledge Engineering* (pp. 525-532).

Chang, S. K., Arndt, T., Levialdi, S., Liu, A. C., Ma, J., Shih, T., & Tortora, G. (2000). Macro University: A framework for a federation of virtual universities. *International Journal of Computer Processing of Oriental Languages, 13*(3), 205-221.

Causen, A., Spanias, A., Xavier, A., & Tampi, M. (1998). A Java signal analysis tool for signal processing experiments. *Proceedings of the 1998 IEEE International Conference on Acoustics, Speech and Signal Processing* (Vol. 3, pp. 1849-1852).

Chang, W. F., Wu, Y. C., Chiu, C. W., & Yu, W. C. (2003). Design and implementation of a Web-based distance PLC laboratory. *Proceedings of the 35th Southeastern Symposium on System Theory* (pp. 326-329).

Concepcion, A. I., Ruan, J., & Samson, R. R. (2002). SPIDER: A multi-agent architecture for internet distributed computing system. *Proceedings of the ISCA 15th International Conference on Parallel and Distributed Computing Systems* (pp. 147-152).

Dey, A. K. (2000). Enabling the use of context in interactive applications. *Proceedings of the 2000 Conference on Human Factors in Computing Systems* (pp. 79-80).

DMATEK Co. Ltd. (n.d.). Retrieved from http://www.dmatek.com.tw/ (2005).

Dorca, F. A., Lopes, C. R., & Fernandes, M. A. (2003). A multiagent architecture for distance education systems. *Proceedings of the 3rd IEEE International Conference on Advanced Learning Technologies* (pp. 368-369).

Dow, C. R, Lin, C. Y., & Hsu, F. W. (2002). A mobile agent-based virtual language learning laboratory. *Proceedings of the International Conference on Chinese Language Computing* (pp. 98-103).

Dow, C. R., Lin, C. Y., Shen, C. C., Lin, J. H., & Chen, S. C. (2002). A virtual laboratory for macro universities using mobile agent techniques. *The International Journal of Computer Processing of Oriental Languages, 15*(1), 1-18.

Gan, W. S., Chong, Y. K., Gong, W., & Tan, W. T. (2000). Rapid prototyping system for teaching real-time digital signal processing. *IEEE Transactions on Education, 43*(1), 19-24.

IBM's Java Aglet. (n.d.). Retrieved from http://www.trl.ibm.com/aglets/ (2005).

Lange, D. B., & Oshima, M. (1998). *Programming and deploying Java mobile agents with aglets*. Boston: Addison Wesley.

Mousavinezhad, S. H., & Abdel-Qader, I. M. (2001). Digital signal processing in theory and practice. *Proceedings of the 31st ASEE/IEEE Frontiers in Education Conference*.

Pham, V. A., & Karmouch, A. (1998). Mobile software agents: An overview. *IEEE Communications Magazine, 36*(7), 26-37.

Silva, A., Silva, M. M., & Delgado, J. (1998). *AgentSpace: A next-generation mobile agent system*. Lecture Notes in Computer Science.

Silva, L. M., Soares, G., Martins, P., Batista, V., & Santos, L. (1999). *Comparing the performance of mobile agent system: A study of benchmarking*. Technical Report, JAMES Project.

Sudmann, N. P., & Johansen, D. (2001). Supporting mobile agent applications using wrappers. *Proceedings of the 12th International Workshop on Database and Expert Systems Applications* (pp. 689-695).

Texas Instrument. (n.d.). Retrieved from http://www.ti.com.tw/ (2005).

Wu, H. T., Hsiao, T. C., Chen, C. L., Su, C. M., Su, J. C., & Jiang, J. C. (2001). An integrated teaching and learning DSP lab system. *Journal of Science and Technology, 10*(1), 29-36.

Section IV Educational Technologies

Chapter X

Interactive E-Learning

Claude Ghaoui, Liverpool John Moores University, UK

W. A. Janvier, Liverpool John Moores University, UK

Abstract

This chapter introduces the concept of improving student memory retention using a distance learning tool by establishing the student's communication preference and learning style before the student uses the module contents. It argues that incorporating a distance learning tool with an intelligent/interactive tutoring system using various components (psychometric tests, communication preference, learning styles, mapping learning/teaching styles, neurolinguistic programming language patterns, subliminal text messaging, motivational factors, novice/expert factor, student model, and the way we learn) combined in WISDeM to create a human-computer interactive interface distance learning tool does indeed enhance memory retention. The authors show that WISDeM's initial evaluation indicates that a student's retained knowledge has been improved from a mean average of 63.57% to 71.09% — moving the student from a B to an A.

Introduction

This chapter discusses interaction between the computer interface and the user in e-learning and indicates that the correct use of component parts, as a result changing the way the interface interacts with each student, is likely to enhance his or her memory. Catania (1992) reports that sensory input is mainly derived from iconic (sight) 60%, auditory (hearing) 30%, haptic (touch) 10% — as little derives from olfactory (smell) and gustatory (taste). Driscoll and Garcia (2000), Fleming (2001), Fleming and Mills (1998), Fuller, Norby, Pearce, and Strand (2000), and Murphy, Newman, Jolosky, and Swank (2002) show that everyone has his or her own sensual preference for exchanging ideas, and acquiring and passing on knowledge. Sadowski and Stanney (1999) report that there is a tendency to prefer one sensory input (visual, auditory, or kinaesthetic — tactile/haptic). Fleming's 2001 research shows that most students prefer multi-modal communication. Liu, Pastoor, Seifert, and Hurtienne (2000) assert that multimodal interfaces are more natural and engaging, encouraging a wider use of human senses and perceptual systems and that, latterly, video-games are introducing the Haptic sense, with the mouse and joysticks, and balance through headsets.

Hypothesis

As this chapter's authors, we consider that communication preference (CP) linked to learning styles (LS) interaction is not used in e-learning (Janvier & Ghaoui, 2001, 2002a, 2002b). Our research hypothesis is

Matching neurolinguistic (NLP) language patterns in a distance learning tool (DLT)-interactive/intelligent tutoring system (ITS) will enhance human-computer interface/interaction (HCI) communication and, thus, enhance the storing of and recall of instances to and from the learner's memory.

WISDeM (Web intelligent/interactive student distance-education model) develops this.

Components

Distance Learning Tool

The learner should find a DLT intuitive to use with either an extranet, intranet, or Internet browser with the ideal DLT encompassing self-directed learning (English & Yazdani, 1999), asynchronous and synchronous communication (Phillos, Merisotis, & O'Brien, 1999; Turgeon, 1999; Wang, Jorg, Rubart, & Tietze, 2000), and intelligent interaction[1] to each learner's own profile capable of dynamically changing as the learner develops, offering: relevant links to libraries, system resources and WWW websites, hints, structured answers, tracking every learner's progress and 'learning' from the learner's usage and interactivity (see A'Herran, 2000, for an excellent presentation of the various components usually offered).

A DLT should also exhibit easy-intuitive-flexible-authoring facilities; while this is not required for the student, it is vital for the tutor to be able to make changes fast and easily. The questions that need to be posed for any DLT are:

1. Is authoring easy?
2. Is there an administrative Web database front-end?
3. Can the author create/add/amend/delete content?
4. Can questions and answers be easily created?
5. Is it easy to authorize and control student access?
6. Is online authoring training/support available?

The JCU (2000) report looked for ease of maintenance, flexibility, integration of legacy materials, consistency, a uniform framework, quality of design, and streamlining administrative procedures. Allison, Lawson, McKechan, and Ruddle (2000) suggested that quality of service needs to be addressed for all stakeholders, including students and tutors/authors. Konstandinidis, Ng, and Ghaoui (2000) consider that the number of authoring steps required should be kept low with a simple authoring interface. Technologies (2000) reported that current development authoring DLT programs/modules are experiencing a major shift in thinking: the vision is to create small independent "learning objects" in repositories for modules to be assembled as required.

Interactive Intelligent Tutoring System

Wær (1997) considers that intelligent interfaces must make an improvement: resulting interfaces should be better than other solutions, not just different and technically more advanced. The research area of intelligent interfaces comprises two research complimentary issues: (1) creating an interface design that takes regard of the model's limitations in reasoning power and interaction modalities, and (2) the extension of the reasoning power and presentation for the interface. The roots for research on intelligent interface design lies mainly in cognitive psychology: ITS should try to adapt to and understand the user's way of thinking. Canut, Gouarderes, and Sanchis (1999) consider that emerging multi-agent ITSs have four main components: *learner model, knowledge model, pedagogical model,* and the *interface model.* Nkambou and Kabanza (2001) report that recent ITS architectures have focused on the tutor or curriculum components, paying little attention to planning intelligent collaboration between different components. They suggest that the ideal architecture contains a curriculum model[2], pedagogical model[3], and a learner model[4] (central in ITS).

Sensory Interaction: Neurolinguistic Programming Language Patterns[5]

E-learning multi-modality uses multiple-student-sensory inputs. Cotton (1995) reports that each type of person uses their main preceptor style to store and recall memories: echoic use auditory perception in communication, iconic use visual perception in communication, and haptic communicate with feelings. The NLP model suggests that subjective experience is encoded in terms of three main representation systems: visual, auditory, and kinesthetic (VAK). Practitioners of NLP claim that people have a tendency to prefer one representation system over another in a given context: the visual system includes external images, as well as remembered or constructed internal mental images; the auditory system includes external sounds and remembered or contrived internal sounds and the internal dialogue (i.e., a person talking to themselves on the inside); and the kinesthetic system includes tactile sensations caused by external forces acting on the body and emotional responses (Sadowski & Stanney, 1999). Pasztor (1998) reports that inter-partner rapport is key to effective communication, and that incorporating NLP language patterns and eye-gaze (see also Colburn, Cohen, & Drucker, 2000; Sadowski & Stanney, 1999) in intelligent agents will allow customization of the (virtual) personal assistant to the particular habits and interests of the user, making the system more user-friendly. Pasztor (1998) confirms that introducing the correct sub-modality (VAK) will enable the subject to more easily remember and recall instances.

Figure 1. Communication preference & learning styles flow chart used to establish the student's CP (visual, auditory, or kinaesthetic preference) and LS

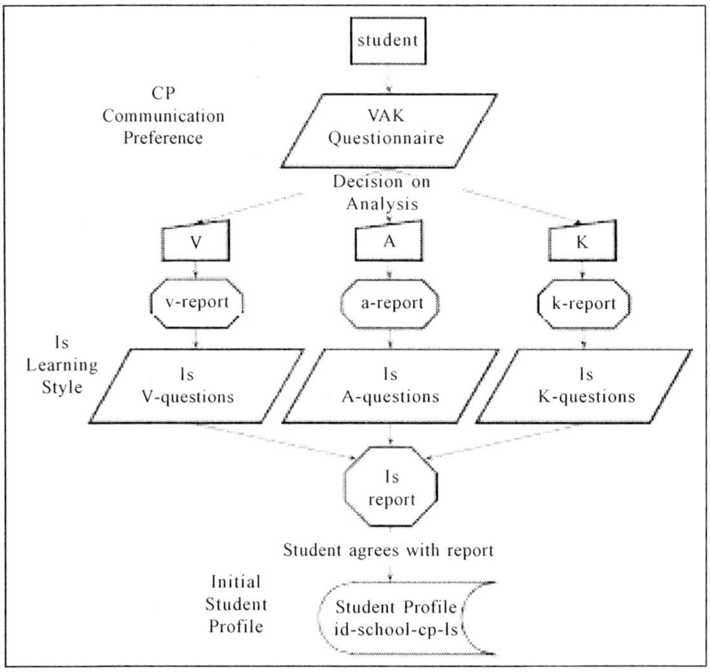

Psychometric Test: Communication Preference

Fleming (2001) suggests four sensory-modality categories that reflect students' experiences are used for learning. Named VARK[6], these include: *visually*-orientated students prefer information input via their eyes, in charts, graphs, flow charts, and symbolic representation; *aural*-orientated students prefer hearing information; *read/write*-orientated students prefer information displayed as words; and *kinaesthetic*-orientated students prefer to learn by doing, simulating real-world experience and practice. His research shows that the number of multi-modal students in a class can range from approximately 50%-90%, depending upon context. Borchert, Jensen, and Yates (1999) state that the VARK psychometric tests reveal how students prefer to receive and process information, but not necessarily how they learn best, and Driscoll and Garcia (2000) report that results from student class profiles using VARK indicate that their *learning styles are firmly in place by the time a student is 18 and may well differ substantially from what their tutors perceive or assume.*

Psychometric Test: Personality Type Indicator

MBTI® (Myers & Myers, 1995) is a self-report personality inventory designed to provide information about your Jungian psychological type preferences[7]. Murphy and colleagues' (2002) research shows that MBTI® is more widely used by educators in the U.S. than any other tool and that the system is widely used around the world in many languages. MBTI® has four preference categories

1. **Interpersonal communication:** Extroversion focuses outwardly on and gains energy from others; introversion focuses inwardly and gains energy from ideas and concepts
2. **Information processing:** Sensing focuses on the five senses and experience; iNtuition focuses on possibilities, future use, the big picture
3. **Information evaluation:** Thinking focuses on objective facts and causes and effect; Feeling focuses on subjective meaning and values
4. **Decision style:** Judgment focuses on timely, planned conclusions and decisions; Perception focuses on the adaptive process of decision making

Most researchers see information processing as the most important of the four categories in terms of implications for education (Borchert et al., 1999).

Figure 2. Personality types (extrovert, introvert, sensing, intuitive, feeling, thinking, perceptive, judgmental) comparative results

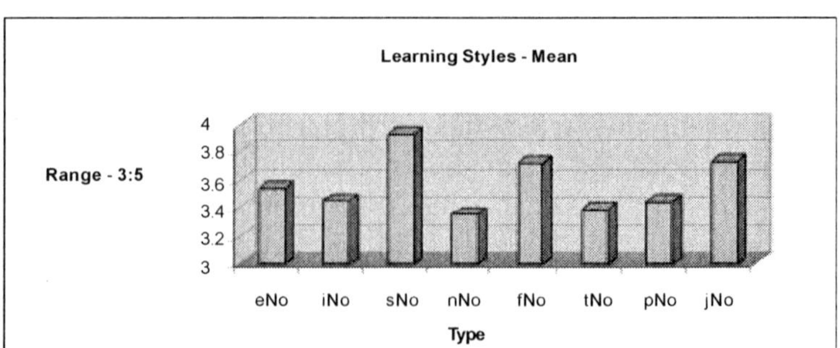

Figure 3. Sixteen learning styles distribution: E = extrovert, I = introvert, S = sensing, N = intuition, F = feeling, T = thinking, P = perception, and J = judgment

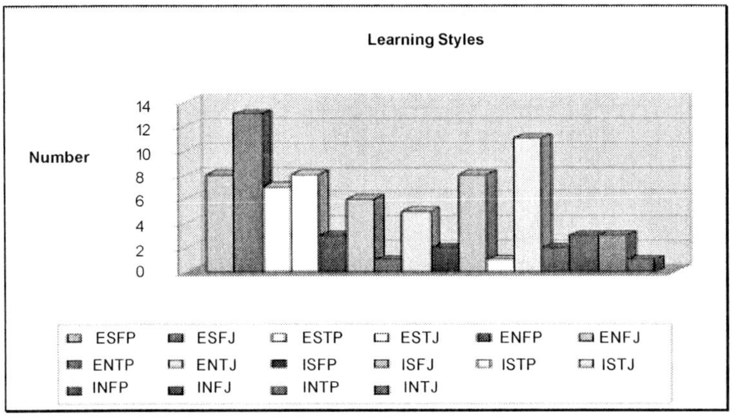

Figure 4. Comparative Gain in Student Retained Knowledge

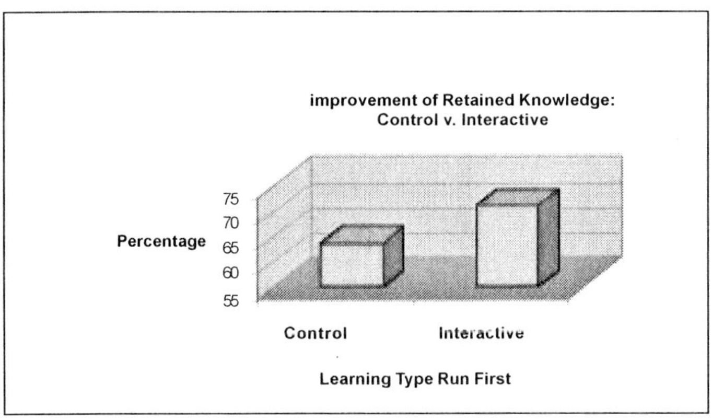

Tool, "WISDeM"

WISDeM has been developed as a generic DLT with an ITS section; it initially uses two psychometric tests to establish the student model (SM) BEFORE the module is accessed. The SM represents the student's CP + LS[8] + Novice-Expert[9] factor (NE) (Biggs, 1994; Handley, 2002). The DLT uses HTML, DynamicHTML, CSS Style, JavaScript, Active Server Pages, and Structured Query Language, linking to the database using ODBC. The student's DLT includes: university links, registration and login, low-vision user facility, staff information and module content (overview, specification, main topics, coursework, exam papers, revision (multi-choice question and answer (Q&A)), tutorials, courses (additional information)), resources, download, evaluation, feedback, forum, mail-list, student registration, search, help, MS NetMeeting).

WISDeM Interactive Tutorial Design

The multi-choice Q&A interactive interface and SM are dynamically changed in real time as the student progresses through the module topics. The interface provides feedback based on the SM and motivational requirements. The tutorial is designed with two sections, topic revision and course revision. Topic revision allows the student to either LEARN or TEST knowledge for any released topic, thus promoting memory rehearsal[10] (it offers either a learning[11] or an intelligent interactive testing[12] tool). Course revision picks a random multi-choice question from all the released topics; it does not provide interactivity and therefore provides a good test of long-term retained knowledge.

Scenario

A new learner, Jo, connects to WISDeM, selects his school and module, and then uses his university registration ID, password, and module selection to log on. The system checks if he is new or existing. If the former, the CP question/answer screen is opened where Jo is asked to complete the CP questionnaire by selecting only those statements with which he agrees: his visual, auditory, or kinaesthetic preference is established. When completed, the LS question/answer screens are activated. The questions/answers are couched using his NLP language pattern as ascertained from the CP answers. The resulting learner profile is saved in the learner profile repository, and the module front page is opened (see Figure 1).

Jo experiments with 'topic learning' and finds that he can open any topic using the hyperlinks at the top of the table — each topic opens with the first question with three answers. He goes back to topic 1, question 1 and reads the header message. He now reads the question and clicks the bibliography link to check if he has the correct reading material for in-depth learning; he likes the way each answer is expanded with feedback, providing him with information about the answer: why it is incorrect or correct. He notes that the color coding allows him to easily understand the various parts of the page. He clicks the next question button and reads this question. Here he sees that there is a link to a diagram; he clicks the link and remembers that it was used in his lecture. Jo continues to use topic learning until he has reached the end of the questions and answers. *Note:* Each question, answer, and feedback includes a suitable NLP language pattern subliminal text message[13] (Catania, 1992; Gustavsson, 1994) header designed to activate Jo's preferred sensory communication channel (VAK).

Jo opens topic testing to see how well he has remembered the material. He answers the first question, reads the feedback, and notes that his selected answer was correct. He now proceeds to use the facilities and answer questions, and watches his progress for about an hour before leaving the system. When he returns he logs in again and is pleased to note that the system picks up where he stopped; he completes revision for topic 1. He likes the way he can control feedback output, see all the feedback to each answer. He also finds that the header messages and information page act as a reminder to enable to him plan his revision.

Evaluation

The evaluation formed two parts: Part 1: Evaluate the LOGON that required the student to report on the results from two psychometric tests. Part 2: evaluated the interactive ITS multi-choice Q&A section of WISDeM.

Part 1 had 93 responders (82 male, 11 female): 68.09% visual, 27.66% auditory, 4.26% kinaesthetic. The average time to complete logon and complete the short questionnaire was 15 minutes; 64.29% were extrovert and 35.71% introvert (Extrovert | Introvert: 54/39, Sensing | iNtuitive: 65/28, Feeling | Thinking: 47/30, Perception | Judgment: 30/63). Each type was rated from 0 to 5; the mean rating for the dominant type, from a possible rating of 3 to 5, was E=3.56 | I=3.49, S=3.97 | N=3.25, F=3.67 | T=3.51 and P=3.50 | J=3.73 (see Figure 2). The largest LS was ISTJ — 16.678%, with the second being ESFJ — 15.48% (see Figure 3).

Part 2 had 72 students log into the system. The average time taken for the evaluation/exercise was 84 minutes, varying from 50 minutes to 140 minutes. The mean mark for control subjects was 63.57%, and the mean mark for interactive subjects was 71.09% (see Figure 4). Comparing the mean gain made by students: those who completed the non-interactive Q&As first gained 21.67%; those who completed the interactive Q&As first gained 25.00%. The NE factor was substantially better for the interactive students as compared with the non-interactive students (6.75 : 3.75). In analyzing the use of button and link facility between the two types (interactive and non-interactive interfaces) of topic learning and topic testing, there was little difference noted in comparing the same buttons for each system. Overall, the interactive students used the facility buttons 10.21 times each, as compared with 8.93 each for the non-interactive students. There was an additional use of buttons for the interactive-student; the mean usage for each was: header messages link = 0.50, change feedback response = 0.75, header message = 0.75, answer feedback = 1.00, and statistical report = 0.88. These links are not available for the non-interactive student.

Conclusion

The initial evaluation results indicate that WISDeM's interactive system is likely to make a significant improvement to student learning and memory. The interactive system produced more rehearsal from students than the control system and improved their marks; it was easier and more interesting to use with greater facilities to research and rehearse knowledge. There was a general belief in the system, "that it did indeed assist knowledge retention." This in itself is an important factor for the students' psyche. As compared with the neutral system, the interactive system held interest longer and was more capable of interacting at the student's own level than the control system.

References

A'Herran, A. (2000, September). *Research & evaluation of online learning systems.* Paper presented at ALTC-2000, UMIST Manchester, UK.

Allison, C., Lawson, H., McKechan, D., & Ruddle, A. (2000). *Quality of service issues in distributed learning environments.* St Andrews, Scotland: School of Computer Science, University of St Andrews.

Biggs, J. (1994). Student learning research and theory—where do we currently stand? In G. Gibbs (Ed.), *Improving student learning—theory and practice,* Oxford Centre for Staff Development (pp. 1-13). Hong Kong: University of Hong Kong.

Borchert, R., Jensen, D., & Yates, D. (1999). *Hands-on and visualization modules for enhancement of learning in mechanics: Development and assessment in the context of Myers Briggs Types and VARK learning styles.* Paper presented at the ASEE Annual Conference, Charlotte, NC.

Canut, M.F., Gouarderes, G., & Sanchis, E. (1999). The Systemion: A new agent model to design intelligent tutoring system. In S.P.L.a.M. Vivet (Ed.), *Artificial intelligence in education—frontiers in artificial intelligence and applications* (pp. 54-65). IOS Press.

Catania, A.C. (1992). *Learning—remembering* (3rd ed.). Prentice-Hall International Editions.

Colburn, R.A., Cohen, M.F., & Drucker, S.M. (2000). *The role of eye gaze in Avatar mediated conversational interfaces*. Retrieved September 2002, from http://www.itpapers.com/cgi/PSummaryIT.pl?paperid=10265&scid=431, http://citeseer.nj.nec.com/colburn00role.html

Cotton, J. (1995). *The theory of learning—an introduction*. London: Kogan Page.

Driscoll, S.A., & Garcia, C.E. (2000). *Preferred learning styles for engineering students*. Paper presented at the ASEE Annual Conference, St. Louis, MO.

English, E., & Yazdani, M. (1999). Computer-supported cooperative learning in a virtual university. *Journal of Computer Assisted Learning, 15,* 2-13.

Fleming, N. (2001). *Teaching and learning styles: VARK strategies.*

Fleming, N.D., & Mills, C. (1998, May). *Not another inventory, rather a catalyst for reflection. VARK for teachers, VARK study strategies.* Paper presented at the AAHE's Focus on Learning, Atlanta, GA.

Fuller, D., Norby, R.F., Pearce, K., & Strand, S. (2000). Internet teaching by style: Profiling the online professor. *Educational Technology & Society, 3*(2), 71-85.

Gustavsson, B. (1994, March 21-22). *Technologizing of consciousness—problems in textualizing organizations.* Paper presented at the Workshop on Writing, Rationality, and Organization, Brussels.

Handley, K. (2002, September 26-27). *Comparison of novice and expert learner's perception of instructional feedback in computer-based training to develop managerial problem-solving skills.* Paper presented at the HCT2002 Workshop—Tools for Thought: Communication and Learning Through Digital Technology, Brighton, UK.

Janvier, W.A., & Ghaoui, C. (2001, September 26-27). *Searching for WISDeM, the Holy Grail of intelligent distance education.* Paper presented at the HCT2001 Workshop—Information Technologies and Knowledge Construction: Bringing Together the Best of Two Worlds, University of Sussex, Brighton, UK.

Janvier, W.A., & Ghaoui, C. (2002a, September 26-27). *WISDeM: Communication preference and learning styles in HCI.* Paper presented at the HCT2002 Workshop—Tools for Thought: Communication and Learning Through Digital Technology, Brighton, UK.

Janvier, W. A., & Ghaoui, C. (2002b, November 1-4). *WISDeM—student profiling using communication preference and learning styles mapping to teaching styles.* Paper presented at the APCHI 2002—5th Asia Pacific Conference on Computer Human Interaction, Beijing, China.

JCU. (2000). *Online systems: Research and evaluation.* Retrieved September 2002, from http://www.tld.jcu.edu. au/general/syrvey_re/recs.html

Konstandinidis, V., Ng, E. H., & Ghaoui, C. (2000). *Dynamic reference to support authoring of Web-based material.* School of Computing and Mathematical Sciences, Liverpool John Moores University, UK.

Liu, J., Pastoor, S., Seifert, K., & Hurtienne, J. (2000, November 5-8). *Three-dimensional PC: Toward novel forms of human-computer interaction.* Paper presented at the SPIE International Symposium on Information Technologies, Boston.

Murphy, E., Newman, J., Jolosky, T., & Swank, P. (2002). *What is the Myers-Briggs Type Indicator (MBTI)®.* Retrieved October 2002, from http://www.aptcentral.org/training/aptcheck.pdf

Myers, I. B., & Myers, P. B. (1995). *Gifts differing: Understanding personality type.* Palo Alto, CA: Financial Times, Prentice-Hall.

Nkambou, R., & Kabanza, F. (2001). *Designing intelligent tutoring systems: A multi-agent planning approach.*

Pasztor, A. (1998). Subjective experience divided and conquered, communication and cognition. In E. Myin (Ed.), *Approaching consciousness, Part II* (pp. 73-102). Retrieved from http://citeseer.nj.nec.com/pasztor98subjective .html

Phillos, R., Merisotis, J., & O'Brien, C. (1999). *What's the difference? A review of contemporary research on the effectiveness of distance learning in higher education.* Institute for Higher Education Policy.

Sadowski, W., & Stanney, K. (1999). *Measuring and managing presence in virtual environments.* Retrieved January 2002, from http://vehand.engr.ucf.edu/handbook/Chapters/Chapter45.html

Technologies, T. C. f. L. (2000). *The design, development and delivery of Internet-based training and education.* Retrieved from http://teleeducation. nb.ca/media/reports.shtml

Turgeon, A. J. (1999). *Implications of Web-based technology for engaging students in a learning society.* Retrieved from http://www.adec.edu/user/resource/turgeon-implications.html

Wær, A. (1997). *What is an intelligent interface? Introduction seminar.* Retrieved June 2002, from http://www.sics.se/~annika/papers/intint.html

Wang, W. H., Jorg, M., Rubart, J., & Tietze, D. (2000). *Supporting cooperative learning of process knowledge on the World Wide Web.*

Endnotes

1 **Intelligent interaction:** Individual student-profiles dynamically changing as the student develops, tracking individual progress and '*learning*' from the student's usage/interactivity

2 **Curriculum model:** Curriculum objects describing subject matter from a domain, pedagogical and didactical point of view, and course object — describing one particular course

3 **Pedagogical model:** Tutorial actions, lesson planner, and multimedia presentation generation

4 **Learner model:** Learner model, didactic resource, and GUI interface

5 **Neurolinguistic programming language patterns:** For example, in text or speech, using words and descriptions that are 'visual' for visual subjects, 'auditory' for auditory subjects, and 'emotional' for kinaesthetic subjects

6 **VARK:** The VARK psychometric test now covers multi-modality as a preference

7 **Jungian psychological type preferences:** Carl G. Jung was a Swiss psychiatrist (1875-1961) who identified certain psychological types (extroversion/introversion, judgment/perception)

8 **Learning styles** (in WISDeM)**:** Derived from the 16 personality types developed using Carl Jungian and MBTIÒ (Myers & Myers, 1995) principles

9 **Novice expert:** This factor copes with the changing requirements as a novice becomes more experienced and requires less support. It varies from 0 to 8 (novice to expert), has an initial default of 3, and is incremented for each correct answer or decremented for each incorrect answer; it is set to default for each new topic.

10 **Memory rehearsal:** Retention of an instance (sensual input) is improved with rehearsal moving that instance from short-term memory to long-term memory, provided that the perceptual filters allow retention

11 **Topic learning:** This provides information for each module topic, allowing the student to develop knowledge. It covers: Q&As for each topic, select any topic's Q&As, see the relevant bibliography, select next question. Each answer gives feedback, indicating the reason why it is correct or incorrect.

12 **Topic testing:** This allows the student to test retained knowledge. It provides a running % total (carried forward), Q&As for each topic, see ques-

tion specific bibliography, see correct answer, restart current topic at Q1, restart revision at Topic1/Q1, select next question, see any topic correct answers, view analysis report or statistical report, progress is saved, the student starts where he/she last stopped.

13 **Subliminal text messaging:** Subliminal images and text (instance input that the conscious mind does not observe but the subconscious does) can have a powerful effect on memory and cognitive memory. "Unconscious words are pouring into awareness where conscious thought is experienced, which could from then on be spoken (the lips) and/or written down" (Gustavsson, 1994).

This work previously appeared in the International Journal of Distance Education Technologies, 2*(3), 26-35, copyright 2004.*

Chapter XI

Using Ontology as Scaffolding for Authoring Teaching Materials

Jin-Tan Yang, National Kaohsiung Normal University, Taiwan

Pao Ta Yu, National Chung-Cheng University, Taiwan

Nian Shing Chen, National Sun-Yat-Sen University, Taiwan

Chun Yen Tsai, National Kaohsiung Normal University, Taiwan

Chi-Chin Lee, National Kaohsiung Normal University, Taiwan

Timothy K. Shih, Tamkang University, Taiwan

Abstract

The purpose of this study is to conduct teachers to author a teaching material by using visualized domain ontology as scaffolding. Based on a content repository management system (CRMS), mathematics ontology to support teachers for authoring teaching materials is developed. Although the domain ontology of mathematics at secondary school level in Taiwan provides structured vocabularies for describing domain content, those teachers who want to create a knowledge-rich description of domain knowledge, such as required by the "Semantic Web," use ontology that turns out to provide only part of knowledge required. In this chapter, we examine problems related to capturing the learning resources or learning objects (LOs) on a CRMS. To construct ontology for a subset of mathematics course descriptions, the representation requirements by resource description framework/resource description framework schema (RDF/RDFS) was implemented. Furthermore, a visualized online authoring tool (VOAT) is designed for authoring teaching materials on the Web. Finally, discussion and future research are addressed.

Introduction

Learning objects (LOs) (Wiley, 2001) are a promising way to create modules of reusable learning content associated with metadata (Yang & Tsai, 2002). The high-quality content, composed by learning objects, has been proven to be the most important requirement for a successful e-learning activity. However, developing educational resources such as a teaching material frequently requires significant efforts from teachers as well as support from a team of skilled professionals. To respond to the stern realities of high development costs and restricted budgets, developing learning object repositories offers a robust and sustainable strategy.

Learning objects in a content repository management system (CRMS), a SCORM-compliant learning object repository, can be used to support effective search mechanisms and provide advantages for teachers and course developers. A digital course is generally presented as hierarchical for flexibility in terms insertion and deletion. The amount of LOs on CRMS has dramatically increased as time proceeds. It raises an issue that a teacher might have trouble to deal with LOs while he/she uses keywords or form-based slots to acquire LOs on a CRMS.

Several initiatives are trying to resolve practical difficulties related to reuse of learning object technology. These arise in the indexation and retrieval of material (ARIADNE, 2001), creation of new learning content based on individual learning requirements, or development of standards, specifications and tools (ADL, 2002; IMS, 2000; LTSC, 2001). Stimulated by these initiatives, several computer-based training vendors have implemented their own tools, which have begun to provide teachers with wide range of LOs. Up to date, it, however, is still far away for teachers to author their teaching material since guiding authoring is not always supported.

We address the problem of capturing knowledge needed for indexing and retrieving information using highly structured semantic descriptions in this study. Such structured descriptions can be much richer than the traditional "set of terms approach." In fact, they come nearer to a description in natural language, often considered to be the ideal way of describing and indexing teaching material. In order to circumvent the problems of ambiguity in natural language descriptions and queries, structured descriptions should be limited to a fixed set of predefined structures and a set of closed vocabularies. Ontology has a set of closed terms and relations among those terms for simple inference.

In this chapter, we assume that the structured descriptions are created by a human annotator using specialized tools. Two related problems arise in this approach: (1) how can a teacher be supported during processes of authoring teaching materials, and (2) where do domain terms or ontology for filling in a structured description come from? The solution to these problems that we pursue in this chapter is to implement mathematics at secondary school level of Taiwan by domain ontology to support rich structured descriptions.

This chapter is structured as follows. Firstly, we review literature on various alternative approaches to teaching material indexing and retrieval and the requirements that they pose on vocabularies. Secondly, we give brief description of methodology of this study. Thirdly, results of this study are demonstrated. Finally, some problems arising in using domain ontology as conducting strategy are also included in the conclusion.

Literature Review

In this section, four major issues on learning object retrieval are reviewed, brief description CRMS in e-learning ecology, ontology as scaffolding for authoring teaching material, and RDF/RDFS for secondary school mathematics in Taiwan.

Retrieval of Learning Object

A LO should have at least one specifiable educational purpose or context and could also be used in different contexts while it is used and reused by different teachers. The biggest difference between a LO and an object is whether concerning learning perspective or not.

There are several paradigms for retrieval of LO in terms of use (Aroyo, Dicheva, & Cristea, 2002)

- **Text-based retrieval:** There are two keyword search methods: with free vocabulary like "Google" or with a closed vocabulary like thesaurus-based search. The latter search method is that the query is composed of a (possibly tree-structured or Boolean-structured) set of terms. The index usually consists of an unordered set of terms. The indexing and retrieval process must be supported by tools to browse or to select terms from the limited vocabularies.
- **Field-based retrieval:** Typically, a metadata schema is defined that describes the elements (fields) and some indications are given what values can be assigned to a particular field. The most widely used schema is the Dublin Core metadata template (Dublin Core Metadata Initiative, 1999) for describing documents in general. In field-based retrieval, users can retrieve an item by a set of attribute-value pairs, not by a set of keywords.
- **Structure-based retrieval:** To improve the support for indexing a mapping is required from the fields to particular parts of the thesaurus, such that the indexer is only presented with terms that are relevant for a particular field.

Where the field-based approach essentially uses a flat structure of attribute-value pairs, the structure-based approach allows more complex descriptions involving relations. The structure-based approach introduces a large degree of complexity in the indexing process. Relational descriptions can vary widely between different categories of objects. A LO can have components and can be described by a complex subject matter structure. A solution to the problem of complexity of the indexing process is to use contextual information to constrain the relations and terms presented to the indexer. In this study, knowledge requirements are with respect to existing structure-based terms to create knowledge-rich LO descriptions by a mathematics ontology.

CRMS in an E-Learning Ecology

In an e-learning ecology, learning management system (LMS) and learning content management system (LCMS) are responsible for dealing with learners and content respectively. In Figure 1, LCMS consists of authoring tool, administrative tools, and learning object repository (LOR). Each learning object may have been created from scratch or by re-purposing existing knowledge documents in other formats because separating content from programming logic and code in LOs allows each of LO can be reused many times or different purposes. Once the content providers like teachers developed a LO, then they might put it in a LOR. Content is typically maintained in a centralized content repository by the form of small, self-describing, uniquely identifiable objects, or learning objects, each of which satisfies one or more well-defined learning objectives (Yang & Tsai, 2003). Through the share of LOs in LOR, the reuse of LOs can be enacted. In contrast, a LMS primarily focuses on competencies, learning activities, and the logistics of delivering learning activities. In Figure 1, we name our LCMS as CRMS (content repository management system).

To avoid that teachers author their teaching materials from scratch every time, CRMS was designed for compulsory education teachers in Taiwan. CRMS can be used to motivate teachers as authors of teaching material since those existing LOs in CRMS are reusable. In other words, those teachers can author teaching

Figure 1. The ecology between LCMS and LMS

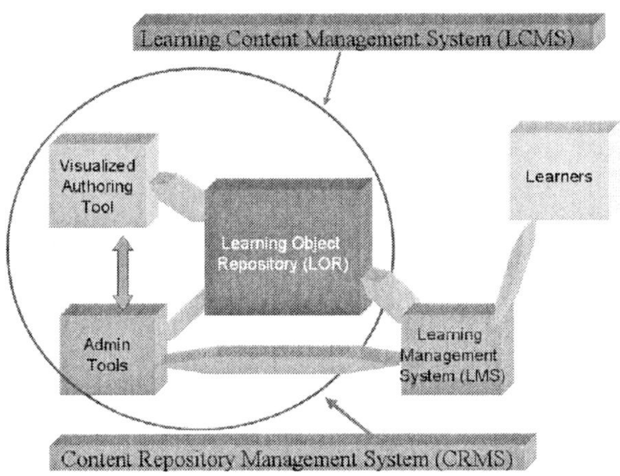

Figure 2. Hierarchical structure of a sample teaching material assembled by LOs

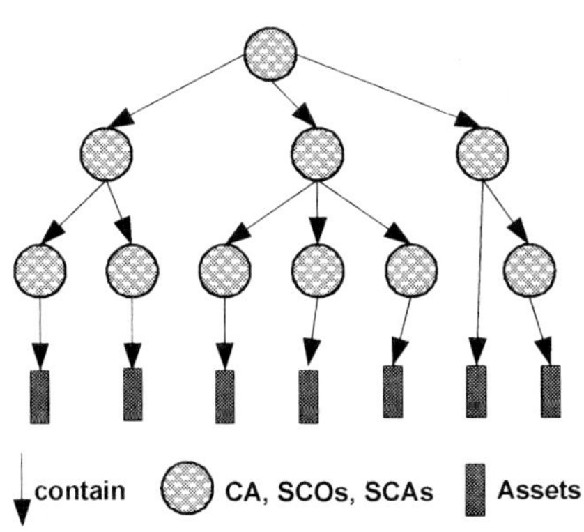

materials by searching, and editing in an effective way while provided by reusable LOs and visualized online authoring tool (VOAT) on CRMS. Figure 2 shows that a teaching material consists of LOs assembled in hierarchical structure. In the highest three levels, the information is organized in XML format for later parsing as tree-like structure. In the lowest nodes, the physical content units such as SCO (sharable content object), SCA (sharable content assets), and, assets are organized in an appropriate way.

Providing CRMS, a central database that each of LOs is either dispensed to users individually or used as a component to be assembled in an appropriate context of educational setting. To encourage teachers to reuse existing LOs in lower cost and higher efficiency, a scaffold as outlines of domain contents should be provided in visualized format. The advantage of this approach is that the integrity of a course can be easily assembled. The core technology of implementing this purpose is to encode an LO by XML which allows to define domain and task specific extensions. With those XML descriptions, a LO can be re-structured easily. CRMS has many functions shown in Figure 3. Those functions consist of "Classified retrieval," "Conducting retrieval," "My Package," and so forth in Figure 3. Those administrative functionalities can be composed by a series of actions. For example, a teacher wants to author a teaching material unit. The typical processes are shown as follows

1. To search LO or content package (CP) by a set of keywords or natural language
2. To choose those LOs or CPs from visualized result set
3. To put those suitable LOs or CPs for authoring into "My package"
4. To author teaching materials by VOAT
5. To pack those teaching materials as the content package in ZIP format that will be delivered on ADL's (run-time environment)

Figure 3. The CRMS with functionalities illustrated

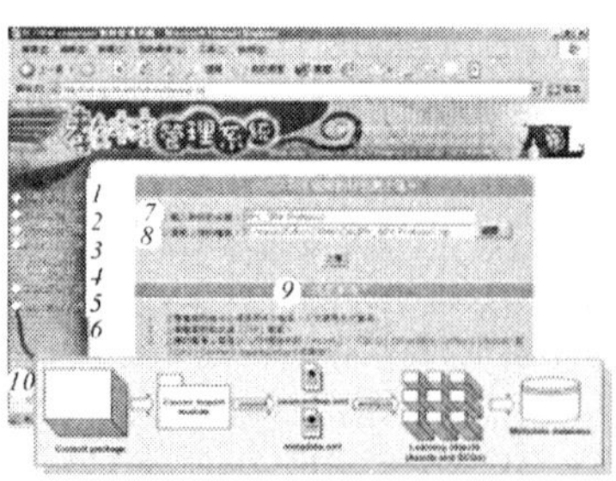

1 Classified retrieval *2* Conducting retrieval
3 My Package *4* Normalized importing
5 Normalizing import *6* Account management
7 Name of imported file
8 Selected CP to be uploaded
9 Points of Attentions
10 Transformation processes of importing a CP

Ontology for Mathematics at Secondary School Level in Taiwan

Ontology is a formal, explicit specification of a shared conceptualization (Gruber, 1995). Ontology might be a document or file that formally defines the relations among terms. The most typical kind of ontology for the Web has a taxonomy and a set of inference rules (Brickley & Guha, 2000). Ontology can be viewed as a document or file that formally defines the relations among terms. The most typical kind of ontology is defined in terms of taxonomy of terms and a set of inference rules. Any knowledge-based system consists of at least two fundamental parts: domain knowledge and problem-solving knowledge. Ontology mainly plays a role in analyzing, modeling, and implementing the domain knowledge (Studer, Benjamins, & Fensel, 1998).

Ontology is a key enabling technology for the Semantic Web. They interweave human understanding of symbols or terms with their machine, process ability. Originally, ontology was developed in artificial intelligence to facilitate knowledge sharing and re-use. Ontology, however, have become popular with different disciplinary such as knowledge management, natural language process, and knowledge representation. The reason why ontology is becoming popular is largely due to what they promise: a shared and common understanding of a domain that can be communicated between people and application systems.

Defined as "specifications of a shared conceptualization of a particular domain," ontology provides a shared and common understanding of a domain that can be communicated across people and application systems, and thus facilitate knowledge sharing and reuse. Ontology aims at machine-process of information resources accessible to agents. Currently, the Web is an incredibly large, mostly static information source. The main burden in information access, extraction, and interpretation still rests with the human user. Document management systems now on the market have severe weaknesses (Fensel & Harmelen, 2001):

- **Searching information:** Human browsing and reading is required to extract relevant information from information sources while agent programs do not have the common sense knowledge required to extract such information from textual representations, and they fail to integrate information spread over different sources.
- **Maintaining overloading information:** Handling weakly structured text sources is a difficult and time-consuming activity when such sources become large. Keeping such collections consistent, correct, and up-to-date requires mechanized representations of semantics that help to detect anomalies.

- **Machine-accessible representation of the semantics of these information sources:** Automatic document generation would enable adaptive Web sites that are dynamically reconfigured according to user profiles or other aspects of relevance. Generation of semi-structured information presentations from semi-structured data requires a machine-accessible representation of the semantics of these information sources.

This chapter describes semantic Web-based knowledge management architecture. Teachers can get the supporting from domain ontology while they author their content knowledge. Those teachers can choose what scope of content they want to include while domain ontology provided and displayed in a hierarchical structure. This kind of guiding gives a scaffold for authoring a teaching material.

RDF/RDFS Example for Mathematics Courses

A course can be represented as an aggregation. For example, a mathematics course at secondary school levels of Taiwan consists of four subparts. One for each descriptor forms a group. However, one requirement with respect to the use of RDFS/RDF was that a general RDF-aware browser should be able to interpret as much as possible the resulting course-item description. From this point of view, the representation of a mathematics course template consisting of subparts with their own closed set of descriptors is machine-accessible provided by those XML descriptions. To get domain ontology of mathematics, In Figure

Figure 4. An example of RDF for RDFS graph shown in Figure 5

```
<rdf:RDF
xmlns:rdf='http://www.w3.org/1999/02/22-rdf-syntax-ns#'
xmlns:rdfs='http://www.w3.org/2000/01/rdf-schema#'
 >
<rdfs:Class rdf:ID="function of degree of one">
<rdfs:subClassOf rdf:resource="# function"/>
</rdfs:Class>
<rdfs:Class rdf:ID="function of degree of zero">
<rdfs:subClassOf rdf:resource="# function"/>
</rdfs:Class>
<rdfs:Class rdf:ID="function of degree of two">
<rdfs:subClassOf rdf:resource="# function"/>
</rdfs:Class>
<rdfs:Class rdf:ID=" four fundamental operations of arithmetic of polynomial /">
<rdfs:subClassOf rdf:resource="# function"/>
</rdfs:Class>
```

Figure 5. Using RDFS graph to present relations of mathematics ontology

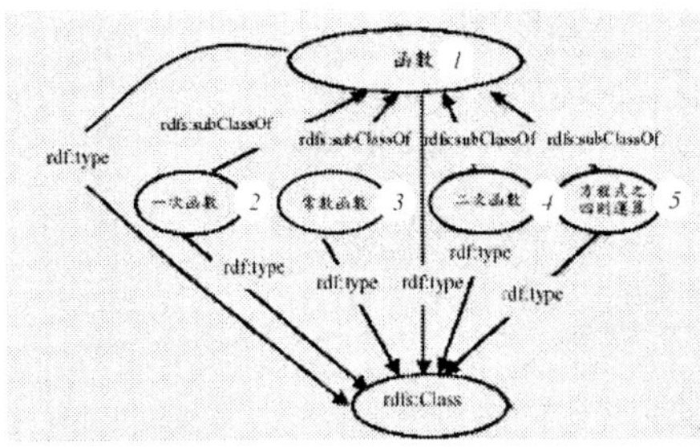

1 Function
2 Function of degree of one
3 Function of degree of zero
4 Function of degree of two
5 Four fundamental operations of arithmetic of polynomial

5, there is only an indirect link from the course instance to the descriptor triple of RDF representation. The root structure is "function" in this study. Also, the whole structure can be described in RDF shown in Figure 4.

As defined a meta-class descriptor with the descriptor groups as subclasses, mathematics course slots were defined as instances of the appropriate course-descriptor subclass. One of the reasons we prefer Prot´eg´e as RDFS editor is that it supports treating instances as classes and vice versa. Not allowing this is in fact a weakness of many description-logic languages, which adhere to a strict separation. Martin (1997) considers class/instance flexibility as a central requirement for adequate conceptual modeling. In addition to the course descriptors and their value sets, there is also a considerable amount of mathematics knowledge about relationships between descriptor values.

System Architecture and VOAT

In this section, a framework of authoring processes of teaching materials and VOAT architecture are described in detail.

A Framework of Authoring Processes of Teaching Materials

Based on CRMS, teachers can author their teaching materials by ontological supporting. The whole architecture of this study is shown as Figure 6. In the upper-left side of Figure 6, teachers can disassemble their teaching material into

Figure 6. System architecture

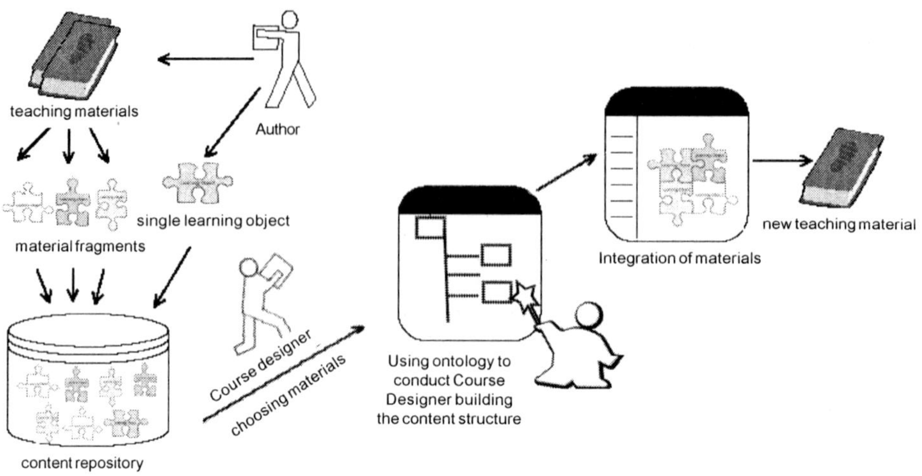

CRMS. In contrast, teachers also can author new teaching materials by ontological support shown as right side of Figure 6.

Using ontological support, the content of secondary mathematics can be constructed as Figure 9. In the root level is secondary mathematics that consists of four components such as "number," "algebra," "geometry," and "statistics." It is worthwhile to mention that RDFS allows multiple inheritances.

VOAT Architecture

VOAT (see Figure 7) is plug-in module in the CRMS. It is a Web-based GUI and offers teachers to authoring teaching materials easily. Seven components have been implemented in terms of authoring teaching materials. VOAT consists of ontology conducting module, editing metadata module, and content package downloading module. The major functionality of three modules are described as follows

1. **Ontology conducting module:** A RDFS will be invoked if teachers enter the related mathematics ontology through GUI dialogue. Then, the detail information will be displayed recursively until the last level.

Figure 7. The VOAT architecture

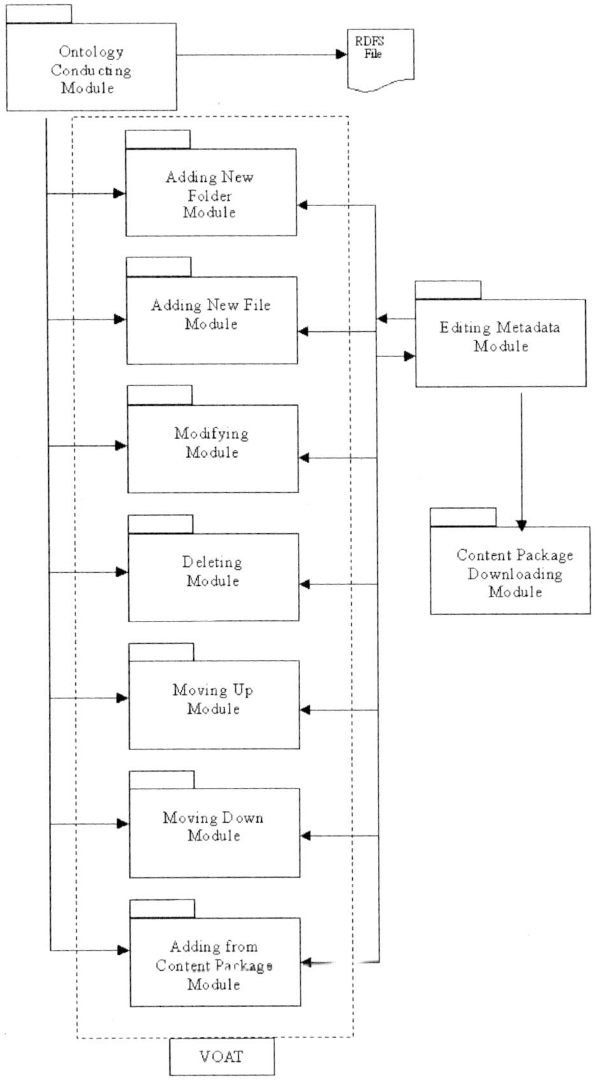

2. **Editing metadata module:** Providing the GUI, teachers can edit those metadata as they edit a course outlines. The functionalities include adding a new folder or file, content package; deleting a node such as file or folder; arranging the location of files or folders.

Figure 8. Ontological support for searching LOs or CPs

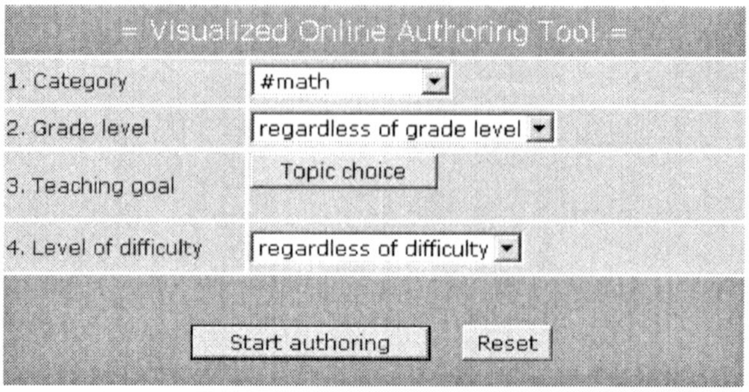

3. **Package downloading module:** Once teachers authored their CP, a new "Manifest. xml" file is created and included in a CP. Then, the CP can be downloaded to local computer for later content modifications or be sent to any platform that is SCORM-compliant LMS.

Research Results

To illustrate results of this study, two cases are demonstrated orderly. In the former case, a scenario of authoring mathematics course is presented. In the latter case, an ontological map is constructed based on the Delphi approach.

Ontological Supporting in the Processes of Authoring Teaching Materials

A teacher fills course requirements such as "category," "grade level," "teaching goal," "level of difficulty of teaching material" in Figure 8. There are four actions can be selected. Firstly, a teacher must choose one kind of categories such as language, natural science and living technology, and so on, in the list box. Secondly, he or she can choose the grade level for his or her teaching. Thirdly, he or she can decide one of course topics and continually asks teaching material information in which an ontological support is given. Finally, he or she can select the level of difficulty of teaching material in the list box.

Figure 9. Expansion of teaching goal under algebra choice

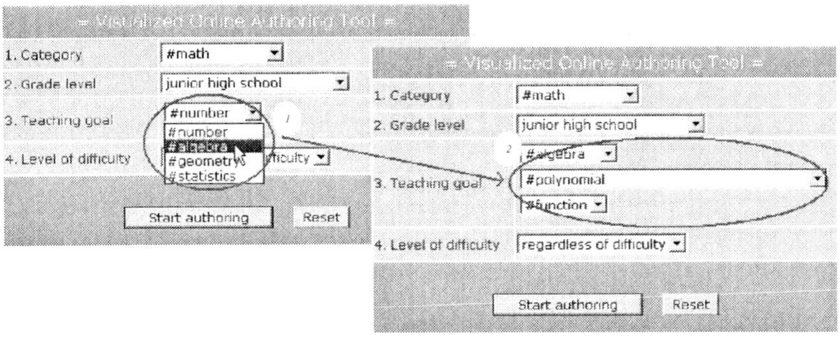

1 Hierarchical domain ontology supported by RDF/RDFS
2 Hierarchical domain ontology goes deeply as expansion of teaching goal occurred

Figure 10. The course outlines shown in a hierarchical structure

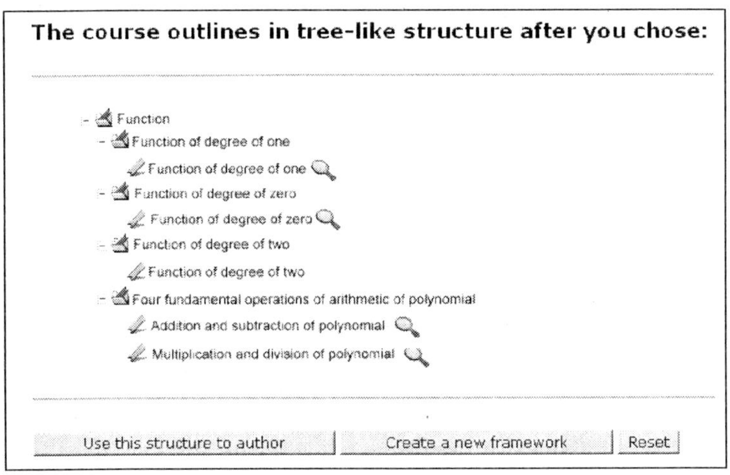

To clarify the processes of how to narrow down the specified topic under the ontological support, we present some steps of the scenario as follows

1. The left side of Figure 9 shows that four subsets such as "number," "algebra," "geometry," and "statistics." Similarly, the right side of Figure 9 shows the continuous processes under teachers' needs. The process is guided by mathematics ontological support.

Figure 11. The actions of VOAT in authoring a math teaching material

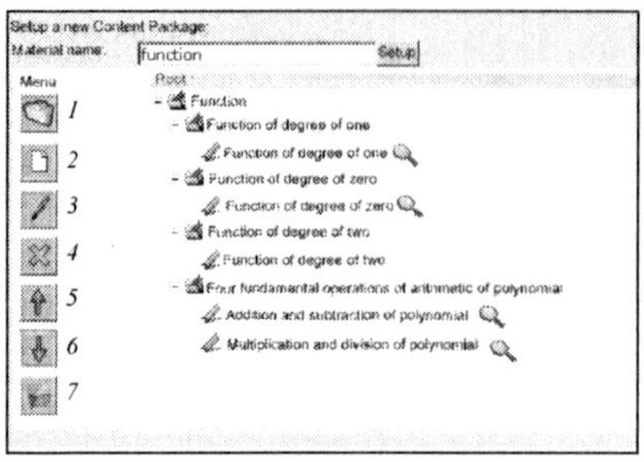

1 Creating a directory
2 Adding a new LO
3 Modifying an existing LO
4 Deleting an existing LO
5 Moving up a LO
6 Moving down a LO
7 Adding a new CP from "My package"

Figure 12. A mathematics course is delivered at ADL's LMS

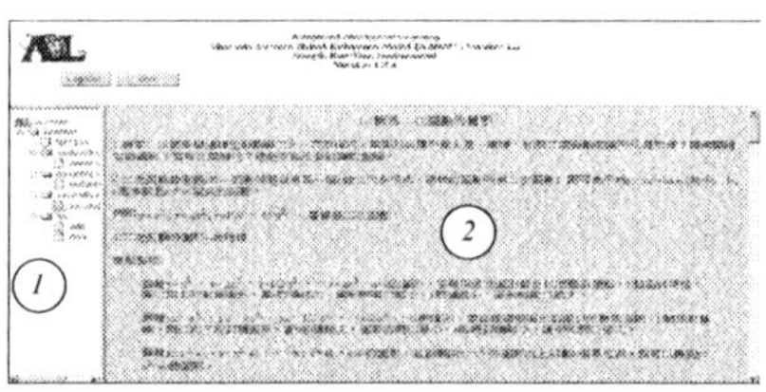

1 With the "choice" option, course outlines are shown at right side of windows

2 Content widows on functions

2. A searching agent locates those related LOs and puts in appropriate locations based on ontological supporting in CRMS. Figure 10 shows that snapshots of course outlines in tree-like structure after a teacher chose by dialogues.
3. **Visualized Online Authoring tool (VOAT):** Based on the SCORM's specifications, the final course material will be packed as Content Aggregation (CA) in a zip file format for delivery purpose. A CA defines the content structure that provides the mechanisms for defining the sequence of content objects presented to its learners. The VOAT in Figure 11 provides a visualized icons and interactive dialogue for teachers sequentially. The VOAT provides seven functionalities. The atomic operation is explained in Table 2. Using the VOAT tool, teachers can author their teaching material within short time since the procedures of each action have been designed sequentially. The final step is to pack all LOs as a zip file that can be delivered by ADL's LMS.
4. **Course delivery by ADL's RTE 1.2.1:** Once a CA is generated, it can be executed in the ADL RTE 1.2.1. Figure 12 shows the snapshot of course delivery.

Summarily, ontological support as a scaffold in VOAT plays guide for teachers to reuse previously written content. Therefore, it is an effective strategy to reduce the cost of LOs. Through the dialogues with automatic processing of authoring teaching materials by searching engine of CRMS, it prevents teachers from great burden of authoring a teaching material from scratch.

Building Ontology for Filling in Structured Descriptions

Ontological design engineering is concerned with the principled design, modification, application, and evaluation of ontology. Holsapple and Joshim (2002) point out that five approaches to ontological design: inspiration, induction, deduction, synthesis, and collaboration. These may be used in the initial design of ontology or the modification of a design. Hybrids of the approaches are possible. In this study, we adopt the Delphi approach to attain mathematics ontology. The Delphi approach requires experts to respond to a series of questions quantitatively and with comments. The summary scores and comments are fed back to the experts for second or more rounds of responses until consensus is satisfied by a group of domain experts. New issues may be added on the second round and some issues may be deleted iteratively.

The sequences of summary and revision allow the experts such as university professors or experienced mathematics teachers at secondary school levels to contemplate their responses and revise their opinions. The Delphi approach leads toward a consensus as ideas are shared and revised. Those experienced teachers and mathematics professors give insightful recommendations to construct the mathematics ontology in Figure 13.

A mathematics ontology is developed by the Delphi approach and satisfies a number of criteria

Figure 13. Ontology of secondary mathematics by Dephi's approach

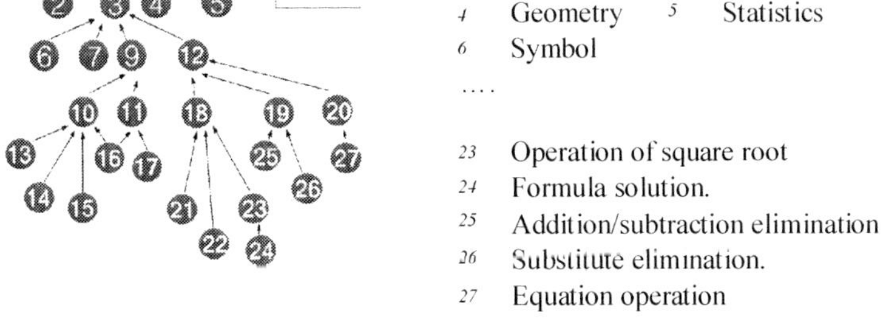

Figure 14. Ontology of Figure 13 built based on (Protégée 2000)

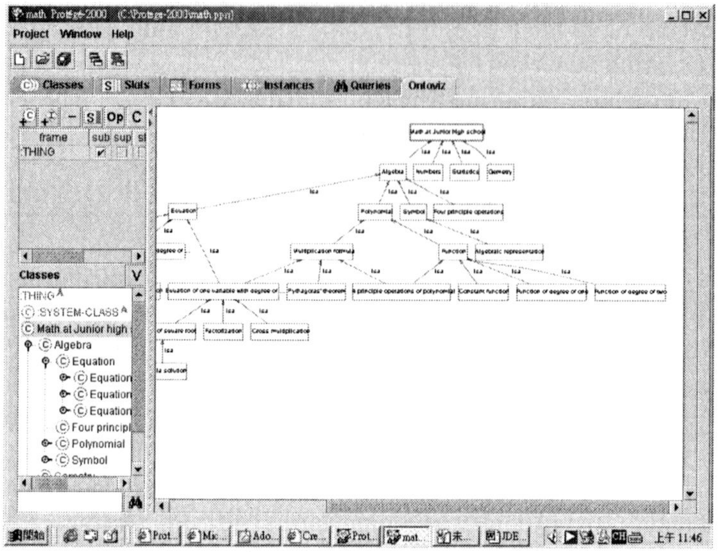

1. The mathematics ontology has a strict sub/super-class hierarchical structure.
2. The mathematics ontology is based on unique concepts rather than on natural-language terms.

The mathematics ontology is represented in a RDF/RDFS format. Also, the ontology was developed in three steps

1. **Building description template of mathematics course at secondary school level:** what kind of information does a teacher need to know taxonomy of mathematics content
2. Linking the course properties to specific subsets that can be used as values for course properties
3. Describing additional domain knowledge, in particular about constraints between course-property values such as "extended," "is-a," or "is-part" relation

Ontological commitment is important for teachers at secondary school level when they are communicating about the mathematics domain, even though they do not necessarily have the same experiences, theories, or prescriptions about mathematics.

Furthermore, this study developed ontology for describing and retrieving mathematics course. We use Prot′eg′e-2000 as ontology editor with RDFS as the underlying representation language (Noy, Fergerson, & Musen, 2000). The mathematics course concepts are represented as a Prot′eg′e class and the descriptors as template slots of this class. Prot′eg′e slots are translated into RDFS properties; the qualifiers are translated into sub-properties. This representation handles a long unstructured list of course descriptors.

Figure 14 shows the template we developed for describing ontology of mathematics course by Ontovize software. The structure of course content can be described by "descriptors." The right side of Figure 14 displays the RDFS of domain ontology on mathematics at secondary school level. It shows that RDFS is a graph structure rather than a tree structure. It is worthwhile to mention is that Ontovize cannot display Chinese characters in appropriate way.

Discussions and Recommendations for Future Study

With supports from learning object repositories, teachers can take some LOs to assemble their lesson plans quickly and easily because they don't need to write it from scratch and get the scaffold from ontological support. Fully making use of the LOR efficient and ontological support as scaffold is need to offer learners and content providers to be willing to use it quickly. This study offers knowledge acquisition by mathematics domain ontology of secondary school level in Taiwan. Although many of the issues raised have been discussed and solved in knowledge acquisition theory, "Semantic Web" is doing task "machine processing" XML document through RDF/RDFS annotations (Berners-Lee, 1998). One of ways to reach this goal is to annotate large amounts of information resources with knowledge-rich metadata from ADL's SCORE specifications.

In this chapter, we adopt that annotations on teaching material are based on ADL's SCORM metadata structure and develop mathematics domain ontology of at secondary school levels. A Delphi approach was designed to generate succinct mathematics ontology. The result was completed and approved by the group of faculty and senior mathematics teachers. Building ontology for large domains, such as medicine, arts, or educational courses, is a costly affair.

However, many domains have been built that can be a basis for the construction of whole ontology in the years to come.

Mathematics concepts and their relationships are further characterized in terms of axioms and constraints that may be expressed more or less formally. In this study, mathematics terms are used in offering insights, describing practices, and discussing investigations pertaining to the conduct of knowledge management. Furthermore, constructing ontology process, additional knowledge such as task ontology should be added to the basic hierarchical structure of concepts derived from mathematics experts.

It is worthwhile to mention, it is important to clearly make the following distinction in terms of building and applying ontology: on one hand, there is the ontology itself, which specifies concepts used in a domain of endeavor, concepts whose existence and relationships are true by definition or convention. On the other hand, there are empirical facts about these concepts and relationships. They are not part of the ontology, although they are structured by it. They are subject to context, observation, testing, evaluation, or modification. In this study, we adopt the Dephi approach to get the mathematics ontology from experts among university professors and senior mathematics teachers at secondary school level. The ontological support really helps teachers to author their own content easily since they can re-assemble a new content package in VOAT. For the future research, other semantic Web oriented languages, such as OIL should be applied for solving some advanced issues such as asking and answering questions, making assertions, or monitoring the processes of assembling a teaching material.

References

ADL. (2002). *Advanced distributed learning*. Retrieved from http://www.adlnet.org

ARIADNE. (2000). *Alliance of remote instructional authoring and distribution networks for Europe*. Retrieved from http://ariadne.unil.ch

Aroyo, L., Dicheva, D., & Cristea A. (2002). *Ontological support for Web courseware authoring*.

Berners-Lee, T. (1998). *Semantic Web road map*. Retrieved from http://www.w3.org/DesignIssues/Semantic.html

Brickley, D., & Guha, R. V. (2000). *Resource description framework (RDF) schema specification 1.0*. Candidate recommendation, W3C Consortium. Retrieved from http://www.w3.org

Decker, M., Erdmann, & Klein, M. (2000). OIL in a nutshell. In *Knowledge engineering and knowledge management: 12th International Conference EKAW2000, Juan-les-Pins* (LNAI 1937, pp. 1-16). Berlin; Heidelberg, Germany: Springer-Verlag.

Dublin Core Metadata Initiative. (1999). *Dublin Core netadata element set Version 1.1: Reference description.* Retrieved from http://dublincore.org/documents/1999/07/02/dces/

Fensel, D., & van Harmelen, F. (2001, March/April). OIL: An ontology infrastructure for the Semantic Web. *IEEE Intelligent Systems*, 38-45.

Gruber, T. (1995). Toward principles for the design of ontologies used for knowledge sharing. *International Journal of Human and Computer Studies*, *43*(5/6), 907-928.

Holsapple, C. W., & Joshim, K. D. (2002). *Communications of the ACM*, *45*(2), 42-47.

IMS. (2000). *Learning resource metadata specification, Version 1.2.* Retrieved from http://www.imsproject.org/metadata/index.html

Katzman, J., & Caton, J. (2001, May 15). *Evaluating learning content management systems (LCMS)*. Peer3 white paper (pp. 7-13).

LOM. (2000). *LOM Standard, "Draft Standard for Learning Object Metadata.*" IEEE P1484.12/D4.0. Retrieved from http://ltsc.ieee.org / doc/wg12/LOM_Wd4.doc, 2000

LTSC. (2001). *Learning technology standards committee, 2000.* Retrieved from http://ltsc.ieee.org

Martin, J. (1997). *Object-oriented methods: A foundation* (UML ed.). Upper Saddle River, NJ: Prentice Hall.

Noy, N. F., Fergerson, R. W., & Musen, M. A. (2000). The knowledge model of Prot´eg´e-2000: Combining interoperability and flexibility. In *Knowledge Engineering and Knowledge Management: 12th International Conference EKAW2000*, Juan-les-Pins (LNAI 1937, pp. 17-32). Berlin; Heidelberg, Germany: Springer-Verlag.

Studer, R., Benjamins, V. R., & Fensel, D. (1998). Knowledge engineering: Principles and methods. *Data Knowledge Engineering*, *25*(1-2).

Wiley, D. A. (2000). Connecting learning objects to instructional design theory: A definition, a metaphor, and a taxonomy. In D. Wiley (Ed.), *The instructional use of learning objects*. Bloomington: Association for Educational Communications and Technology.

Yang, J. T., & Tsai, C. Y. (2003). *A SCORM-compliant content repository management system for teachers at primary & secondary school levels, ICALT2003,* Athens, Greece.

Chapter XII

The Next Generation of E-Learning: Strategies for Media Rich Online Teaching and Engaged Learning

Daniel Tiong Hok Tan,
Nanyang Technological University, Singapore

Chye Seng Lee,
Nanyang Technological University, Singapore

Wee Sen Goh,
Nanyang Technological University, Singapore

Abstract

In a short span of three years, the Nanyang Technological University (NTU) in Singapore witnessed significant growth in the adoption of e-learning. With the use of professors-friendly e-learning applications, NTU has been able to achieve critical mass buy-in by the academic staff when the e-learning take-up rate achieved 85% of the existing NTU course curriculum. As NTU moves on to celebrate the third year of e-learning, measures were taken with the careful design considerations that aimed to "humanize" e-learning, (i.e., make e-learning interactive and engaging with active collaborations and student learning involvement). This includes the proliferation in the use of the video talking head format synchronized with the lecture presentation, live audio-video delivery, text chat and document annotations of a lecture presentation and delivery. This chapter reviews the processes NTU adopted in adding the human touch to traditional e-learning projects and serves as a good case study for other institutions with a similar aim to achieve interactive and engaged online learning.

Introduction

Nanyang Technological University was established in 1970. It is one of two publicly funded universities in Singapore. Courses offered includes engineering, biological sciences, business, education, accountancy and communication studies. In NTU, the service unit Centre for Educational Development (CED) is responsible for spearheading and facilitating e-learning.

The innovative brand name edveNTUre was created for her e-learning initiative in 2000: "e" represents everything electronic for the knowledge economy, and "ed" stands for education — the purpose of the platform for life-long learning. "Adventure" in a modified form depicts the concept of learning as an experience and journey to explore new frontiers of knowledge, much like a team collaborating synergistically together in new learning environments to discover new frontiers. With the university's name "NTU" embedded, "edveNTUre" symbolizes the e-learning initiative and aspiration for the university. Professors and students feel a sense of identity and affiliation as stakeholders in an environment where they share experiences, knowledge, and experimentations in a new learning paradigm and environment. edveNTUre is accessible at http://edventure.ntu.edu.sg and the current home page is shown in Figure 1.

Figure 1. edveNTUre home page

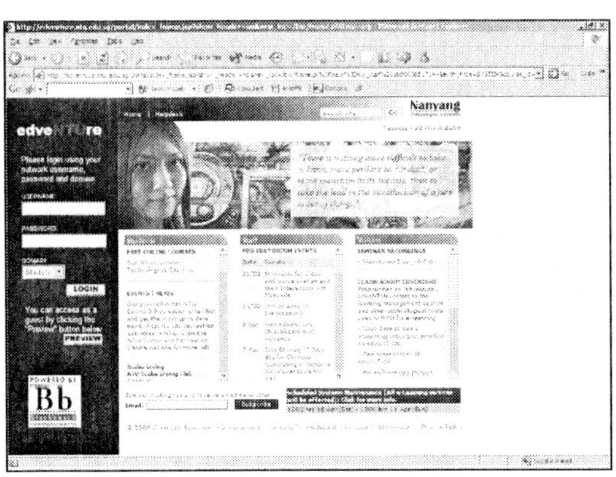

Through the NTU e-learning eco-system, the university hopes to achieve the following business and educational goals

a. To create an eco-system of life-long learning in our students and graduates towards the pursuit and establishment of a national digital knowledge economy.

b. To facilitate, equip and enable the academic staff (who represent the beginning of the e-learning food chain in this local context) to create and enhance content, develop competence and capability to deliver effective learner-centric and pedagogical approaches and methods for the training and development of our students and graduates.

c. To "humanize" e-learning and develop quality interactive and engaging content that will facilitate and enable self-paced learning for students anywhere, anytime on any device.

d. To enhance face-to-face tutorial sessions and enable collaborative learning in such environments through the provision of effective audio-visual tools.

e. To provide robust and reliable e-learning services to a progressive community in content delivery, knowledge management utilizing synchronous and asynchronous modes of teaching and learning. This includes an infrastructure that facilitates fault tolerance systems, disaster recovery-high availability-business continuity systems, content creation and editing tools, online assessment tools, student tracking and progress tools, etc.

When the university embarked on its own e-learning adventure, it undertook a process of due diligence to select a suitable platform and system. It finally adopted an established courseware and learning management platform from Blackboard (http://www.blackboard.com). The Blackboard product was used by over 3,300 institutions worldwide and this large user base will and community would ensure that this courseware management system will continue to evolve, receive community feedback, and provide new tools and better features that would continuously enhance the learning experience for students.

Today, this mission critical service is powered by high end SUN servers (SUN Enterprise 10000 then, and later SUN Fire 15000) running today on Solaris 8.0 with 10 domains on 34 processors, 42 GB system memory and 2.1 TB networked storage. The production and development servers have high network bandwidth (1Giga bits Ethernet link) connectivity. The system architecture facilitate those times when additional compute power is required, e.g., during the pre-examination time window, system resources (processors and memory) could dynamically be re-allocated from one server domain to another without shutting down the system. The current e-learning software platform is Blackboard 5.5.1 Level 3 with Oracle 8.1.6i as the database management system, Apache as the Web server and BEA WebLogic as the portal application. Video-on-demand and Web-casting services are powered by software and hardware systems from SGI, HP, Microsoft, Dell and AcuLearn platforms and products. edveNTUre has enabled and facilitated new paradigms of teaching and learning not possible before in traditional classroom settings.

Launched at an estimated cost of S$1.1 million, edveNTUre enables 23,000 NTU and its distance learning students and 1,300 academic staff to access online resources through innovative means of content creation and knowledge discovery. The e-learning platform allowed dynamic content to be delivered digitally over the campus wired and wireless network to any student, anytime, anywhere and on various devices. edveNTUre complements the traditional lectures through several e-learning tools including discussion forums for collaborative knowledge sharing, personalised learning, dynamic content delivery, and other automated e-teaching tools. This online learning environment will expose the students to new learning approaches as they acquire skills for life-long learning, a critical asset in today's knowledge economy.

Rapid E-Learning Adoption Rate

Within three years of its implementation, nearly 90% of courses in the university have an active online presence (96% adoption rate for under-graduate and 75% for post-graduate courses). The hit rate in the academic year 2003/4 (from July 2003) was over 2.1 million page views per week from a student population of 23,000 and over 1,300 instructors (professors).

Planning for edveNTUre commenced in November 1999. The concept of edveNTUre was that it should be a dynamic e-learning environment that will evolve and facilitate change. The initial target was that by end 2000, there would be 100 courses online. The hardware system and software were delivered in May 2000. Within two months in July 2000 when the academic year 2000/1 began, 200 course sites were online, exceeding the original target by two times. By December 2000, over 800 courses were online. The number of page view (more accurate measurement of utilization than page hits) was 1M/month in January 2001, and 1M/week in July 2002, and recently 2.1M/week in July 2003. In that regard, rather than having timeframe (straightly speaking, this was completed and implemented within 4 months), we have mile-stones of achievements.

Figure 2 illustrates the growth rate of the number of online courses in edveNTUre from Jul 2000 to January 2004.

Figure 2. edveNTUre's growth chart (May 2000 to January 2004)

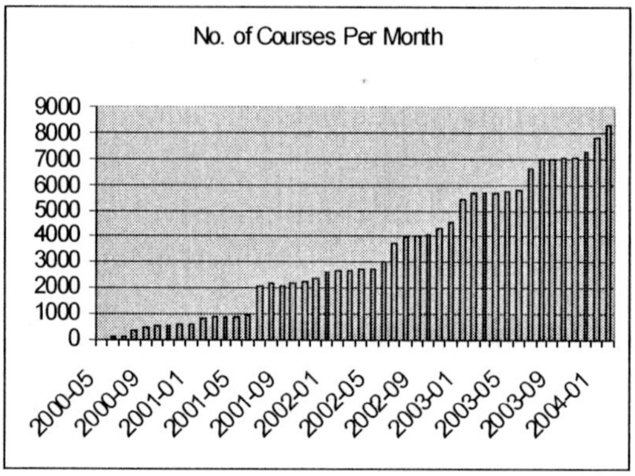

Figure 3 illustrates the high usage level of edveNTUre in terms of the overall number of page views downloaded by all NTU students.

Figure 4 shows a typical usage pattern at the course level. It indicates the edveNTUre e-learning service being used by students throughout the day, with peaks in the morning and late evening. The lull period was in the early morning hours between 3 am and 6 am.

Figure 5 provides the course professor-instructor a good feel of how much time and effort the students spend on course content areas, communication areas (i.e., discussion boards, virtual chat, group pages, e-mail) and student areas (edit home page, assignment drop box, student calendar).

For the purpose of strategic planning, NTU defined arbitrarily Phase I as the period from first roll out in May 2000 up to June 2002. By Phase I, we have

Figure 3. edveNTUre's overall usage graph (May 2000 to January 2004)

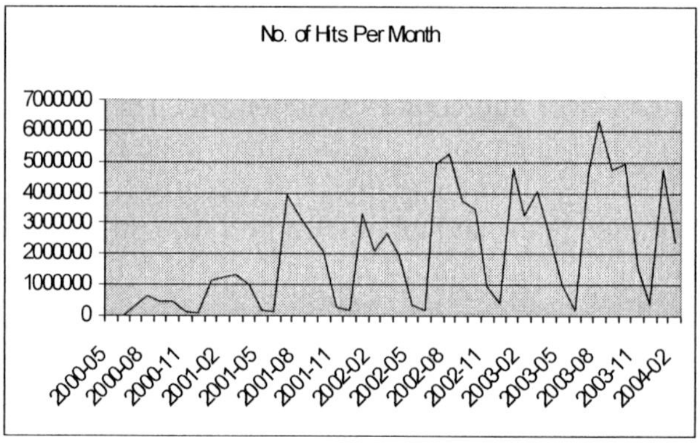

Figure 4. Daily usage pattern of a typical online course

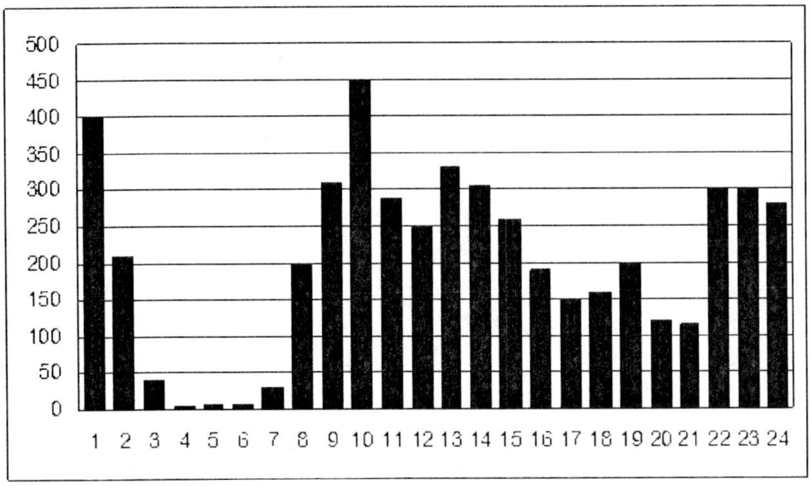

achieved saturation levels for the number of courses, student-learners and academic staff participation. Phase II which began in July 2002 was the beginning of the theme "humaniZing e-learning" and the introduction of active content. As e-learning become more pervasive, it was envisaged that it would be challenging for students to have a significant part of their learning online and expect them to remain engaged for content that are static page-turners. There was, thus, the need to make the content and learning experience of e-learning more engaging and interactive; Phase II emphasized the use of more human elements in the effective "high tech-high touch" delivery of learning online. This

Figure 5. Pie chart showing students' participation of the component services in edveNTUre

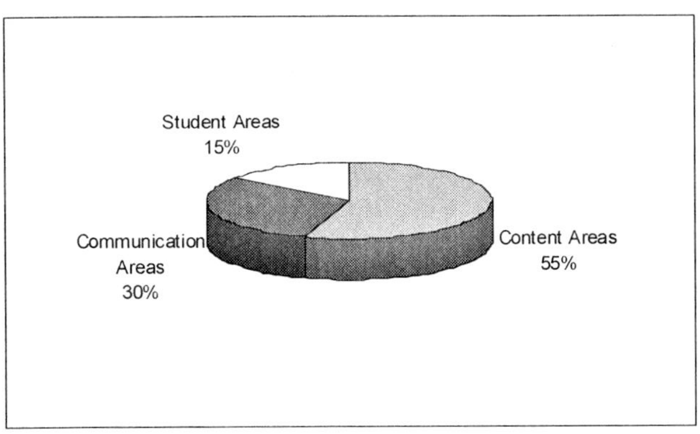

is manifested by the recent introduction of e-learning programs with branding like iNTUition, preseNTUr and aNTUna.

iNTUition (using InterWise ECP 4.2 http://www.interwise.com) is a synchronous learning tool that facilitates virtual classrooms with students and professors not having to be in the same physical location at the same time. preseNTUr is the content creation and editing tools with systems supplied by AcuLearn Systems (http://www.aculearn.com). These systems were chosen for their ease of use, and would greatly facilitate the creation of content quickly and effectively to humanize e-learning. aNTUna is the enablement of mobile-learning on wireless notebook and PDA devices using the product BlackboadToGo operating on the AvantGo (http://www.avantgo.com) system on Solaris OS. Sony Electronics provided the wireless LAN-capable video projectors (FX50 systems) installed in 120 tutorial rooms across campus. These advanced video projectors can be managed centrally and intelligently via this network connection. Through their wireless LAN capability, presentations can be delivered wirelessly through single or multiple projectors via the network locally or distributed widely across the globe.

Barriers to completion were minimal. This was due to the process of due diligence in the planning and deployment of emerging technologies appropriate for e-learning — potential applications were evaluated in depth before the system acquisition. Most of the technologies were acquired, rather than developed in-house. Trying to develop the learning management system or other applications in-house was considered unwise in the light of recent and current e-learning evolution and developments. Acquiring the component systems like aNTUna, preseNTUr and iNTUition and integrating them with edveNTUre would, and have, enabled the university to progress quickly and effectively. In fact, NTU is today regarded as an exemplar and recognized for its leadership in e-learning in the region.

Development Stages of E-Learning in the University

During Phase I, there were no contingency plans for edveNTUre. However, in view of the pervasiveness of e-learning in the university (evidenced by the high page-view rates of 2.1M/week in July 2003), plans were initiated to establish a remote disaster recovery (DR) site. This DR site would serve two purposes. Besides it being a secondary service site, it would also provide system load balancing, especially to students who access edveNTUre off-campus, as well as the growing community of professionals who pursue part-time courses and professional development and continuing education courses.

The general implementation strategy for e-learning involved the following processes

- Careful use and selection of professor-friendly tools. We operated on the axiom that professors are the beginning of the e-learning food chain. If professors do not create an online course, e-learning do not exist.
- Creation of the edUtorium initiative, a staff development program — till date, over 1,000 training places have been taken per year since its launch in April 2001.
- Information sharing sessions to bring awareness to the academic community — professors learn more openly and willingly through such sessions. Champion professors were requested to conduct and lead in such sessions
- Workshop sessions conducted by fellow professors and other educational experts to provide training and enablement.
- Demonstration show-and-tell sessions given by schools, junior colleges (JCs) and polytechnics to the university campus community — these sessions served to provide to the academic community an awareness of developments of IT in education at the earlier portion of the education "supply chain" of students. Professors were impacted by the message that "if this is the experience of their students today (in the schools, junior colleges and polytechnic), these future students would expect more when they become our students within a few years."
- Clinical sessions in which professors can walk-in and speak to technical staff regarding their need for assistance and guidance.
- Establishment of school-based e-learning support team to provide effective first line help (schools refer to the Schools of Electrical & Electronic Engineering, Civil and Environment Engineering, Nanyang Business School, etc.).
- Training sessions were done for students, but they were found to be unnecessary — edveNTUre is also student-friendly!

A faculty development initiative — edUtorium — was established in April 2001 to provide training and support to the teaching staff as they were inducted into e-learning environments. Information sharing sessions, workshops and one-to-one clinical sessions on how to use the learning management system, edveNTUre, were regularly conducted. In addition, a computer based teaching system on

CD-ROM was developed for professors to learn anytime the edveNTUre system. A newsletter — aCEDamia — is also published monthly to share on news, development and best practices of teaching and e-learning for the academic staff.

For students, a manned Help Desk has been made available to support them. An RFI was called in 2002Q4 for Help Desk-Call Centre application to give better support and service to the student-learner community. Training sessions were initially organised for students, but such sessions were found to be unnecessary, as edveNTUre was browser-based. Except suffice for a short 20-minute talk to freshies — edveNTUre has been designed to be user-friendly — short reference guide on edveNTUre is printed and distributed to all freshie students annually.

At a higher administrative level, the e-learning initiative is fully supported and guided by an executive committee called IT-SEED (Steering Executive on Electronic Education) which provides directives and vision for new educational initiatives in NTU. The IT-SEED committee members comprise senior appointment holders and stake-holders, and have the capability to expedite influential action plans efficiently at a campus level. These senior executives also lead an e-learning support team at the departmental or school level. Members of the departmental/school support team are trained technicians who provide first-line and proximity assistance to academic and administrative staff. Problems beyond their first line supportive role are escalated to CED. An online line help-desk application from Parature (http://www.parature.com) ensures efficiencies (quick response and resolution) and effectiveness (tracking of help requests and technical assistance, case management and closure).

With the early success of e-learning, the university president then gave during his convocation speech in 2001 a vision to the university in which our students would learn more and more via online delivery (for lectures) in a blended environment in which students are engaged in face-to-face learning in smaller groups (for tutorial and review-recital sessions). It must be said that such senior management support has been strong and have helped to catapult the fast adoption rate of e-learning by the academic community. Coupled with good and robust technology and a sound strategy for change, results would, and have been, quantifiable.

The outcomes includes reaching saturation levels in the number of courses taught online; all the students learn online in a majority of courses, with the involvement of almost all the teaching staff. However, what counts and a better indicator is the page view rate — this has risen from 1M page-views/month in July 2001 to 1M page-views/week in July 2002, and currently to 2.1M page views/week in July 2003.

Systems are continuously enhanced based on feedback from the user community of professors and students. In such user-centric systems, feedback, requests, and opinions are readily sought and managed.

Adding the Human Touch

With the rapid adoption of e-learning on campus by both professors and students, measures were taken by the CED team to make e-learning interactive and engaging with active professor-to-students/students-to-students active involvement, participation and collaboration.

In using IT for education, the focus should be on teaching, and not IT. A good online course should be one that achieves the pedagogical goals, and not one merely with flashing graphics and animation. E-mail and discussion forums facilitate interaction between the lecturers and students. Students extend their use to project work. However, these useful IT tools are only effective if they reinforce the already good teaching. While integrating IT into teaching, it must be borne in mind that teaching and learning should drive the use of technology, and not vice versa (Aslaksen, 1999; Christudason, 1999). To remind ourselves of this, the word "technology" was morphed into "te@chnology" to maintain that important focus.

Through Audio/Video Mediated Lecture Delivery

Audio/video mediated and multimedia communication can assist students in their learning, when compared with the conventional classroom lecture (Gibbons, Kincheloe, & Down, 1977). In the typical distance learning programmes, course participants do not have regular direct contact with their instructor. This creates a separation between students and teacher and lacks the vital "link" of face-to-face communication between the two parties (Keegan, 1986). Video mediated communication adds that fine touch of humanizing the content delivery. While a student is accessing a piece of e-learning content, a plain and static presentation document would not carry much value with as the learner clicks through all the slides to decipher or extrude the meaning and context behind the key points. However, if the student is able to "see" and "hear" the instructor, he or she would be more engaged to learn as the complementary audio-video elements make learning more engaging and sustainable.

PreseNTUr: For Content Creation

PreseNTUr is an initiative targeted at teaching staff who like to add in a video presentation synchronized with their presentation slides. It is a content creation system based on technology from Aculearn (www.aculearn.com) that enables professors to quickly and easily create content with such a format Such talking head presentation format can, in addition to providing a human touch, also has the capability to pace the learning of the online lessons. Students have different learning rates, as they do for reading. However, when watching the synchronized presentations, they all learn at the same rate of lecture presentation, While the faster learning would find it easily to follow, it helps the slower and weaker learner to learn at a pace, much like the runner-pacer who helps the marathon runner complete the race.

Features that make this tool professor-friendly include the installation of the Aculearn tool as software add-on to the commonly used Microsoft PowerPoint product. There is, hence, no need to learn an additional separate or supplementary content creation tool. Professors can prepare their lesson at their own convenience using a digital video camera and this authoring tool.

The studio set up of PreseNTUr system is shown in Figure 6. Before publishing it, professors can edit, add, delete or rearrange slides. Once concluded, the presentation is then published and uploaded to a server for online delivery to students. The publication process usually takes a few minutes only. Once published, if there is a need to do any amendments to the presentations, that can be done easily on specific slides, and thereafter published. The need not to have to create the whole presentation all over again for each change is a major productivity enhancement when compared with other software tools available.

Figure 6. PreseNTUr setup

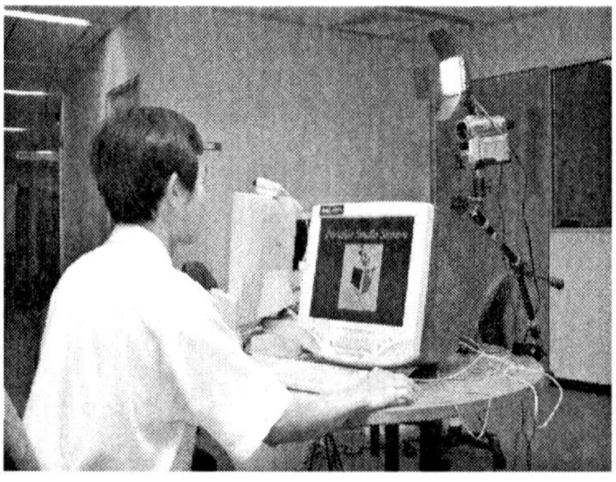

Figure 7. PreseNTUr lecture delivery

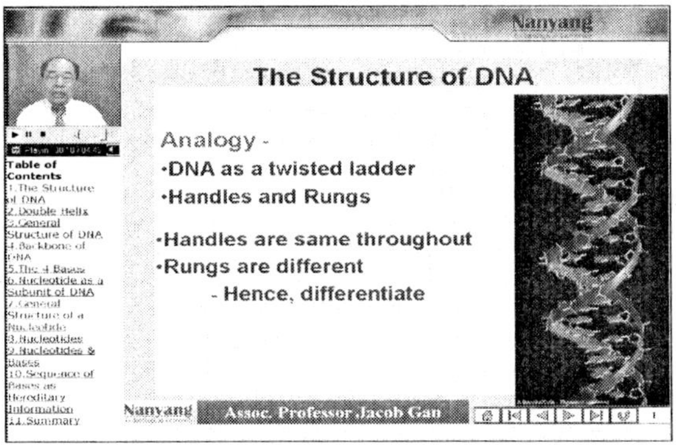

Once the content is published online, the lecture presentations can be accessed any where, any time on the network. The PreseNTUr video mediated lecture delivery is illustrated in Figure 7. One key advantage of this system is that the video mediated delivery can be streamed live onto the PDAs and students can view the content on portable devices via the internally on the campus wireless network or wireless hot-spots or Internet point anywhere in the world.

Breeze: For Low-Bandwidth Media-Rich Content

Macromedia Breeze (http://www.macromedia.com/software/breeze) is a recent multimedia content creation tool that converts the conventional Microsoft PowerPoint slides into the low bandwidth format of the Macromedia Flash animation. It allows voice narration to be synchronized with the PowerPoint slide transitions. It also enables interactive quiz to be incorporated as part of the audio lecture. Like the preseNTUr platform, the key advantage of this software is that the learning curve is almost zero for those who are already familiar with Microsoft PowerPoint. The instructor only needs some training on how to incorporate audio into the lecture delivery. The audio mediated lecture is capable of reaching out to users with low bandwidth connectivity like 56k bps modem dial-up. NTU implemented Breeze to complement PreseNTUr and it is targeted at online lecture delivery that does not require the video talking head. An example of Breeze lecture presentation is shown in Figure 8.

Figure 8. Breeze lecture presentation

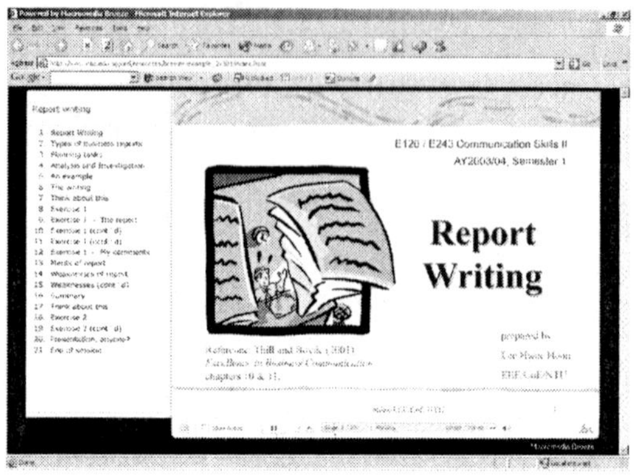

Through Collaborative Community Learning

Using technology to teach is more than just transferring some pen-and-paper classroom tasks and lessons to the PC. It is a question of knowing how to use technology appropriately to do teaching, research and communicate. Instructors must overcome many challenges before they can effectively use technology to educate others. Even if they are technically competent in using the Internet and multimedia tools, instructors may not know how best to employ them in training–today's technology-enabled curricula are very different from traditional, classroom-based programs. The natural tendency for instructors, especially those schooled in conventional models of teaching, is to replace classroom teaching with technology, or use technology to enhance classroom teaching. However, these methods have usually yielded few returns on investments of time and money.

However, in an e-learning environment, it is difficult to guide, direct, and stimulate discussion and learning. There is a lack of spontaneity of live lectures that is instrumental in encouraging student motivation, involvement and development (Christudason, 1999). There is a lack of personal coaching, immediate assistance, and motivation from a mentor who can impart the right knowledge at the earliest time.

Students who are taking online distance learning courses have revealed that they were not sure, at times, that the concepts they learned from the online materials were correct. When they asked among themselves, they were unable to concur with one another. They had tried contacting their lecturer at the remote end (by e-mail and newsgroup discussion) and there was either no reply or a delayed response that did not actually clarify their doubts. At times, many of such unproductive iterations were needed in a typical question & answer exchange. The students also highlighted that they have to be disciplined in order to attend the online lectures on their own. There is a need for good time management and self-motivation to get themselves going.

With the proliferation use of e-learning, there is a gradual change from lecturer-centered to student-centered approaches in the mode of teaching and learning. With the lecturer's role becoming a facilitator of learning, our students are required to participate actively and contribute to their learning. They need to be more disciplined and have greater self-management, and they must know what to learn, how to learn, and have the ability to evaluate their own learning. To do so, we need to change their mindsets, build up their confidence, encourage reflection while self-learning and develop their collaborative skills. There is a need for our students to view things differently, critically and creatively (Pan, 1999). As we would very much like our students to be life-long learners who would constantly upgrade themselves in this knowledge economy, we need to come up with an innovative and practical learning platform that allows them to do e-learning any time, anywhere, and most importantly, e-efficiently and e-effectively.

DeRienzo (2000) highlighted that in online learning, interaction is the key factor and passive "lecturing" is deadly. She suggested the concept of active learning as an alternative to passive learning. Students shall become engaged participants instead of being passive recipients. Professors shall play the role of facilitators, mentors and coaches rather than an information broadcaster. Students shall be evaluated based on their problem solving skills, rather than focusing on how much material they could memorise and regurgitate. The approach adopted shall be objective driven and not content driven.

According to Harasim, Hiltz, Teles, and Turoff (1996), social communications is an essential component of educational activity. According to Galusha (1997), one of the main barriers to online distance education is the feelings of alienation and isolation reported by students, and students' motivation has a major effect on the attrition and completion rates in the course, regardless of institutional setting. It will be difficult for learning to take place when the students do not have a sense of ownership with their individual learning and the spirits of togetherness with their fellow cohorts. In a like manner, Palloff and Pratt (1999) stressed that developing a sense of community among students is one of the critical factors in ensuring the success of online learning. The learning community provides an environment for learning to take place during online sessions (Palloff & Pratt, 1999).

E-learning can bring people together to discuss ideas and share information, and it has the potential for being a highly efficient, effective, innovative form of education and training. Because it provides more flexibility for learners in the ways and times they learn, they should develop more interests in lifelong learning. Instead of having an instructor tell them where to access information, what to do, learners are more likely to share with instructors what they have found and how much information is available. They are also more likely to continue their education and training on their own in future (Porter, 1997, pp. 16-20).

iNTUition: For Virtual Classes

iNTUition, a brand name to infer "in tuition," is an online learning software application whereby the professor can conduct a live lecture or tutorial without the need for a physical classroom environment. It is a user-friendly synchronous teaching and learning tool that enables professors to conduct classes, meetings, seminars and even coaching or mentoring online sessions. The professor and students can attend the live session from anywhere outside the boundary of a traditional classroom, so long that they have access to a network. In other words, they could be located on campus or at home, and could even be physically apart in different time zones.

By logging onto iNTUition (via campus wired or wireless network, or home dial-up/high speed modem), the professor can have the lecture proper conducted online: he could broadcast his teaching materials to all his students in the class, with his voice and video transmission synchronized with his pace of teaching. The students can ask question by clicking the "Ask Question" button on the software application and they can even annotate or write over the presentation whiteboard to illustrate a point. The professor could grant a particular student the floor to become a co-presenter — this is useful when there is a need to do a student presentation. The system also comes with a polling feature that the

Figure 9. iNTUtion online session

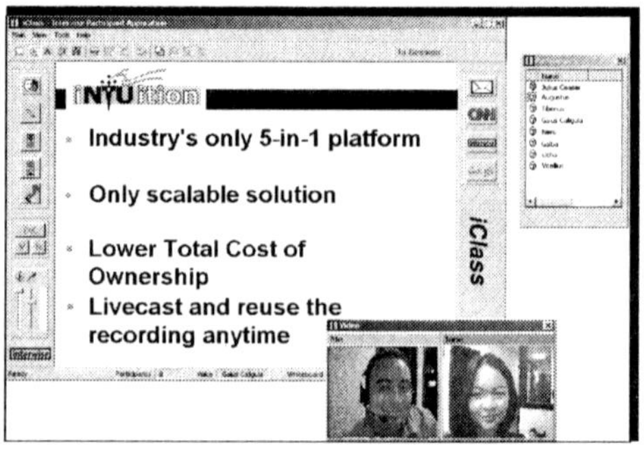

professor may use to ask a quick question and gain immediate feedback. The results will be shown as a percentage histogram. This also allows the professor to adjust his live lecture presentation based on the feedback indicated. There are also indicators from the students' software console to tell the professor in a subtle way that the pace of the lecture is too fast or too slow.

An example of iNTUition online session is shown in Figure 9. iNTUition is an online collaborative system powered by Interwise Enterprise Communication Platform (http://www.interwise.com).

aNTUna: For Mobile Learning

At present, with the proliferation of students' notebook computer/tablet PC ownership and growing usage of our wireless network, edveNTUre is easily available any time, anywhere, to anyone on campus and elsewhere with network access. As part of edveNTUre services, aNTUna, sounds like the "antenna" for radio communication, is a service to embody mobile e-learning applications on portable devices such as personal digital assistants (PDA), handphones and notebook computers. Currently, we have two services under this initiative, namely aNTUna BlackboardToGo! and the aNTUna video projector system.

aNTUna BlackboardToGo!

BlackboardToGo! is the first aNTUna initiative rolled out in the academic year 2002-03. This software application allows content located on edveNTUre Blackboard server to be downloaded to PDAs for off-line browsing. With this application, students are able to revise their lecture materials while they are traveling and on the move. It runs as a supplementary channel to the wide-used Avantgo service commonly used by PDA users for accessing news, information and other reading articles. Lecture materials in Microsoft Word, Excel, PowerPoint and portable document format (PDF) and other file formats can be viewed with the necessary third party tools and viewers.

aNTUna Video Projector

The second aNTUna initiative is the use of wireless video projectors in 60 tutorial rooms (under the first of three phases) on campus Prior to the start of the tutorial session, the professor can locate the networked video projector in the various tutorial room from the convenience of his office PC or notebook computer. He can quickly transfer the relevant teaching material to the video projector remotely via the campus wired or wireless network. With this new setup, he does not have to worry about lugging on his notebook computer and messing around with video-computer screen projection as the essential teaching materials have been pre-loaded onto the networked video projector's storage space.

During the tutorial class, the professor can then do his presentation using a remote controller. In addition, when there is a need for student presentations, they could use their notebook computers to send their presentation document to the video projector in the tutorial room using their PC wireless link. Thereafter, the presentation can be done by the student without the need to connect the monitor cable and sometimes problematic video signal synchronization process that would hold up the class. The professor and students can also access to World Wide Web using the build-in Internet browser that is embedded within the network projector. The ease of convenience that wireless video projector brings helps to cultivate collaborative learning further as both professor and students are now able to "show-and-tell" opinions quickly.

Feedback of the User Community to E-Learning

A recent two-week poll conducted in October 2003 was conducted to gather information on users' satisfaction levels, needs, opinions on additional features as well as general feedback. The purpose for gathering such data was to

1. Gather timely and relevant data for use in evaluation and planning processes
2. Be accountable for the performance of the e-learning portal in the university
3. Enhance the Centre's service to the NTU community by Web-publishing the results

To facilitate the data collection, the survey was administered through the edveNTUre course-site system by batch enrolling all staff and students (1,321 staff members and 21,223 students) into 2 separate course-sites. The surveys, which consisted of 22 questions each (multiple choice and free response), were developed using the survey feature in the course-sites. A portlet module that linked the users directly to the surveys was deployed on the home page of the e-learning portal (my edveNTUre). This module allowed for easy and direct access to the questionnaire, as well as provided daily live updates of the results. E-mails (with direct URL links to the surveys) were also sent to the NTU community to boost the response. An incentive for responding to the survey was a chance to win a ticket to a public educational-cum-entertainment event. 60 tickets (3:1 for student:staff ratio) for the winners were offered, and names of winners drawn daily were updated at the main edveNTUre course-site.

The core questionnaire sections were

- Overall satisfaction levels with edveNTUre
- Usability of edveNTUre
- Desired features of edveNTUre
- Usage patterns
- Improvements/general feedback (free response)

Summary of Results

A total of 141 staff (10.6%) and 2771 (13.0%) students responded to this 2-week survey. It was observed that most of the responses were gathered in the initial days of the survey period (more than two-thirds of the students answered in the first week, and more than half of them answered in the first 2 days). More than half of the staff members responded to an e-mail reminders that contained a direct hyperlink to the survey, but students were less responsive to the e-mail reminder.

The following observations were noted in this survey.

a. **Overall satisfaction, usability, and accessibility of edveNTUre:** A high percentage (87% students, and 88% staff) indicated that they were satisfied or very satisfied with the course site system in edveNTUre. High scores (88% students, 79% staff) were also observed for usability of the e-learning portal. The system also enjoyed high accessibility; 75% of students and 76% of staff indicated that they do not have problems accessing edveNTUre. Eighty-seven percent of the students and 88% of the staff members look forward to using edveNTUre again in future semesters.

b. **Desired features of edveNTUre:** The staff and students hold similar opinions on the use of discussion boards and electronic portfolios. The most significant difference in the views held by the staff and students was in the area of recorded lectures. Ninety-three percent of the students felt that an archive of recorded lectures in the course-site will be useful. This is in contrast to the 27% of staff who share the same view.

c. **Usage patterns:** Sixteen percent of the staff access edveNTUre on a daily basis, but about half (52%) of the students access it as often. About half of the staff members spend an average of less than an hour in a typical week on edveNTUre. The students registered a higher usage level; half of them (51%) spend an average of at least 1-5 hours on edveNTUre each week.

d. **Other observations:** Ninety percent of the students use some form of instant messaging software (e.g., ICQ, Yahoo messenger, MSN), and 1 in 6 students surveyed own a personal digital assistant. About half of the students own a notebook computer, and 1 in 9 staff owns a tablet personal computer.

Details of the survey results are available online. Student results at http://www.ced.ntu.edu.sg/resources/edventure/survey2003/studentsurvey2003.htm, and staff results at http://www.ced.ntu.edu.sg/resources/edventure/survey2003/staffsurvey2003.htm.

Feedback from users, both academic staff and students on the usefulness and usability has been generally positive with regard to the use of edveNTUre. E-learning will aid the objective towards the goal of training the student community to be effective knowledge workers. When they join the workforce, it is hoped that their future employers from business and industry will find them effective in the creation, use, application, and exploitation of knowledge in the digital economy.

The technology has also made it possible for students to learn anytime, anyplace or any device. The augurs well the potential of life-long learning in the digital economy. The process of due diligence in system specification, design and implementation is important and critical for our success. Having an academic to lead the e-learning initiative has been appropriate in our case, though one would venture to surmise the outcome if it was led by IT staff.

Staff and faculty development is important — as they are the beginning of the e-learning food chain, it is important that they are enabled and facilitated in the transition and introduction of e-learning from the traditional teaching environments. In that regard, the edUtorium initiative has been successful with its program of staff orientation, training, faculty development, publications and other support programs.

Mistakes in e-learning can be very expensive — for the institution, its community of professors and students. Some case study has shown a negative perception of its capability and potential due to a wrong choice in platform, policy, or practice. A process of due diligence, therefore, can have significant impact not only of the e-learning initiative, but in the strategic evolution and adoption of e-learning in the institution.

E-learning is evolving and growing. The analysts have projected very optimistic projections in the growth and impact of e-learning as an industry and a component of IT industrial growth. Today, the industry is speaking of standards — a sign of critical mass and maturity of the industry and business. Defining standards is challenging, and can be decisive in how fast the industry will grow further in the future. E-learning has been regarded as the next killer application on the Internet (Moore & Jones, 2001). It has made into the cover of Fortune magazine, as well as creates new industries of publications, content, and management systems. E-learning will enable and facilitate life-long learning — and the way people (young, old, the student, professional and the public) will learn in the future. Although some might argue that some bubbles have burst, the Internet and e-learning has established new modes of learning through the use of technology with an impact that can be seen at every strata of society, but more significantly, at every strata of the educational system.

Conclusion

This chapter outlines the processes NTU adopted in its early initiative and the continual enhancement of the e-learning culture among its constituents in its academic community of staff and students. Today, the use of e-learning is pervasive on the campus and has become mission critical. It recognizes that the use of e-learning will continue to grow, and its direction in the next phase of its growth is governed by the theme of "humaniZing e-learning" to inculcate an online teaching and learning culture that is highly interactive, engaging and collaborative for the professors and students.

References

Aslaksen, H. (1999). *Is IT it?* CDTL Brief (6). Singapore: National University of Singapore, Centre for Development of Teaching and Learning.

Christudason, A. (1999). *Fundamental teaching skills in an IT age.* CDTL Brief (6). Singapore: National University of Singapore, Centre for Development of Teaching and Learning.

Dan, M. (1999). *Effective teaching in distance education.* Washington, DC: ERIC Clearinghouse on Teaching and Teacher Education. (ERIC Document Reproduction Service No. ED 4336528).

DeRienzo, E. (2000). *Teaching in a distance learning environment*. Boston: Massachusetts Institute of Technology, Center for Advanced Educational Services.

Galusha, J. M. (1997). Barriers to learning in distance education. *Interpersonal Computing and Technology: An Electronic Journal for the 21st Century, 5*(3-4), 6-14.

Gibbons, J. F., Kincheloe, W. R., & Down, K. S. (1997). Tutored videotape instruction: A new use of electronics media in education. *Science*, *195*(4283), 1139-1146.

Harasim, L., Hiltz, S. R., Teles, L., & Turoff, M. (1996). *Learning networks.* Cambridge, MA: MIT Press.

Keegan, D. (1986). *The foundations of distance education.* London: Croom Helm.

Moore, C., & Jones, M. (2001) *Comdex: e-Learning takes stage as the next killer app.* Retrieved December 29, 2003, from http://archive.infoworld.com/articles/hn/xml/01/11/15/011115hnelearnmantra.xml

Palloff, R. M., & Pratt, K. (1999). *Building learning communities in cyberspace.* San Francisco: Jossey-Basss.

Pan, D. (1999). Helping students learn in the IT age. *CDTL Brief, 2*(2), 1. Singapore: National University of Singapore, Centre for Development of Teaching and Learning.

Porter, L. R. (1997). *Creating the virtual classroom: Distance learning with the Internet.* Canada: John Wiley.

Storck, J., & Sproull, L. (1995) Through a glass darkly: What do people learn in video conferences? *Human Communication Research*, *22*(2), 197-219.

Chapter XIII

A SCORM-Compliant U-Learning Grid by Employing CC/PP

Ching-Jung Liao, Chung Yuan Christian University, Taiwan

Jin-Tan Yang, National Kaohsiung Normal University, Taiwan

Abstract

In this study, a SCORM-compliant ubiquitous learning grid was constructed by using the grid services technologies combined with CC/PP. The purpose was to let anyone access any information at anyplace, anytime, by any device to learn. Several SCORM-compliant learning management systems collaborated by Globus Toolkit 3.2 grid engine and CC/PP were implemented to provide a content adaptive environment. In the experiment, English learning objects were produced with access to learn and made accessible using PC, Laptop, Tablet PC, PDA, and mobile phones. Results of this study demonstrate the feasibility of the proposed framework.

Introduction

Ubiquitous networks makes it easy for anyone to access any information at anytime from anywhere by using any appliances. One of the important applications on the ubiquitous network is learning. It will make a fast development for the future information society. Recently, electronic learning (e-learning) has become an important media of learning, and ubiquitous learning (u-learning) refers to learning at anytime and anywhere. SCORM (sharable content object reference model) is a standard for e-learning, which most of the learning management systems (LMSs) followed.

However, LMSs suffered several problems. First, e-learning resources are always distributed around several locations, and thus it makes e-learning systems difficult to integrate numerous e-learning resources. Second, most e-learning components are system-dependent, and cannot be combined with other systems. In other words, it means a component programmed by Visual Basic (VB) is difficult to migrate to a Unix-like platform, or communicate with a component hosted on it. Third, the service-level agreements across multiple LOs are insufficient to control workflow collaboration. Fourth, learners still cannot learn with restrictions of time and place. Most LMSs ask learners to use specific client devices to learn. Because of these problems, the ubiquitous learning system is devised to solve these problems based on the grid service core technologies combined with CC/PP (composite capability/ preference profiles), and is called the ubiquitous learning grid (u-learning grid, ULG). This study developed a service-oriented solution of ubiquitous e-learning system based on a ubiquitous learning grid using several SCORM-compliant LMSs. GT3 (The Globus Project) was employed as a grid engine for integrating the LMSs into a ubiquitous learning grid. Client learners can access the LOs from the ULG using PC, Laptop, PDA, and mobile phones.

The remainder of this chapter is organized as follows: related works are discussed in Section 2. Section 3 details the proposed framework of a SCORM-compliant u-learning grid. Section 4 presents and discusses the experimental results. Finally, Section 5 gives conclusions and directions for future research.

Related Works

The works related to our proposed framework is presented here in a way how we leverage existing solutions from grid technologies and public standards to provide the intended open and interoperable LMSs to solve the important SCORM-compliant e-learning system integration issues.

Basic Concepts of Grid Computing

Grid computing owns better abilities of workflow collaboration and sharing resources for integrating e-learning platforms. The sharing resource of grid computing primarily focuses on direct access to computers, software, data, and other resources, as required by various collaborative problem-solving and resource-brokering strategies emerging in industry, science, and engineering (Foster, Kesselman, & Tuecke, 2001).

Currently, grid architecture has demonstrated a shift toward service-oriented concepts. For example, Web service is a key technology in service-oriented technology. A grid service with Web service technologies is a new development trend and gradually obtains enterprise's support. A service can be considered a platform-independent software component, which is described by using a descriptive language and published as part of a directory or registry by a service provider. A service request can then locate a set of services by querying the registry, a process called resource discovery. Moreover, a suitable service can finally be selected and invoked, which called binding. Service-oriented concepts solve the problems associated with "Naming," and employ open standards and protocols to enable the concepts and solutions for enterprise systems to be viewed. A service that follows the specifications of OGSA can be viewed as a grid service (Foster, Kesselman, Nick, & Tuecke, 2002).

Key Points of Applying Grid Services to the U-Learning Grid

The main purpose of applying grid services to the ULG is to facilitate workflow collaboration and share resources. Grid services combined with Web services technologies are a new developing trend and gradually obtain enterprise support. Based on grid technology and Web services, grid services seamlessly gather various and dynamic resources from various places and achieve comprehensive and meaningful sharing of grid resources. According to the aforementioned, grid services have some advantages over Web services in terms of workflow collaboration and resources sharing. Notably, grid services provide a better solution for the problem of learning resource sharing and collaboration for e-learning.

Recently, some researchers have proposed methods for learning resource sharing. For example, Brusilovsky proposed reusable distributed learning activities (Brusilovsky & Nijhavan, 2002). Xu, Yin, and Saddik (2003) proposed a Web services oriented framework for dynamic e-learning systems integration (Xu, Yin, & Saddik, 2003). Pankratius and Vossen applied the concepts of grid computing into the e-learning (Pankratius & Vossen, 2003). Meanwhile, several works have examined how to apply grid service technologies to e-learning. For example, Reklaitis developed a framework based on Globus (The Globus Project) to develop a grid environment for e-learning (Pankratius & Vossen, 2003). Gaeta also developed some concepts for employing grid technologies to integrate learning resources (Gaeta, Ritrovato, & Salerno, 2002. Neumann and Geys describe the relationship between SCORM standard and the learning grid (Neumann & Geys, 2004). Li, Zheng, Ogata, and Yano designed a continuous ubiquitous learning system that integrated different types of e-learning platforms into a ubiquitous learning environment (Li, Zheng, Ogata, & Yano, 2003), but did not use grid service technologies. The main difference between using grid technologies to integrate learning resources and traditional distributing technologies is that a grid can obtain all computational information among the grid nodes, and thus can provide multi-dimensional qualities of services (QoS) for learning platforms.

SCORM, CC/PP, and U-Learning

SCORM is a standard for e-learning which combines XML based technologies to define and describe each e-learning material as a learning object (LO). Different LOs can be inter-recognized so it can exchange among different learning systems that support these standards.

CC/PP is a standard, which can be used to transmit their capabilities and user preferences for various devices. For example: mobile phone, PDA, and so on. It was originally design to be used when a device requests Web content via a browser so that servers and proxies can customize content to the target device. In u-learning grid, it can be used to detect what kind of device connects to the portal so that broker can send the adaptive learning content service to the client device.

Ubiquitous learning should make users be able to learn any information, anytime, anyplace, with any devices. Rogers et al. (2005) proposed u-learning that can integrate indoor and outdoor experiences to improve the learning performance. The main purpose of this chapter is trying to integrate SCORM-compliant LMSs by using grid services technologies combined with CC/PP.

The Framework of U-Learning Grid

This study applied grid services technologies and CC/PP standard to ubiquitous learning. GT3 was used to establish an environment for grid services, which connected several computers. The Los, which is distributed among various SCORM-compliant learning platforms, were packed with different types of services, and these LOs were mapped as the standard grid services. The proposed framework was named the ubiquitous learning grid. Figure 1 shows the system architecture of ULG. The system can be explained in three parts. The left part of Figure 1 illustrates several LO Services supported by different content creators. The LO Services can be either located at different positions or hosted in heterogeneous platforms. These LOs were focused on English learning, and were packed using the SCORM standard. The central part of Figure 1 is u-learning grid portal (ULGP). The right part of Figure 1 illustrates the clients of ULG, which could be mobile devices, for example, tablet PC, laptop, PDA, cellular phone, and so on. The mobile devices could connect to the ULGP to access adaptive services.

Figure 1. The system architecture of u-learning grid

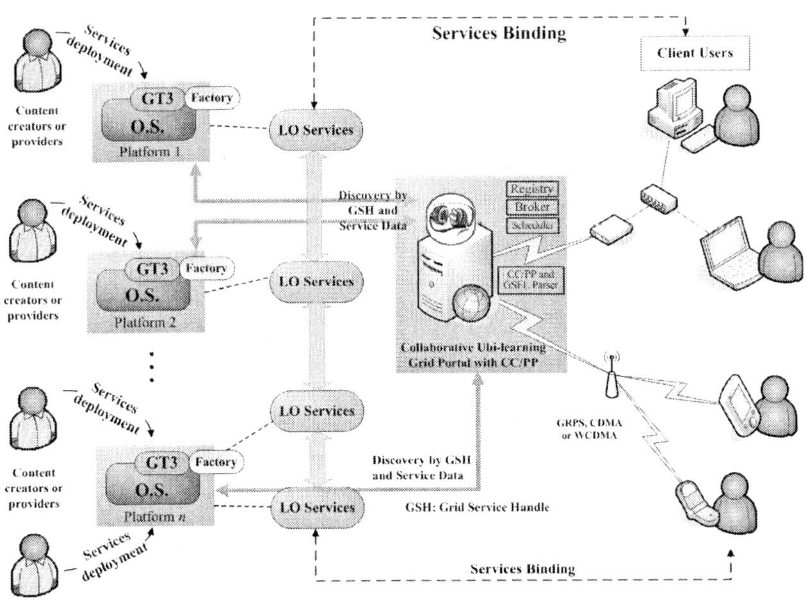

U-Learning Grid Portal

The ULGP contains service registry, service broker, services scheduler, CC/PP parser, and GSFL (Krishnan, Wagstrom, & Laszewski, 2002) parser. The service registry enabled each LO to register here, enabling the service requester to bind services. Since the ULG was constructed under the grid environment, the host computer of each node was peer-to-peer, and information could be shared and exchanged among all of the nodes. In addition, the grid core engine monitored the states of each node and registry services to confirm whether or not they were alive. That is, LO services in ULG are dynamically generated, searched, released, and bound. The host of each node in the ULG could also be the service registry for searching the services. The service broker could be any host in ULG, but cellular phone must assign a gateway to enter the system by GPRS, and then a virtual organization (VO) must be identified to perform this task. Generally, a broker processed the query and registry of learning object services. Service providers register the services with the broker. CC/PP parser was used to parse CC/PP document to obtain the attributes of client devices and implemented by using JSR 188 API. GSFL parser was used to parse the GSFL document and scheduler coordinated the services and their lifecycle management.

The Operation of U-Learning Grid Portal

The operation for accessing the ULGP via mobile phone was shown in Figure 2, where the circle number denoted the steps of process. The procedures described as following

- **Step 1:** All of the e-learning platforms registered their services to ULGP
- **Step 2:** The client user requested and sent header information to ULGP, so that ULGP obtained the device brand and type
- **Step 3:** ULGP found the CC/PP document mapped by the device brand and type. CC/PP document was parsed to get detail attributes of client device
- **Step 4:** The available services could be discovered in registry from the parse results, and then returned the listing to mobile phone
- **Step 5&6:** User chose the services then transmitted the sequence to ULGP for generating the GSFL (Grid Services Flow Language) document and parsed it. The scheduler would coordinate the services via parse results
- **Step 7:** Factory would create and adapt LO services dynamically

Figure 2. The operation for accessing the u-learning grid portal by using mobile phone

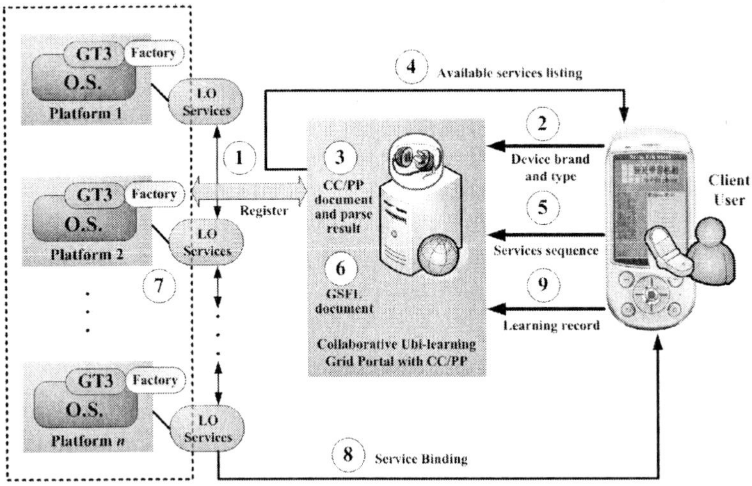

- **Step 8 & 9:** User bound the service to get adaptive content and returned the learning record to update the portfolio after the learning activities were finished

Results and Discussions

In an u-learning grid, GT3 was installed on each node as a grid engine for establishing grid services. The client devices were PC, Laptop, Tablet PC, iPAQ H3950PDA, and several mobile phones, e.g., Nokia 6100, 6610, 7210, Sony Ericsson P900, or Motorola 388C, etc. ULG supported a seamless environment for learners where they could get adaptive content at anytime, anyplace, by using any devices. To describe the experiment of ULG, four learning scenarios were described as follows:

- **Scenario 1:** Thomas can learn by interacting with his teacher at the multimedia classroom in the school. He also can learn by accessing materials from ULG.

- **Scenario 2:** When Thomas is at home, he can learn by using PC with access to ULG. He chose several learning materials (e.g., some words, several sentences, and assessments).

Finally, the learning record can be customized.

- **Scenario 3:** Thomas logs on ULG via cellular phone during his vacation. At this time, ULG supported adaptive content by following his personal learning profile and device attributes. For example, if Thomas connected to ULGP via Nokia 7210 cellular phone, the CC/PP parser will parse the CC/PP document, part list of the parse result was given in Figure 3. From Figure 3, several attributes of client device could be obtained (e.g., browser name, screen size, etc.). The adaptive content could be shown in Figure 5.
- **Scenario 4:** Thomas used his PDA to learn when he was rest at classroom. ULG would provide images with better solution and video/audio materials due to the reason of more powerful ability of computing and display than mobile phones

Figure 3. Part list of the CC/PP document parsing result for Nokia 7210 cellular phone

```
component: BrowserUA
  attribute: BrowserName = Nokia
  attribute: TablesCapable = Yes
  attribute: FramesCapable = No
component: NetworkCharacteristics
  attribute: SecuritySupport = WTLS-2
  attribute: SupportedBearers = GPRS
component: HardwarePlatform
  attribute: BitsPerPixel = 12
  attribute: TextInputCapable = Yes
  attribute: OutputCharSet = ISO-8859-1
  attribute: NumberOfSoftKeys = 2
  attribute: Keyboard = PhoneKeypad
  attribute: ColorCapable = Yes
  attribute: ScreenSize = 128x128
  attribute: Vendor = Nokia
  attribute: InputCharSet = US-ASCII
  attribute: SoundOutputCapable = Yes
  attribute: StandardFontProportional = Yes
  attribute: ScreenSizeChar = 18x5
  attribute: Model = 7210
  attribute: ImageCapable = Yes
  attribute: PixelAspectRatio = 1x1
```

Figure 4. One of the learning contents displayed on the Laptop or PC

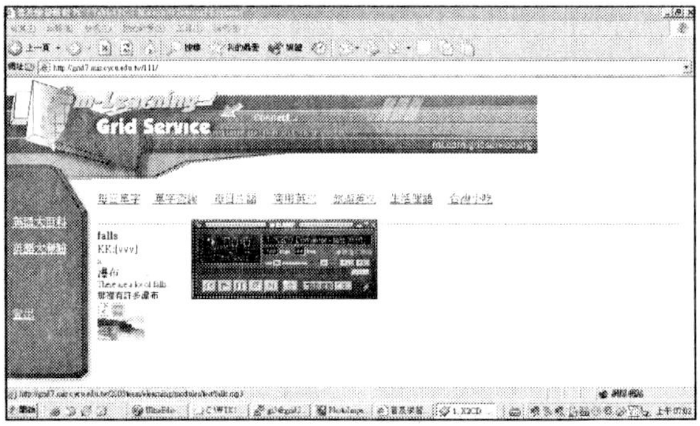

Figure 5. A series of learning contents displayed on the Nokia 7210 mobile phone

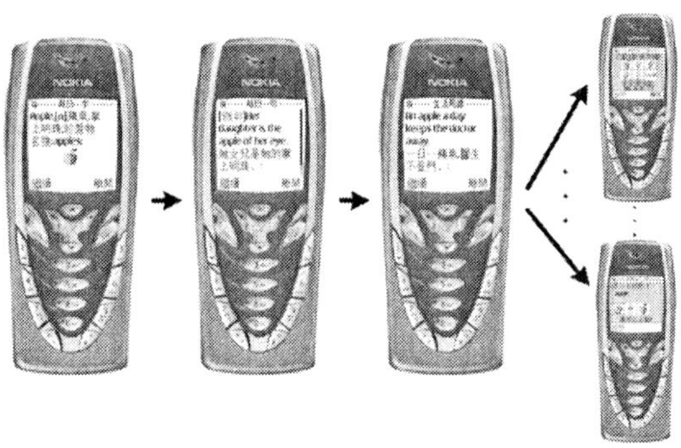

Figure 6. Two of the learning contents displayed on the iPAQ H3950 PDA

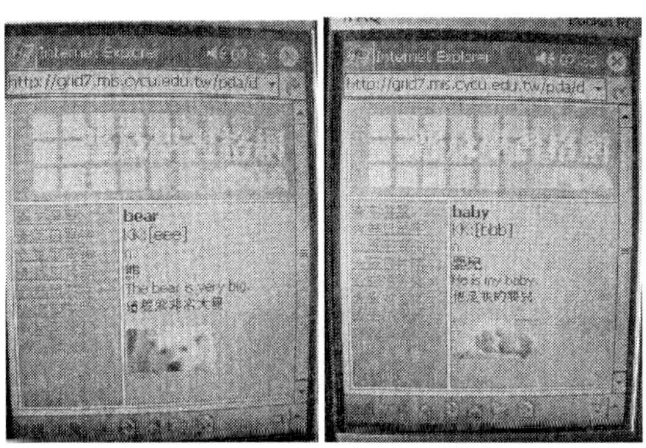

Figures 4-6 showed that learning content accessed by PC or laptop, mobile phone Nokia 7210, and iPAQ H3950 PDA, respectively. The advantages of u-learning grid are the workflow collaboration, content adaptation, and SCORM-compliant LMSs integration.

Conclusion

This study proposed a SCORM-compliant u-learning grid by employing CC/PP for solving the difficulties of sharing learning resources distributed on different LMSs and helping learners to learn at anytime, anywhere, by using any devices to get adaptive content. Furthermore, the proposed framework produces learning objects wrapped by SCORM standard that can be used effectively for collaboration and reuse. The ULG is based on grid services technologies combined with CC/PP, mobile devices and relevant technologies to support ubiquitous learning. Several SCORM-compliant learning management systems collaborated by GT3 grid engine and CC/PP were implemented to provide a ubiquitous learning grid. During our experiment, we produce English learning objects that can be learned and accessed by using PC Laptop PDA and mobile phones. Results of this study demonstrate the feasibility of the proposed framework. In the future, the ontology can be attached on ULG to improve the adaptive capability and flexibility.

Acknowledgment

The authors would like to thank the National Science Council of the Republic of China, Taiwan for financially supporting this research under Contract No. NSC 93-2213-E-033-030.

References

Brusilovsky, P., & Nijhavan, H. (2002, October). A framework for adaptive e-learning based on distributed reusable learning activities. *Proceedings of E-Learn 2002*, Montreal, Canada (Vol. 1, pp. 154-161).

Foster, I., Kesselman, C., Nick, J., & Tuecke, S. (2002). Grid services for distributed system integration. *Computer, 35*(6), 37-46.

Foster, I., Kesselman, C., & Tuecke, S. (2001). The anatomy of the grid enabling scalable virtual organizations. *International Journal of Supercomputer Applications, 15*(3), 200-222.

Gaeta, M., Ritrovato, P., & Salerno, S. (2002, September). Implementing new advanced learning scenarios through GRID technologies. *Proceedings of the 1st LeGE-WG International Workshop on Educational Models for GRID Based Services*, Lausanne, Switzerland.

Krishnan, S., Wagstrom, P., & Laszewski, G. (2002, July). *GSFL: A workflow framework for grid services.* Retrieved from http://www-unix.globus.org/cog/papers/gsfl-paper.pdf

Li, L., Zheng, Y., Ogata, H., & Yano, Y. (2001, November 7-11). Using constructionism for ubiquitous learning environment design. *Proceedings of E-Learn 2003—World Conference on E-Learning in Corporate, Government, Healthcare, and Higher Education*, Phoenix, AZ (pp. 599-602).

Neumann, F., & Geys, R. (2004, April 27-28). SCORM and the learning grid. *Proceedings of the 4th International LeGE-WG Workshop — Towards a European Learning Grid Infrastructure: Progressing with a European Learning Grid*, Stuttgart, Germany.

Pankratius, V., & Vossen, G. (2003, October). Toward e-learning grids: Using grid computing in electronic learning. *Proceedings of IEEE Workshop on Knowledge Grid and Grid Intelligence,* Saint Mary's University, Halifax, Nova Scotia, Canada (pp. 4-15).

Reklaitis, V., Baniulis, K., & Masevicius, A. (2002, December). Towards e-learning application architecture based on GLOBUS framework. *Proceedings of Euroweb 2002 Conference*, St Anne's College Oxford, UK.

Rogers, Y., Price, S., Randell, C., Fraser, D. S., Weal, M., & Fitzpatrick, G. (2005, January). Interaction design and children: U-learning integrates indoor and outdoor experiences. *Communications of the ACM, 48*(1), 55-59.

Xu, Z., Yin, Z., & Saddik, A. E. (2003, May). A Web services oriented framework for dynamic e-learning systems. *Proceedings of CCECE 2003–CCGEI 2003*, Montreal, Canada (pp. 1-4).

Chapter XIV

A Distance Learning System for Teaching the Writing of Chinese Characters Over the Internet

K. T. Sun, National University of Tainan, Taiwan

D. S. Feng, National University of Tainan, Taiwan

Abstract

This chapter proposes an intelligent tutoring system (ITS) for teaching students to write Chinese characters over the Internet. Since each Chinese character is like a picture, knowing the correct stroke orders can enable a person to write characters more easily. Accordingly, primary schools in Taiwan teach the correct orders in which strokes should be made when writing Chinese characters. In the proposed system, students can use a pen (or drag the mouse) to write Chinese characters on a digital board through a browser such as Microsoft Internet Explorer. For realizing the situation of student's writing behavior, a neuron-based student model was designed *to learn the writing style of each student. When a wrong stroke order is used, a short animated cartoon is displayed to show the error to the student, and the reason for the error will be explained. An intelligent tutoring module selects a Chinese character that is similar to the character written with the wrong stroke order, to teach the student again. Several databases and rule-bases are used to store important information such as the correct stroke orders and the structure of each Chinese character, the screen positions of each stroke, the writing behavior of each student, the rules of inference by which training characters are selected, and the error codes (types). This system has been in development since 1996, and includes 2734 Chinese characters (taught in primary schools). It has been used in elementary schools, and by thousands of students. Educational research reveals that over 82% of primary school students had some problems in using the correct stroke orders when writing Chinese characters, and the improvement exhibited by the experimental group was significant ($F = 25.331$, $p < .005$). The proposed system has been verified as being of high value in teaching students to write Chinese characters.*

Introduction

Around 4,000 Chinese characters are commonly written, and they have a wide variety of shapes and stroke orders. Each Chinese character is like a picture, and each stroke has a special shape, direction, and position. Chinese characters can be written more easily if the correct stroke order is used (Bjorksten, 1994; Lam, et al., 2001; Law, Ki, Chung, Ko, & Lam, 1998; McNaughton & Ying, 2000; Yao, et al., 1997). Additionally, the written characters are then more understandable and beautiful. Accordingly, the correct stroke orders of the characters should be learned before Chinese characters are written. Primary schools in Taiwan therefore teach correct stroke order of each Chinese character (as defined by the Ministry of Education, Taiwan, ROC, 1996). However, a teacher cannot verify the correctness of the stroke orders of characters written by every student in a class of 30. Therefore, an intelligent tutoring system (ITS) (Anderson, 1988) is required to help students learn the correct stroke orders of Chinese characters.

CAI (computer-assisted instruction) has been developed over the last two decades. Several good systems, such as the declarative model SCHOLAR (Carbonell, 1970; Carbonell & Collins, 1974), the black-box model SOPHIE-I (Brown & Burton, 1978), the qualitative model SOPHIE-III (Brown, Burton, & de Kleer, 1982), the glass-box expert model GUIDON (Clancey, Barnett & Cohen, 1982), the procedural knowledge model BUGGY (Brown, & VanLehn,

1980) and the neuron-based ITS (Sun, Huang, & Wang, 1997) have been proposed. Most CAI systems are run only on personal computers. Users cannot operate the CAI system on the Internet, and researchers therefore have not been able to collect much data on the use of the CAI system. Therefore, "designing a CAI system on the Internet" has become extremely important in the field of distance learning. Moreover, "applying artificial intelligence to the CAI systems" is also critical for designing an effective learning system. These two issues were considered in the design of the proposed ITS, which combines the newly developed AI technique "neural network" (Lippmann, 1987; Sun, & Fu, 1992; Sun, & Fu, 1993) with the WWW programming techniques "Active X control" and "ODBC" (Denning, 1997; Microsoft, 1997) so it can provide an effective environment for learning the stroke orders of Chinese characters on the Internet. Similar CAI systems have recently been proposed (Lam, 2001). However, they can only be run on local PCs, and not on the Internet; also, they only "click" the strokes of the Chinese character and so cannot detect if a stroke is made in the wrong direction. (The rules about the directions of strokes are not included.) The "click" operation is very different from actual writing behavior. The proposed system includes and all writing rules and checks that they are followed as students write each stroke of a Chinese character.

Section 2 introduces the system architecture of the proposed ITS. Section 3 clarifies the pertinent artificial intelligence techniques. Section 4 presents experimental results and Section 5 draws conclusions.

System Architecture

The proposed ITS includes seven major parts — the user interface, the student model, the intelligent tutoring module, the instruction/test module, the explanatory module, the data- and rule-base module and the multimedia animated cartoon engine (as depicted in Figure 1). Figure 2 presents the architecture of the proposed ITS executed on the Internet.

Each Chinese character displayed on the user interface is specified by the pixel-locations on the screen (represents by X- and Y- coordinates). Each stroke is recorded as two to six (X, Y) positions, according to the complexity of the stroke. The first position refers to the initial part of the stroke, the final position to the final part of the stroke; the others are the intermediate turn-positions in the stroke (Figure 3). For example, the stroke " ㇇ " in the lower-right part of the Chinese character "伶" (Figure 3) is recorded as (123, 183), (198, 178) and (175, 228), referring to the first, the intermediate and the final positions, respectively.

Figure 1. Main structure of the proposed ITS for teaching the stroke orders of Chinese characters

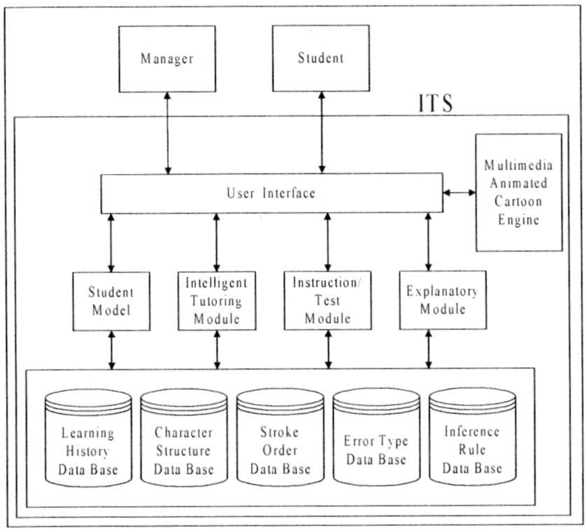

Figure 2. Architecture of the ITS executed on the Internet

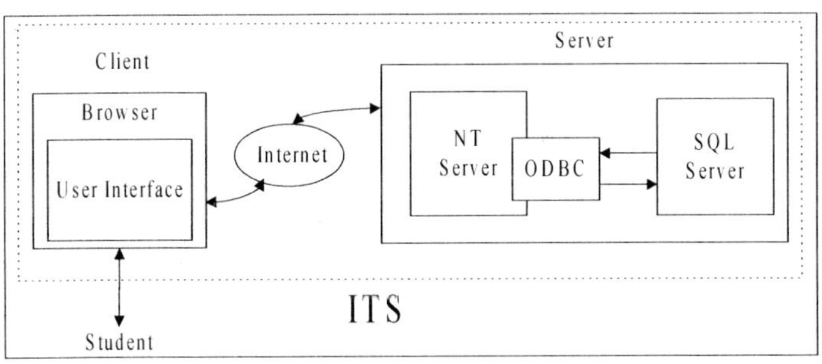

Figure 3. Method for coding position of a Chinese character on the screen

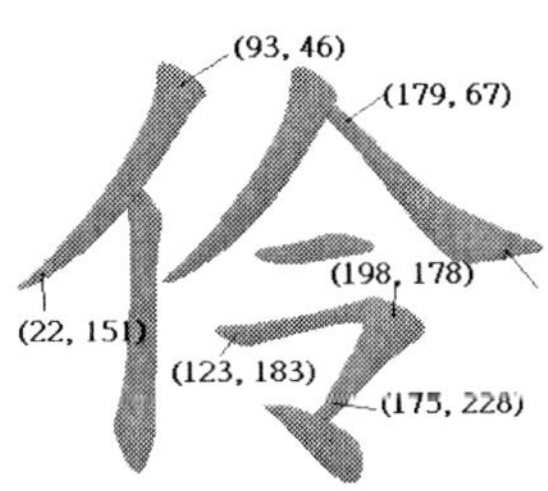

Figure 4. Method for coding the directions of strokes in Chinese characters

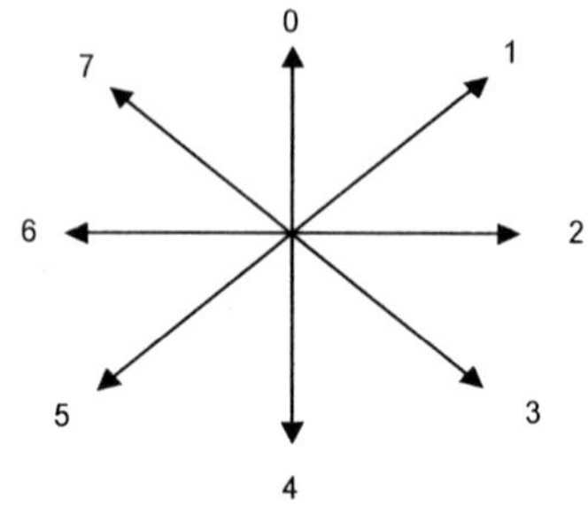

Therefore, the stroke orders of a Chinese character can be recorded as a sequence of (X, Y)-positions. Additionally, the "direction" of each stroke must also be considered. Eight directions are defined to represent each stroke in a Chinese character (Figure 4).

The direction of each stroke is determined by connecting the first position to the final position of each stroke. This direction is compared with eight directions (Figure 4), the closest of which is used to represent the direction of this stroke. If a stroke is written from the upper-right to the lower-left, its direction is "↙" and is coded as "5." For example, the Chinese character 天 (tian1; day) is written (according to the following sequence of directions); →, →, ↙ and ↘ for the strokes 一 , 一 , 丿, and ㇏, respectively, and the directional codes are 2, 2, 5 and 3. For ease of operation, the interface of the system is designed to operate using a pen, a mouse, or a touch panel monitor. When a student writes a Chinese character on the browser (or drags the mouse), the dragged part is

Figure 5. User interface of the proposed ITS for writing Chinese characters on the Internet (The darker part is the stroke being written by the user)

displayed in a different color (Figure 5), corresponding to the writing of a character on paper using a pen. The stroke orders of the written characters will be recorded in the history database and learned by the student model. If the written stroke orders are correct, then a congratulatory cartoon, produced by the multimedia animated cartoon engine, is displayed as a reward (Figure 6). Then another Chinese character, with a different stroke order, is generated for instruction. However, an incorrectly written stroke order will cause a warning cartoon to be displayed (Figure 7), and the explanatory module automatically responds with an explanation of the error to help the student understand his or her mistake. Then, the intelligent tutoring module will respond with a Chinese character that is similar to the character written with the wrong stroke order, to enable the student to rewrite and relearn his strokes. The user interface shows seven functions (as shown on the right of Figure 5). The basic effects of each function are as follows

Figure 6. A congratulatory cartoon rewards the student

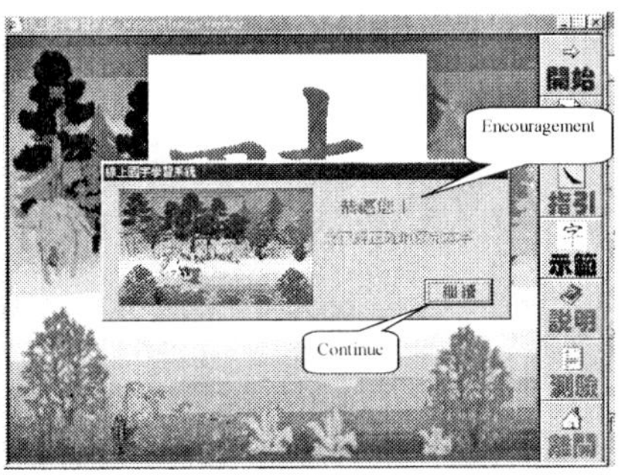

Figure 7. A warning cartoon and an error message help to correct the student

Figure 8. User-login interface

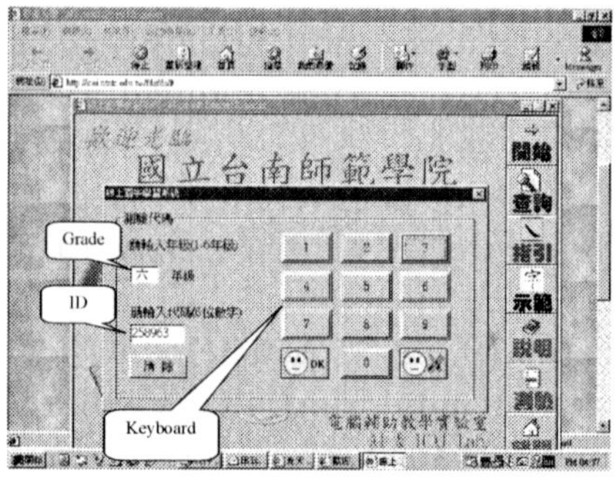

- **Function (1)**  : Initiates the instruction/test module and displays an interface that allows the user to key in his or her grade and ID (Figure 8). Then, the user can select a lesson from the menu (Figure 9). The system includes 12 volumes, 2734 Chinese characters, taught for 12 semesters by primary schools in Taiwan.

- **Function (2)**  : Retrieves the records from the history database and shows the number of errors of the ten most recently written Chinese characters (Figure 10). The returned information includes the ten most recently written Chinese characters, and the digit after each character represents the number of stroke errors made by the student when writing this character. The digits are also recorded in the learning history database and are used by the explanatory module.

Figure 9. Course selection interface

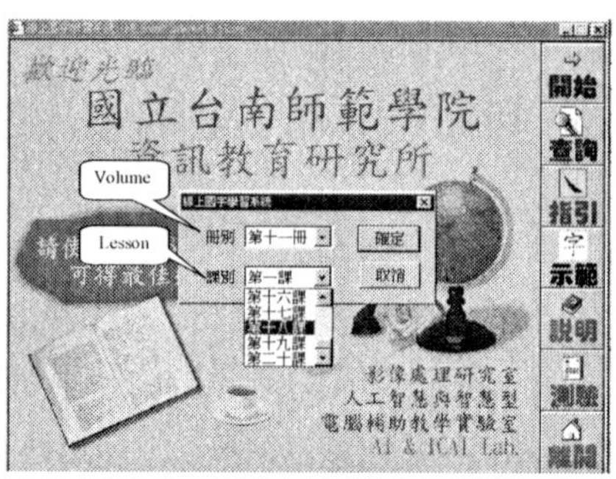

Figure 10. The pop-up window presents the number of errors of recently written Chinese characters, and the digit specifies the number of stroke errors

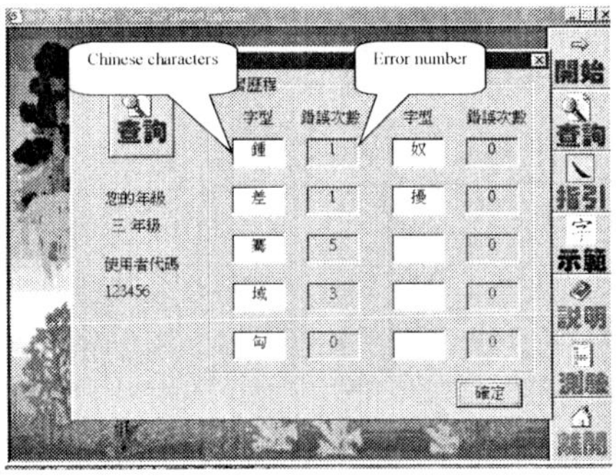

- **Function (3)**  **:** Directs the next stroke during the writing of a Chinese character. The next stroke will be written and shown by the system and disappears after three seconds. The student can then rewrite and learn the correct stroke order by following this direction.
- **Function (4)**  **:** Demonstrates the stroke order of the displayed Chinese character. After three seconds, the written strokes will disappear and then the student can write this Chinese character with the correct stroke order by following the demonstration.
- **Function (5)**  **:** Calls an online help that explains how to use the system.
- **Function (6)**  **:** Enters a test mode, as does function (1) except that functions (3) and (4) are disabled. Users do not receive any instruction while writing the Chinese characters. However, when a test is finished, a score will be given to the student and the stroke orders of writing behavior becomes training data for the neural network of the student model (as detailed in Section 3).
- **Function (7)**  **:** Used to exit the ITS, and if the student wants to practice/learn again, he or she must re-log in by keying in a user ID and password.

Two parts of this system are developed using artificial intelligence techniques. The first is the student model (Anderson, 1983) that was designed and developed using a neural network (NN) (Lippmann, 1987). The student model is used to learn the writing behavior of the student. The system can simulate internally this behavior and predict the stroke orders of unlearned characters. If the student writes a character with the wrong stroke order, then the student is likely to use the wrong stroke orders when writing some unlearned characters that are similar to this character. Accordingly, the characters predicted by the NN to be written incorrectly by the student are used to test and teach the student, to correct wrong writing behavior. The student is only required to practice a small subset of Chinese characters but to write thousands of Chinese characters. For example, the Chinese characters 未 and 末 have the same stroke orders, and so can be used to correct the writing behavior when one of these two characters is written incorrectly.

The second part of this system that uses artificial intelligence is the tutoring module, implemented by a rules-based system (Rich, 1983). The tutoring module analyzes the writing behavior of the user and outputs the error message when an incorrect stroke order is detected. An incorrect stroke order may include many factors (such as for example, a wrong direction or wrong sequence). An intelligent tutoring module will select a Chinese character with characteristics similar to those of the one written with an incorrect stroke order, to teach the student. The selected character is used to test the student. Therefore, the student isn't required to write several Chinese characters unassociated the wrong stroke order. Students learn efficiently when learning on this system.

Applied Artificial Intelligence Techniques

In the proposed ITS, two artificial intelligence techniques, involving a neural network (NN) and an inference engine (a rule-based system), are used to develop the student model and an intelligent tutoring module.

Student Model

Figure 11 presents the architecture of the NN used to learn the writing behavior of a student. The proposed NN is a multi-layer perceptron (MLP) structure (Rumelhard, Hinton, & Williams, 1986) whose inputs are the correct stroke orders of a Chinese character shifted left in each period. The desired output for the neuron in the "target" position is the written stroke order and set to be one. The initial stroke begins from this position, and the inputs are shifted left in the subsequent period to learn the next written stroke of the character, and so on.

Figure 11. Architecture of NN for learning the writing behavior of a student

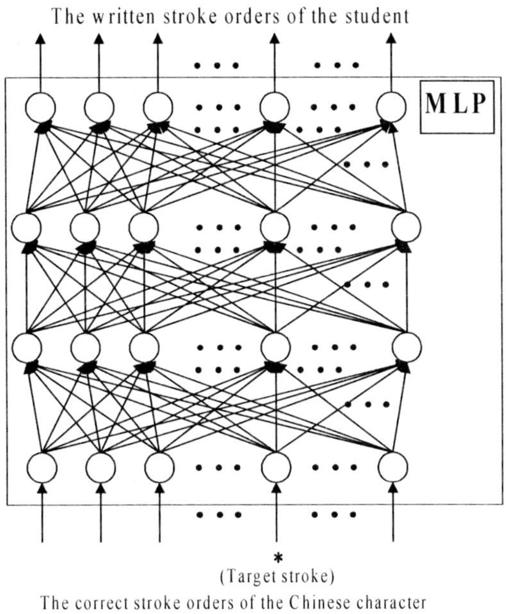

The learning and shifting processes for each stroke will continue until all strokes are trained and learned by the NN. The outputs include the orders of all of the strokes of the Chinese characters. Therefore, each stroke direction and the sequence of the strokes must be considered. For example, the Chinese character "森" has three strokes 一 , _ and _ , in the same direction "→", corresponding to the output neurons, $\rightarrow^1$, $\rightarrow^2$ and $\rightarrow^3$.

The upper index j of each output neuron D^j represents the sequence of strokes with the direction D. The upper "木" in the Chinese character "森" is written first, followed by the lower-left "木", and then the lower-right "木". The stroke order of "森" is "→, ↓, ↙, ↘, →, ↓, ↙, ↘, →, ↓, ↙, ↘," and the directional codes are "2, 4, 5, 3, 2, 4, 5, 3, 2, 4, 5, 3." Suppose the direction of the stroke "—" written by a student is incorrect, and that he writes it in the direction "←" rather than "→." The directional codes of "森" would then be written by this student "6, 4, 5, 3, 6, 4, 5, 3, 6, 4, 5, 3." The desired output of the first training pattern is "←"; that the value "1" is set to output neuron "$\leftarrow^1$" and the others are set to "0".

Figures 12 (a)-(d) present the first four training patterns (the stroke orders of the Chinese character 森) used by the NN to learn the Chinese character "森." The NN must learn 12 strokes (training patterns) for "森." The learning

Figure 12a. First training pattern (Start from the target position "")*

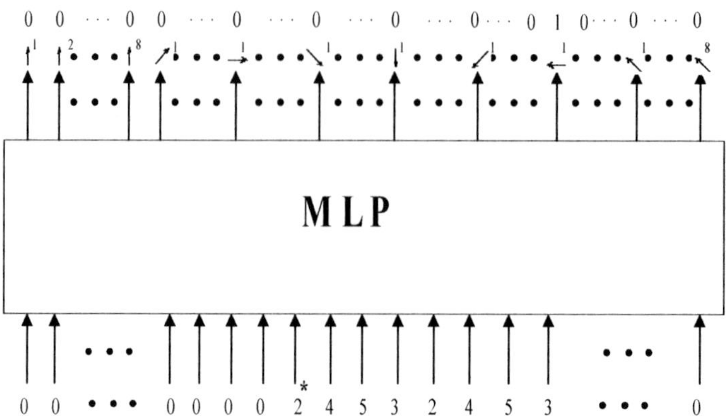

Figure 12b. Second training pattern (Shift one position to the left of the input in (a))

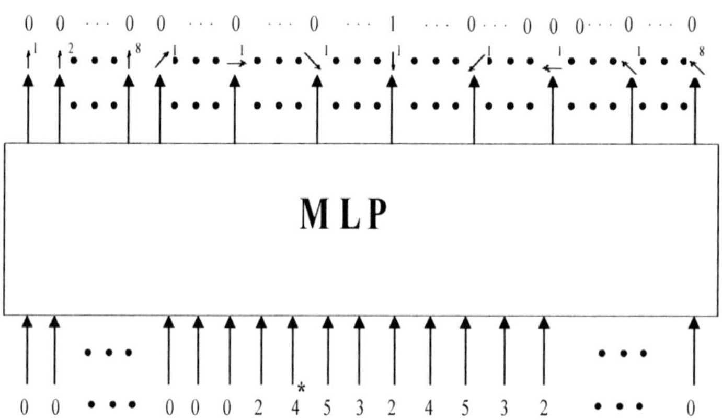

technique (delta learning rule) (Rumelhard, Hinton, & Williams, 1986) is applied to learn the student's writing behavior. Then, a similar input pattern generates the same output. For example, if a student writes a similar Chinese character "林," then the written direction codes could be "6, 4, 5, 3, 6, 4, 5, 3" (an error in the direction of stroke "—") rather than "2, 4, 5, 3, 2, 4, 5, 3." Experiments confirmed that when the input "2, 4, 5, 3, 2, 4, 5, 3" is applied to the NN, a sequence of outputs "6, 4, 5, 3, 6, 4, 5, 3," which can correctly predict the way in which the strokes are written by the student, is generated (Huang, 1999). Restated, the neuron-based student model can successfully learn the writing behavior of a student.

Figure 12c. Third training pattern (Shifted one position to the left of the input in (b))

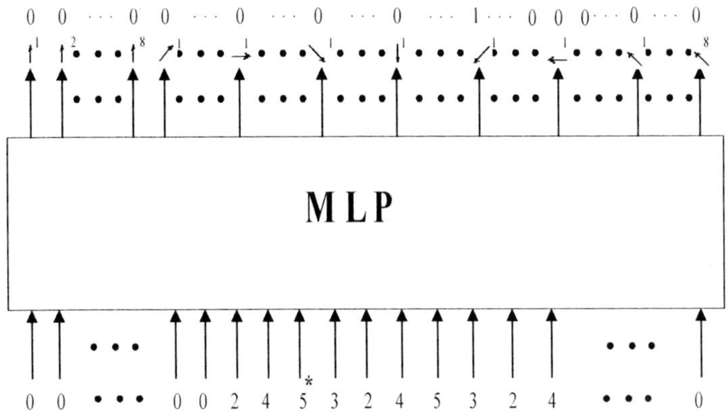

Figure 12d. Fourth training pattern (Shifted one position to the left of the input in (c))

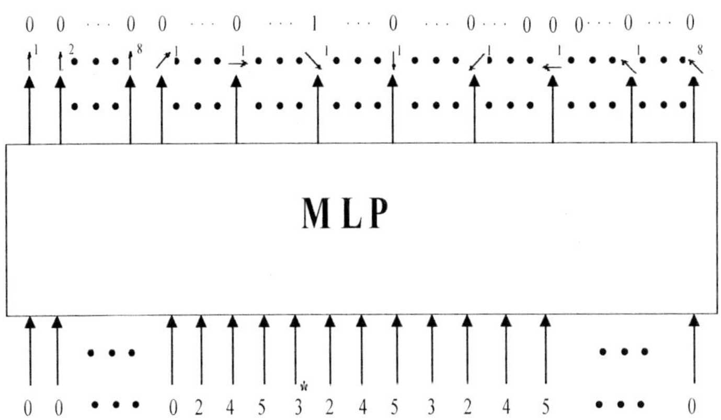

When a student finishes the learning activities of this system, the NN is used to learn the writing behavior of this student by adapting the weights of NN in the background of the system. The adaptation of weights takes about 20 minutes. After the NN has learned a student's writing behavior, it will generate the same output when the student tries to write an unwritten Chinese character with a stroke order similar to that of a previously learned character. Experimental results indicate that the neural network method successfully predicts the wrong stroke orders of unlearned characters (correct ratio > 95%) which will be written by the student (Huang, 1999). When the student next logs in to the system, the student model can select some unlearned Chinese characters with the wrongly written stroke orders to test the student. This system is very useful in increasing the efficiency of remedial teaching.

Intelligent Tutoring Module

Seventeen major rules, defined by the Ministry of Education, Taiwan, ROC, govern the writing of Chinese characters. A rule-base is constructed by combining these rules and the directions of the strokes. All writing errors were analyzed herein and grouped into three different types.

The first type of error is called *structure error*. Since many Chinese characters contain two or more "sub-characters," each is often a Chinese character. For example, the Chinese character "味" is comprised of two sub-characters "口" and "未," which are also Chinese characters. The sub-character "口" is written first and the sub-character "未" is then written. If a student wrote the sub-character "未" first and then wrote the sub-character "口" a *structure error* would occur, even though the stroke sequence is correct for each sub-character.

The second type of error is a *sequence error*. For the Chinese character "未", the correct stroke order is "一 , 一 , 丨 , ノ , ㇏." If a student writes the strokes in the sequence "一 , 丨 , 一 , ノ , ㇏", then a *sequence error* occurs.

The third type of error is the *direction error*. For the Chinese character "未", the correct direction of the stroke "一" is "→." If a student writes the stroke "一"in the direction "←," then a *direction error* occurs.

After a student has written a Chinese character, the system checks for these three types of error. The corresponding type-error-codes are generated. These three type-error-codes are then combined into a single error code to specify fully the wrong writing behavior of a student. Three databases are used to select Chinese characters that have the similar structure according to the error code. An inference engine was designed to analyze the selected Chinese characters using inference rules. The designed inference rules are applied to select a Chinese to retrain the student and correct his or her writing behavior. Figure 13 depicts the operating flow of the inference engine for the Chinese character "吐" with the maximum amount of information of the error code that specifies the wrong stroke orders in the writing of the Chinese word "味." Accordingly, the student can learn the correct the stroke orders of Chinese characters in an intelligent and efficient environment.

Figure 13. Operating flow of the inference engine in the ITS

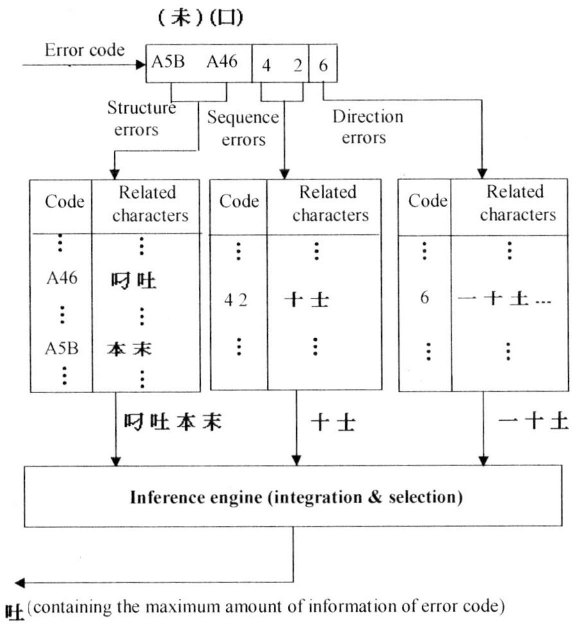

Experiment Results

The prototype of this ITS was presented at the 1997 Children's Information Show (from December 1-30, 1997, sponsored by the National Science Committee, Taiwan) in Taipei and Kaohsiung. More than 1000 people operated the prototype system, and the data collected indicate that stroke orders are written incorrectly over 80% of characters (Table 1).

Some educational studies followed these shows. From February to May 1998, 300 students were randomly selected from primary schools to use this system to learn the stroke orders of Chinese characters (Sun, Chen, Fang, & Wang, 1998). The experimental results revealed that over 82% of the 300 students made at least one mistake. The main reason is that teachers cannot determine whether the students' stroke orders are correct by checking the written characters on the paper. Therefore, teachers cannot correct the wrong patterns of students. Hence, an intelligent tutoring system is required. Another educational study involved two groups of 24 primary school students each. One group was the control group and the other was the experimental group. The results indicated

Table 1. Statistics on the written Chinese characters, obtained during the 1997 Chinese Children's Information Show

	Written Chinese characters (partial)							
	件	什	任	上	扒	扣	味	未
Total written No.	1017	994	984	978	1024	1142	1106	1143
Incorrect written No.	289	231	788	148	256	273	237	195
Incorrect ratio (%)	28.4	23.2	80.1	15.1	25.0	23.9	21.4	17.1

Table 2. Statistics on learning to write Chinese characters by the experimental group and the control group

		Pre-test	Post-test	Difference
Experimental Group	Average	70.6250	86.7917	16.1667
	N	24	24	24
	SD	11.1738	10.1852	4.1564
Control Group	Average	68.2500	78.6250	10.3750
	N	24	24	24
	SD	13.4915	14.4397	3.8086
Total	Average	69.4375	82.7083	13.2708
	N	48	48	48
	SD	12.3131	13.0318	4.9019

Table 3. Analysis of covariance in Table 2

Source of Variation	Sum of Squares	df	Mean Square	F
Main Effects	402.521	1	402.521	25.331**
Residual	730.958	46	15.890	
Total	1133.479	47		

***$p < .005$

showed that the experimental group achieved much better learning of Chinese characters (see Table 2). Statistical software SPSS (SPSS, 1999) was used to conduct an analysis that showed that the learning achievements of experimental group were significantly better than those of the control group ($F = 25.331, p < .005$, shown in Table 3) after the proposed ITS was applied (Feng, 2000). This result confirms that the proposed ITS is very useful in helping students to learn Chinese characters.

Conclusion

This work presents an ITS to help students to learn and write Chinese characters using the correct stroke orders. This system won the Best Product Award of the International Conference on Computer-Assisted Instruction (ICCAI'99) in Taiwan. The system includes several new approaches for learning Chinese characters, involving Chinese character analysis, neural networks and inference engines; it also includes the programming technique for writing Chinese characters on WWW. The system can instruct students to write Chinese characters using correct stroke orders over the Internet. Additionally, two artificial intelligence techniques were designed to improve the effect and power of this ITS, and help students to determine the correct stroke orders of Chinese characters more intelligently and efficiently. Experiments results revealed that over 82% of the 300 students made at least one mistake, confirming that an ITS is required to assist students to learn the correct stroke orders of Chinese characters. This study also shows educational research that the designed ITS can efficiently help students to learn Chinese characters. The proposed ITS is a very useful tool and contributes greatly to the education of Chinese children.

Acknowledgments

This research was supported by the National Science Council of Taiwan, ROC, under grant NSC 87-2411-H-024.

References

Anderson, J. R. (1983). *The architecture of cognition.* Cambridge: Harvard University Press.

Anderson, J. R. (1988). The expert module. In M. C. Polson & J. J. Richardson (Eds.), *Foundations of intelligent tutoring systems* (pp. 21-53). Lawrence Erlbaum.

Bjorksten, J. (1994). *Learn to write Chinese characters.* Ann Arbor, MI: Edwards Brothers.

Brown, J. S., & Burton, R. R. (1978). Multiple representations of knowledge for tutoring reasoning. In D. G. Bobrow & Allan Collins (Eds.), *Representation and understanding studies in cognitive science* (pp. 311-349). New York: Academic Press.

Brown, J. S., Burton, R. R., & de Kleer, J. (1982). *Knowledge engineering and pedagogical techniques in SOPHIE I, II, and III. Intelligent Tutoring Systems.* London: Academic Press.

Brown, J. S., & VanLehn, K. (1980). Repair theory: A generative theory of bugs in procedural skills. *Cognitive Science, 4*, 379-426.

Carbonell, J. R. (1970). AI in ICAI: An artificial intelligence approach to computer assisted instruction. *IEEE Transactions on Man-Machine Systems, 11*, 190-202.

Carbonell, J. R., & Collins, A. M. (1974). Natural semantics in AI. *IJCAI, 3,* 344-351.

Clancey, W. J., Barnett, J. J., & Cohen, P. R. (1982). Applications-oriented AI research: Education. *The Handbook of Artificial Intelligence* (Vol. 2). Los Altos, CA: William Kaufmann.

Denning, A. (1997). *Active X control inside out.* Microsoft Press.

Feng, D. S. (2000). *The performance evaluation of ITS for learning Chinese characters in primary schools.* Unpublished master's thesis, National Tainan Teachers College, Taiwan, ROC.

Huang, C. U. (1999). *An intelligent computer-assisted instruction system for the stroke orders of Chinese characters: A study on student model.* Unpublished master's thesis, National Tainan Teachers College, Taiwan, ROC.

Lam, H. C., Ki, W. W., Chung, A. L. S., Ko, P. Y., Ho, A. H. S., & Pun, S. W. (2001). Designing CALL for learning Chinese characters. *Journal of Computer Assisted Learning, 17*, 115-128.

Law, N., Ki, W. W., Chung, A. L. S., Ko, P. Y., & Lam, H. C. (1998). Children's stroke sequence errors in writing Chinese characters. *Reading and Writing: An Interdisciplinary Journal, 10,* 167-192.

Lippmann, R. P. (1987). An iIntroduction to computing with neural nets. *IEEE ASSP magazine, 4,* 4-22.

McNaughton, W., & Ying, L. (2000). *Reading & wWriting Chinese.* Japan: Charles E. Tuttle Co.

Microsoft. (1997). *The Visual C++ MFC Library Reference*, Part1 and Part2. Microsoft Press.

Rich, E. (1983). *Artificial intelligence.* New York: McGraw-Hill Book.

Rumelhard, D. E., Hinton, G. E., & Williams, R. J. (1986). Learning internal representations by error propagation. *Parallel Distributed Processing: Explorations in the Microstructure of Cognition.* Cambridge: MIT.

SPSS (1999). *SPSS.* Retrieved from http://www.spss.com/products/

Sun, K. T., Chen, Y. H., Fang, T. S., & Wang, C. I. (1998). An intelligent tutoring system for teaching the stroke order of Chinese characters. *Proceeding of the 6th International Conference for the Advancement of Computing in Education (ICCE'98)* (Vol. 2, pp. 346-348). Beijing, China.

Sun, K. T., & Fu, H. C. (1992). A neural network implementation for traffic control problem on crossbar switch networks. *International Journal of Neural Systems, 3*(2), 209-218.

Sun, K. T., & Fu, H. C. (1993). A hybrid neural network model for solving optimization problems. *IEEE Transactions on Computers, 42*(2), 218-227.

Sun, K. T., Huang, C. U., & Wang, C. I. (1997). An intelligent computer-assisted instruction system for the stroke order of Chinese characters. *Proceedings of the National Computer Symposium 1997*, Taiwan (pp. A115-120).

Yao, T. C., Liu, Y., Ge, L., Chen, Y. F., Bi, N. P., & Wang, X. (1997). *Integrated Chinese—Traditional Chinese edition textbook.* Boston: Cheng & Tsui Company.

Section V
Future Directions

Chapter XV

Future Directions of Multimedia Technologies in E-Learning

Timothy K. Shih, Tamkang University, Taiwan

Qing Li, City University of Hong Kong, Hong Kong

Jason C. Hung,
Northern Taiwan Institute of Science and Technology, Taiwan

Abstract

In the last chapter, we discuss how advanced multimedia technologies are used in distance learning systems, including multimedia authoring and presentation, Web-based learning, virtual environments, interactive video, and systems on mobile devices. On the other hand, we believe pedagogic theory should be incorporated into the design of distance learning systems to add learning efficiency. Thus, we point out some suggestions to the designers of future distance learning systems.

Introduction

Distance learning, based on styles of communication, can be categorized into synchronized and asynchronized modes. The advantages of distance learning include flexibility of time and space, timely delivery of precisely presented materials, large amount of participants and business opportunity, and automatic/individualized lecturing to some degrees. Both synchronized and asynchronized distance learning systems rely on multimedia and communication technologies. Due to its commercial value, distance learning is becoming a killer application of multimedia and communication research. We discuss current distance learning systems based on the types of multimedia technologies used and point out a few new research directions in the last section.

Multimedia Presentations and Interactions

Authoring and playback of multimedia presentations are among the earliest applications of multimedia technologies. Before real-time communication and video-on-demand technologies, multimedia presentations were delivered to kids and distance learning students on CD ROMs. The advantage of multimedia presentation over traditional video tapes is due to interactivity. Multimedia presentations allow one to select "hot spots" in individualized topology. Techniques to realize this type of CD ROM presentations allow a rich set of media coding and playback mechanisms, such as images, sounds, and animations (including video and motion graphics). Successful examples include MS PowerPoint, Authorware Professional, Flash, and others.

With the development of communication technologies, multimedia computing focuses on efficient coding mechanism to reduce the amount of bits in transmission. Synchronization among media became important. Inner stream synchronization is implemented in a single multimedia record, such as the interleaving coding mechanism used in a video file, which includes sound track and motion picture track. Another example of inner stream synchronization and coding is to merge graphics animation with video stream (Hsu, Liao, Liu, & Shih, 2004). On the other hand, inter stream synchronization is more complicated since both the client (i.e., user) side and the server (i.e., management system) side need to work together. Inter stream synchronization allows packages (e.g., sound and image) to be delivered on different paths on a network topology. On the client side, packages are re-assembled and ensured to be synchronized. Another example of a recent practical usage of inter stream synchronization is in several commercial systems allowing video recording to be synchronized with MS PowerPoint presentation or Flash. Some systems (Shih, Wang, Liao, & Chuang, 2004) use an underlying technology known as the advanced streaming format (ASF) of Microsoft. ASF allows users or programs to embed event markers. In a playback system on the client side, users can interrupt a vide presentation, or jump to another presentation section. The video presentation can also use markers to trigger another presentation object such as to bring up a PowerPoint slide (converted to an image) or another multimedia reference. In order to deliver a synchronized presentation, an ASF server needs to be installed on the server machine.

ASF provides a preliminary technology for video-on-demand (or lecture-on-demand). In order to support multiple clients, it is necessary to consider bandwidth allocation and storage placement of video records. Video-on-demand systems (Hua, Tantaoui, & Tavanapong, 2004; Mundur, Simon, & Sood, 2004 allow a video stream to be duplicated and broadcast in different topology on multiple channels, to support multiple real-time requests in different time slots. In addition, adaptive coding and transmission mechanism can be applied to video-on-demand systems to enhance overall system performance.

Video-on-demand allows user interactions to select video programs, perform VCR-like functions, and choose language options. Interactive TV (Liao, Chang, Hsu, & Shih, 2005) further extends interactivities to another dimension. For instance, the users can select the outcome of a drama, refer to specification of a commercial product, or answer questions pre-defined by an instructor. The authoring and playback system developed in Liao, Chang, Hsu, and Shih (2005) takes a further step to integrate video browser (for interactive TV) and Web browser. Thus, distance learning can be implemented on set-top box.

Web-Based Distance Learning and SCORM

Most multimedia presentations can be delivered online over Internet. And, Web browser is a common interface. HTML, XML, and SMIL are the representation languages of learning materials. Typically, HTML is used in the layout while other programming languages (such as ASP) can be used with HTML to retrieve dynamic objects. As an extension to HTML, XML allows user defined tags. The advantage of XML allows customized presentations for different Web applications, such as music and chemistry, which requires different presentation vocabularies. In addition, SMIL incorporates controls for media synchronization in a relatively high level, as compared to inner stream coding technologies. HTML-like presentations can be delivered by Web servers, such as Apache and MS IIS.

Although Web browsers are available on different operating systems and HTML-like presentations can be reused, search and reuse of course materials, as well as their efficient delivery, are key issues to the success of distance learning. In order to achieve reusability and interoperability, a standard is needed. The advanced distributed learning (ADL) initiative proposed the sharable content object reference model (SCORM) (The Sharable Content Object Reference Model, 2004) standard since 2000. Main contributors to SCORM include the IMS Global Learning Consortium, Inc., the Aviation Industry CBT (computer-based training) Committee (AICC), the Alliance of Remote Instructional Authoring & Distribution Networks for Europe (ARIADNE), and the Institute of Electrical and Electronics Engineers (IEEE) Learning Technology Standards Committee (LTSC). The SCORM 2004 (also known as SCORM 1.3) specification consists of three major parts

- **The content aggregation model (CAM):** Learning objects are divided into three categories (i.e., assets, sharable content objects (SCOs) and content organizations). The contents of the learning objects are described by metadata. In addition, CAM includes a definition of how reusable learning objects are packed and delivered.
- **The run-time environment:** In order to deliver learning objects to different platforms, a standard method of communication between the learning management system (LMS) and the learning objects is defined.
- **The sequencing and navigation:** Interactions between users (i.e., students) and the LMS are controlled and tracked by the sequencing and navigation definitions. This also serves as a standard for defining learner profiles, as well as a possible definition for intelligent tutoring.

The SCORM specification clearly defines representation and communication needs of distance learning. To realize and promote the standard, a few SCORM-compliant systems were implemented (Chang, Chang, Keh, Shih, & Hung, 2005; Chang, Hsu, Smith, & Wang, 2005; Shih, Lin, Chang, & Huang; Shih, Liu, & Hsieh, 2003). However, common repository for SCORM learning objects, representation of learner records, and intelligent tutorial mechanisms to facilitate sequencing and navigation are yet to be identified. On the other hand, most existing SCORM-compliant LMSs fail to support the newest specification, except the prototype provided by ADL.

Virtual Classroom and Virtual Lab

Web-based distance learning supports asynchronized distance learning in general. Usually, distance learning programs rely on Web browsers to deliver contents, collect assignments from students, and allow discussion using chat room or e-mails. These functions can be integrated in a distance learning software platform such as Blackboard (http://www.blackboard.com/) and WebCT (http://www.Webct.com/). On the other hand, real-time instruction delivery can be broadcast using video channels, or through bi-directional video conferencing tools (Deshpande, & Hwang, 2001; Gemmell, Zitnick, Kang, Toyama, & Seitz, 2000). Real-time video communication requires sophisticated network facilities and protocols to guarantee bandwidth for smooth transmission.

In addition to online delivery of instruction, lab experiments can be realized using remote labs or virtual labs (Auer, Pester, Ursutiu, & Samoila, 2003). Remote lab uses camera and advanced control technologies to allow physical lab instruments to be accessed by students using Internet. Virtual lab may or may not include physical experimental instruments. Emulation models are usually used. In most cases, assessment of experiment outcomes from software emulation is compared with those from physical devices.

Virtual reality (VR) and augmented reality techniques can also be used in distance learning (McBride & McMullen, 1996; Shih, Chang, Hsu, Wang, & Chen, 2004). Most VR systems use VRML, which is an extension of XML for 3-D object representations. The shared-Web VR system (Shih, Chang, Hsu, Wang, & Chen, 2004) implements a virtual campus, which allows students to navigate in a 3-D campus, with different learning scenarios. Behaviors of students can be tracked and analyzed. The incorporation of game technologies points out a new direction of distance learning, especially for the design of courseware for kids. With wireless communication devices, ubiquitous game technologies can be used for mobile learning in the near future.

Mobile Learning

Wireless communication enables mobile learning. With the capability of multimedia technologies on wireless connected notebook computers, PDAs, and even cellular phones, system developers are possible to implement distance learning systems on mobile devices (Meng, Chu, & Zhang, 2004; Shih, Lin, Chang, & Huang, 2004). The challenges of deploying course materials on small devices, such as cellular phones, include the limited display space, slow computation, and limited memory capacity. On a small display device, reflow mechanism can be implemented (Shih, Lin, Chang, & Huang, 2004). The mechanism resizes contents into a single column layout, which can be controlled using a single scroll bar on PDAs or cellular phones. To cope with small storage, pre-fetching technique on subdivided course contents can be used. Thus, the readers can download only the portion of contents of interesting.

To realize learning management systems on wireless network connected devices, a distributed architecture needs to be designed between the server and the client (e.g., PDA). SOAP is a communication protocol very suitable for the architecture. SOAP packages are messages that can be sent between a client and server, with a standard representation envelope recommended by the W3C (http://www.w3.org/). The advantages of the protocol include platform independency, accessibility, and implementation efficiency. In addition, in order to maintain the status of each individual learner, learner profiles needs to needs to be defined. Yet, SCORM contains only a preliminary description of learner profile definition. The representation of course contents should also consider how to enable small packages to be delivered on a remote request. Cashing mechanism and hand shaking protocol are important issues yet to be developed. In addition, in some occasion for situated learning, location awareness is necessary for situated collaborative learning.

On the other hand, synchronized distance learning on mobile devices requires efficient real-time streaming due to the limited bandwidth of current wireless communication systems (Liu, Chekuri, & Choudary, 2004. Even as 3G mobile communication technologies are available, smooth video streaming requires a broader channel and a robust error resilience transmission mechanism.

Hybrid Interactive Systems and Pedagogical Issues

Whether learning activities are implemented on mobile devices or PC clients, efficient collaboration is the key issue toward the success of learning. A SCORM-based collaborative learning LMS is developed in Chang, Lin, Shih, and Wang (2005). The system allows learning activities among students to be synchronized based on the Petri net model. The instructor is able to supervise the collaboration behavior among a group of students. Whether or not it is SCORM compliant, a distance learning platform should support collaboration in either synchronized or asynchronized manner. At least, a CSCW-like system should be implemented to support the need of collaboration.

Recently, personalized Web information delivery has become an interesting issue in data mining research. A distance learning server is able to analyze student profiles, depending on individual behaviors. Learner profiles can be stored and analyzed according to traversal sequences and results from tests. This type of distance learning system is based on the self-regulation principles of the social cognitive theory (Bandura, 1986). A system using this approach should allow students to plan on their study schedule based on individual performance (Leung, & Li, 2003), while the underlying intelligent mechanism can guide students to a suitable study schedule, which can be reviewed by an instructor. To facilitate user friendliness, self-regulation can be incorporated with Web-based interfaces and mobile devices. To some degree of the usage of artificial intelligence (Shih & Davis, 1997), an intelligent tutorial system is able to generate individualized lectures (Leung & Li, 2003).

We realize that, it is possible to design an integrated learning environment to support the application of the scaffolding theory (Zimmerman & Schuck, 1989). Scaffolding, proposed by L. S. Vygotsky, was viewed as social constructivism. The theory suggests that students take the leading role in the learning process. Instructors provide necessary materials and support. And, students construct their own understanding and take the major responsibility. Between the real level of development and the potential level of development, there exists a zone of proximal development. This zone can be regarded as an area where scaffolds are needed to promote learning. Scaffolds to be provided include vertical and horizontal levels as a temporary support in the zone of proximal development. The scaffolding theory is essential for cognitive development. It also supports the process of social negotiation to self-regulation. There are three properties of the scaffold

- The scaffold is a temporary support to ensure the success of a learning activity.
- The scaffold is extensible (i.e., can be applied to other knowledge domains) and can be used through interactions between the learner and the learning environment.
- The scaffold should be removed in time after the learner is able to carry out the learning activities independently.

The scaffolding theory indicates three key concepts. Firstly, in the zone of proximal development, the relationship between the scaffolds providers and the receivers are reciprocal. That means that the instructor and students negotiate a mutual beneficial interactive process. Secondly, the responsibility is transferred from the instructor to the student during the learning process. Depending on the learning performance, the instructor gradually gives more control of the learning activities to the student for the ultimate goal of self-regulation. Finally, the interaction facilitates the learners to organize their own knowledge. Scaffolding also encourages the use of language or discourse to promote reflection and higher-order thinking.

Pedagogical principles are not multimedia technology. However, the developers of distance learning system should be aware of the concept.

Summary

This chapter summarizes multimedia technologies for distance learning systems. While we were looking for the essential needs of professional educators and students, in terms of "the useful multimedia distance learning tools," we have found that lots of tools were developed by computer scientists. Most of these tools lack of underlying educational theory to show their usability. However, software is built for people to use. In spite of its advanced functionality and outstanding performance, any system will be useless if no one uses it. Thus, we believe the specification of a distance learning system should be written by educational professionals, with the help of computer scientists.

From the perspective of multimedia and Internet computing, there are a few challenging research issues to make distance-learning systems more colorful and useful. We highlight a few here

- **Interactive TV:** Video-on-demand technologies should be highly integrated with interactive TV and set-top box devices, which should be extended to incorporate different modals of interaction. A sophisticated bi-directional inter stream synchronization mechanism needs to be developed.
- **Standards:** The most popular standard is SCORM. However, the definition of user profile, federal repository, and adaptive techniques for mobile devices are yet to be investigated.
- **High communication awareness:** Video conferencing tools should be integrated with awareness sensors, to bring the attentions on interested video area to users.
- **Virtual and remote lab:** A standard development specification for creating virtual or remote labs is not yet developed. The standard should allow reusable lab components which can be assembled to facilitate different varieties of lab designs.

- **Adaptive contents for mobile learning:** Different mobile devices should have different functional specifications to guide a central server to transmit device and user dependent media for efficient learning.
- **Intelligent tutoring:** User profile dependent tutoring based on intelligent technology applied on Web technology should be used. Pedagogical considerations can be applied on intelligent tutoring.

Among the developed platforms for distance learning, an assessment mechanism, especially the one based on educational perspective, should also be proposed. It is the hope that the multimedia research community can work with educational professionals and the distance learning industry together, to develop a standard distance-learning framework for the success of our future education.

References

Auer, M., Pester, A., Ursutiu, D., & Samoila, C. (2003, December). Distributed virtual and remote labs in engineering. *International Conference on Industrial Technology ICIT 2003,* Slovenia (pp. 1208-1213).

Bandura, A. (1986). *Social foundations of thought and action: A social cognitive theory.* Englewood Cliffs, NJ: Prentice-Hall.

Chang, F. C., Chang, W., Keh, H., Shih, T. K., & Hung, L. (2005). Design and implementation of a SCORM-based courseware system using influence diagram. *International Journal of Distance Education Technologies, 3*(3), 82-96.

Chang, W., Hsu, H., Smith, T. K., & Wang, C. (2005). Enhancing SCORM metadata for assessment authoring in e-learning. *Journal of Computer Assisted Learning, 20*(4), 305-316.

Chang, W., Lin, H. W., Shih, T. K., & Wang, C. (2005, March 28-30). Applying Petri nets to model SCORM learning sequence specification in collaborative learning. *Proceedings of the 19th International Conference on Advanced Information Networking and Applications*, Taiwan.

Deshpande, S. G., & Hwang, J. (2001, December). A real-time interactive virtual classroom multimedia distance learning system. *IEEE Transactions on Multimedia, 3*(4), 432-444.

Gemmell, J., Zitnick, L., Kang, T., Toyama, K., & Seitz, S. (2000, October-December). Gaze-awareness for video conferencing: A software approach. *IEEE MultiMedia, 7*(4), 26-35.

Hsu, H. H., Liao, Y. C., Liu, Y.-J., & Shih, T. K. (2004). Video presentation model. In S. Deb (Ed.), *Video data management and information retrieval* (pp. 177-192). Hershey, PA: Idea Group Publishing.

Kien, A., Hua, M. A., Tantaoui, & Tavanapong, W. (2004, September). Video delivery technologies for large-scale deployment of multimedia applications. *Proceedings of the IEEE* (Special issue on Evolution of Internet Technologies towards the Business Environment), *92*(9), 1439-1451.

Leung, E. W. C., & Li, Q. (2002). Media-on-demand for agent-based collaborative tutoring systems on the Web. *IEEE Pacific Rim Conference on Multimedia 2002* (pp. 976-984).

Leung, E. W. C., & Li, Q. (2003). A dynamic conceptual network mechanism for personalized study plan generation. *ICWL 2003* (pp. 69-80).

Liao, Y., Chang, H., Hsu, H., & Shih, T. K. (2005). Merging web browser and interactive video: A hypervideo system for e-learning and e-entertainment. *Journal of Internet Technology, 6*(1), 121-131.

Liu, T., & Choudary, C. (2004, October). Realtime content analysis and adaptive transmission of lecture videos for mobile applications. *Proceedings of the 12th ACM International Conference on Multimedia*, New York.

McBride, J. A., & McMullen, J. F. (1996, January). Using virtual reality for distance teaching a graduate information systems course. *Proceedings of the 29th Hawaii International Conference on System Sciences 1996* (Vol. 3, pp. 263-272).

Meng, Z., Chu, J., & Zhang, L. (2004, May). Collaborative learning system based on wireless mobile equipments. *IEEE Canadian Conference on Electrical and Computer Engineering CCECE 2004* (Vol. 1, pp. 481-484).

Mundur, P., Simon, R., & Sood, A. (2004, February). End-to-end analysis of distributed video-on-demand systems. *IEEE Transactions on Multimedia, 6*(1), 129-141.

The Sharable Content Object Reference Model. (2004). *ADL Co-Laboratory*. Retrieved from http://www.adlnet.org/

Shih, T. K., Chang, Y., Hsu, H., Wang, Y., & Chen, Y. (2004). A VR-based shared Web system for distance education. *International Journal of Interactive Technology and Smart Education (ITSE), 1*(4), 4.

Shih, T. K., & Davis, R. E. (1997, April-June). IMMPS: A multimedia presentation design system. *IEEE Multimedia* (pp. 67-78).

Shih, T. K., Lin, N. H., Chang, H., & Huang, K. (2004, June 27-30). Adaptive pocket SCORM reader. *Proceedings of the 2004 IEEE International Conference on Multimedia and Expo (ICME2004)*, Taipei, Taiwan.

Shih, T. K., Liu, Y., & Hsieh, K. (2003, July 6-9). A SCORM-based multimedia presentation and editing system. *Proceedings of the 2003 IEEE International Conference on Multimedia & Expo (ICME2003)*, Baltimore.

Shih, T. K., Wang, T., Liao, I., & Chuang, J. (2003). Video presentation recording and online broadcasting. *Journal of Interconnection Networks* (Special issue on Advanced Information Networking: Architectures and Algorithms), *4*(2), 199-209.

Zimmerman, B. J., & Schuck, D. H. (1989). *Self-regulated learning and academic achievement.* New York: Springer-Verlag.

About the Authors

Timothy K. Shih is a professor at the Department of Computer Science and Information Engineering, Tamkang University, Taiwan, ROC. He is a senior member of IEEE and a member of ACM. His current research interests include multimedia computing and networking, distance learning, and content-based multimedia information retrieval. He was a faculty of the Computer Engineering Department at Tamkang University in 1986.

Jason C. Hung is an assistant professor of the Department of Information Management at Northern Taiwan Institute of Science and Technology, Taiwan, ROC. His research interests include multimedia computing and networking, distance learning, e-commerce, and agent technology. From 1999 to date, he was a part time faculty in the Computer Science and Information Engineering Department at Tamkang University. Dr. Hung earned BS and MS degrees in computer science and information engineering from Tamkang University (1996 and 1998, respectively). He also earned a PhD in computer science and information engineering from Tamkang University (2001). Dr. Hung has published over 50 papers and book chapters, as well as participated in many international academic activities, including the organization of many international conferences. He is the founder and workshop chair of the International Workshop on Mobile Systems, E-commerce, and Agent Technology (MSEAT2002, MSEAT2003, MSEAT2004, and MSEAT2005). He is also the executive manager of the *International Journal of Distance Education Technologies* (Idea Group Publishing, www.idea-group.com).

* * *

Jin-Yu Bai was born in 1980. He earned BS and MS degrees in information engineering and computer science from Feng Chia University, Taiwan, ROC (2002 and 2004, respectively). Currently, he is a software engineer in the Inventec Appliances Corp., Taiwan. His research interests include mobile agents, fault tolerance, and mobile computing.

Leonard Barolli earned BE and PhD degrees from Tirana University and Yamagata University (1989 and 1997, respectively). From April 1997 to March 1999, he was a JSPS post doctor fellow researcher with the Department of Electrical and Information Engineering, Yamagata University. From April 1999 to March 2002, he worked as a research associate in the Department of Public Policy and Social Studies, Yamagata University. From April 2002 to March 2003, he was an assistant professor in the Department of Computer Science, Saitama Institute of Technology (SIT). From April 2003 to March 2005, he was an associate professor and presently is a full professor in the Department of Information and Communication Engineering, Fukuoka Institute of Technology (FIT), Japan. Dr. Barolli has published more than 100 papers in referred journals and international conference proceedings. He was editor of the *IPSJ Journal* and has served as a guest editor for many international journals. Dr. Barolli has been a PC member of many international conferences. He was PC chair of AINA-2004 and is PC chair of ICPADS-2005. He also is serving as general co-chair of AINA-2006. His research interests include ad-hoc networks, sensor networks, P2P systems, network traffic control, fuzzy control, genetic algorithms, agent-based systems and distance learning. He is a member of SOFT, IPSJ, IEEE Computer Society, and IEEE.

Nian Shing Chen has been a professor in the Department of Information Management, National Sun-Yat-Sen University, Taiwan, ROC, since 1996. He is currently a visiting scholar at Griffith Institute for Higher Education, Griffith University, while on sabbatical leave. His research areas include computer networks, knowledge management, and the use and development of online and wireless technologies to enhance e-learning.

Chyi-Ren Dow earned BS and MS degrees in information engineering from National Chiao Tung University, Taiwan (1984 and 1988, respectively), and MS and PhD degrees in computer science from the University of Pittsburgh (1992 and 1994, respectively). Currently, he is a professor in the Department of Information Engineering and Computer Science, Feng Chia University, Taiwan, ROC. His research interests include mobile ad-hoc networks, network agents, learning technologies, and embedded systems.

Khalil El-Khatib earned his BS in computer science from the American University of Beirut (AUB) in 1992. From 1992 to 1994, he worked as a research assistant in the Computer Science Department at AUB. In 1996, he earned an MSc in computer science from McGill University and joined the High Capacity Division at Nortel Networks as a software designer. After two years, he joined the Distributed System Research Group at the University of Ottawa as a PhD candidate under the supervision of Professor G. V. Bochmann. His research work includes QoS for multimedia applications, personal mobility, IP telephony, feature interaction for VoIP, and ubiquitous computing. He joined the National Research Council Canada in February 2002, as a member of the Network Computing Group, researching into security and privacy issues for the Internet and ubiquitous computing environments.

D. S. Feng earned an MS in computer science and information education from National Tainan Teachers College, Tainan, Taiwan, ROC (2000). Since 1992, he has been a primary school teacher in Ping-Tung. His current research interests are computer-assisted learning and neural networks.

Norihiro Fujii earned a BE in electrical and electric engineering from the Osaka Institute of Technology (1980) and an ME in IT professional course from Hosei University, Japan (2001). He worked for Nippon Data General Corporation and ADVANTEST Corp. He is now a PhD candidate of Hosei University in computer and information sciences. He is currently researching and developing an environment for parallel and distributed processing systems. His research interests include the Web services and its use for eLearning. He is a member of the IEEE, the IEICE, and the IPSJ.

Claude Ghaoui earned her PhD in computer science at Liverpool University, UK (1995), specializing in hypermedia and electronic publishing on the World Wide Web. She joined the School at Liverpool JMU in 1995 as a senior lecturer. Her current research centers on human-computer interaction and multimedia, and she has keen research interest in the application of ICT to education and promoting flexible learning. In 1997 she chaired EuroMicro on Interface Design in Budapest, Hungary. She was the program chair for the Euromicro Workshop on Multimedia & Telecommunications 2000 (Masstricht, The Netherlands), and was the deputy program chair for the Euromicro Workshop on Multimedia and Telecommunications 2001 (Poland). She has numerous publications on e-learning, and several books by Idea Group Publishing (Hershey, PA). These include *Usability Evaluation of Online Learning Programs* and *E-Education Applications: Human Factors and Innovative Approaches*.

Gwo-Jen Hwang is currently a professor in the Department of Information and Learning Technology at the National University of Tainan, Taiwan, ROC. Dr. Hwang earned a PhD from the Department of Computer Science and Information Engineering at National Chiao Tung University in Taiwan. His research interests include e-learning, computer assisted testing, expert systems, and mobile computing. Dr. Hwang has published nearly 40 papers in such professional journals as *IEEE Transactions on Education*, *IEEE Transactions on Systems Man and Cybernetics*, *Computers & Education*, *Journal of Information Science and Engineering*, and the *International Journal of Distance Education Technologies*, among others.

W. A. Janvier graduated from Liverpool John Moores University (LJMU), UK (2000) with a degree in computer science. His research concentrated on distance learning tools, intelligent tutoring systems, psychometric tests, communication preference, learning styles, and neurolinguistic programming. Prior to studying at LJMU, he ran a dress manufacturing and finance business, then joined the life industry where he was in management. He was a licensed seminar speaker for both Allied Dunbar and J. Rothschild Assurance.

Qun Jin is a tenured full professor at the Networked Information Systems Laboratory, Department of Human Informatics and Cognitive Sciences, Faculty of Human Sciences, Waseda University, Japan. He has been engaged extensively in research works on computer science, information systems, and Internet computing. His recent research interests cover human-centric ubiquitous information systems, service-oriented computing, semantic P2P networking and services, information management and sharing, groupware, and e-learning support. He earned a BSc in process control from Zhejiang University, China, an MSc in computer science from Hangzhou Institute of Electronic Engineering and the Fifteenth Research Institute of Ministry of Electronic Industry, China, and a PhD in computer science from Nihon University, Japan (1982, 1984 and 1992, respectively). He worked at Hangzhou Institute of Electronic Engineering (1984-1989), INES Corporation (1992-1995), Tokushima University (1995-1999), and the University of Aizu, Japan (1999-2003). During the summer of 1997, he was a short-term scholar in the Department of Electrical and Computer Engineering, Boston University. Since April 2003, he has been at the current position.

Nobuhiko Koike earned BE and ME degrees in electrical engineering from the University of Tokyo, Japan (1970 and 1972, respectively). He earned a PhD from Tokyo University in 1991. He was formerly with C&Research Laboratories of NEC Corporation, where he was engaged in the design and development of parallel machines including a parallel logic simulation machine, HAL, a parallel circuit simulation machine, Cenju, and massively parallel machines Cenju-3 and Cenju-4. From 1996-1999, he served as the general manager of the newly founded C&Research Laboratories, NEC Europe, located in Germany. Since 2000, he has been a professor with the Faculty of Computer and Information Sciences, Hosei University, Japan. His current research areas include parallel computer architecture and its applications in scientific and intelligent computing. He is a member of the IEICE of Japan and the Information Processing Society of Japan. He received the Best Paper Award in 1985, the 25th Anniversary Best Paper Award in 1985, and the 30th Anniversary Best Paper Award in 1990 from the Information Processing Society of Japan.

Larry Korba is the group leader of the Information Security Group of the National Research Council Canada in the Institute for Information Technology. He is currently involved in several projects related to security and privacy. His research interests include privacy protection, network security, and computer supported collaborative work.

Akio Koyama earned BE and PhD degrees from Yamagata University, Japan (1987 and 1998, respectively). From April 1999 to March 2002, he was an assistant professor at Faculty of Computer Science and Engineering, University of Aizu. Since April 2002, he is been an associate professor with the Faculty of Engineering, Yamagata University. Dr. Koyama has published about 70 papers in refereed journals and international conference proceedings. His research interests include network agent systems, distance learning systems, high-speed network protocols, routing protocols and mobile communication systems. He is a member of IEEE Computer Society, IPSJ, and IEICE.

Tosiyasu L. Kunii is currently a professor and IT institute director at Kanazawa Institute of Technology, Japan, an honorary visiting professor with the University of Bradford, and a professor *emeritus* of the University of Tokyo and of the University of Aizu. He was a professor of Hosei University from 1998 to 2003. Before that he served as founding president and professor of the University of Aizu dedicated to computer science and engineering as a meta discipline (1993-1997). He had been a professor with the Department of Computer and Information Science at the University of Tokyo from June 1978 until March 1993, after serving as an associate professor at the Computer Centre of the University of Tokyo (October 1969). He was a visiting professor at the University of California at Berkeley in 1994 and the University of Geneva in 1992. He earned a BSc in 1962, an MSc in 1964 and a DSc in 1967 all from the University of

Tokyo. He received the 1998 Taylor L. Booth Education Award of IEEE Computer Society. He is a fellow of IEEE and IPSJ. He has published over 50 books and over 300 refereed papers in computer science. Dr. Kunii was founder and editor-in-chief of *The Visual Computer: A International Journal of Computer Graphics* (Springer-Verlag, 1984-1999), and *International Journal of Shape Modeling* (World Scientific) (1994-1995), and was associate editor of *IEEE Computer Graphics and Applications* (1982-2002). He is associate editor-in-chief of *The Journal of Visualization and Computer Animation* (John Wiley & Sons, 1990-) and is on the editorial board of *Information Systems Journal* (1976-), and *Information Sciences Journal* (1983-).

Chi-Chin Lee is a computing teacher at Chien Chen Senior High School (CCSH), Taiwan. She earned a Bachelor of Information and Computer Education at the National Taiwan Normal University and a master's degree in information and computer education at the National Kaohsiung Normal University, Taiwan, ROC. Her research interests include e-learning systems, authoring tools, and computer-assistant learning.

Qing Li earned a BEng degree from Hunan University (Changsha, China), MSc and PhD degrees from the University of Southern California (Los Angeles, USA), all in computer science. He is currently an associate professor at the City University of Hong Kong, as well as a guest professor of the Zhejiang University, and an adjunct professor of the Hunan University. His research interests include database modeling, multimedia retrieval and management, and e-learning systems. Dr. Li has published over 190 papers in technical journals and international conferences in these areas, and is actively involved in the research community by serving as a guest and associate editor to several technical journals, programme committee chair/co-chair, and as an organizer/co-organizer of major international conferences. Currently he serves as the chairman of the Hong Kong Web Society, and is a counselor of the Database Society of Chinese Computer Federation, as well as a steering committee member of the international WISE Society.

Yi-Hsung Li was born in 1979. He earned BS and MS degrees in information engineering and computer science from Feng Chia University, Taiwan, ROC (2001 and 2003, respectively). He is currently a graduate student for the PhD degree in the Department of Information Engineering and Computer Science, Feng Chia University, Taiwan. His research interests include personal communications, mobile computing, learning technologies, and network agents.

Ching-Jung Liao is currently an assistant professor in the Department of Management Information Systems at Chung Yuan Christian University, Taiwan, ROC. He was director of Department of Information Management, Computer and Communication Center, and Enterprise-Academic Cooperation Center at the Overseas Chinese Institute of Technology (2000-2003). He earned BS and MS degrees in computer science and biomedical engineering from Chung Yuan Christian University, and a PhD of information engineering and computer science from Feng Chia University. He has been a guest scientist in the Institute of Informatics of Technical University of Munich, Germany. His current research interests include grid computing, parallel and distributed computing, e-learning, pervasive learning, and ubiquitous computing. He is a member of IEEE, ACM, and AAEC.

Jianhua Ma is a professor with the Department of Digital Media, Faculty of Computer and Information Sciences, Hosei University, Japan. Prior to joining Hosei University in 2000, he had worked for 7 years at the National University of Defense Technology (NUDT), 3 years at Xidian University in China, and 5 years at the University of Aizu in Japan, respectively. He earned BE and ME degrees in communication systems from NUDT, and a PhD in information engineering from Xidian University (1982, 1985 and 1990, respectively). His research interests include ubiquitous intelligence, pervasive computing, trusted autonomic computing, mobile multimedia, P2P networks, collaborative systems, multi-agents, context aware services, distance learning, etc. He has published more than 100 academic papers in journals, books and conference proceedings. He received the Certificate of Appreciation from IEEE Computer Society in 2004. He is an editor-in-chief of *Journal of Ubiquitous Computing and Intelligence (JUCI)*, *Journal of Mobile Multimedia (JMM)*, and *Journal of Autonomic and Trusted Computing (JoATC)*, and an assistant editor-in-chief of *International Journal of Pervasive Computing and Communications (JPCC)*.

Wee Sen Goh is a manager at Nanyang Technological University (NTU), Singapore, where he heads the design and media team at the University's Centre for Educational Development. Prior to joining NTU, he served as an IT head and a physics lecturer in a junior college, where his team was responsible for driving the adoption of technology in the institution. His interactive courseware has won national innovation awards, and he was also responsible for user-interaction and visual design for the college corporate portal. In NTU, Wee Sen provides consultancy to faculty on the design and Web/multimedia projects. He has conducted large-scale user studies, and evaluates media technologies. He has taught workshops on Web usability, Flash-based applications, and presented on search optimization strategies and Web information architecture. His current pursuits revolve around the domains of user experience, and interactive design. Wee Sen has an MSc in knowledge management from NTU, and an MA in theoretical physics from Cambridge University, UK.

Chye Seng Lee is the deputy director (emerging technologies), Centre for Educational Development, Nanyang Technological University (NTU) in Singapore. He is responsible for the evaluation and implementation of educational technologies for the academic community, and he helps to spearhead the development of eLearning and distance learning in NTU. He also leads an IT team that manages the mission critical online services hosted at the University's E-Learning Operation Centre. Chye Seng earned his Bachelor of Applied Science (computer engineering) and Master of Science (info studies) from NTU, and a Graduate Diploma in business administration from the Singapore Institute of Management. His research interests include emerging educational technologies, intelligent search agents, parallel computing, creative thinking and online content delivery.

K. T. Sun earned a BS in information science from Tunghai University, Taiwan (1985) and MS and PhD degrees in computer science and information engineering from National Chiao-Tung University, Taiwan, ROC (1987 and 1992, respectively). From 1992-1996, he was a research associate in Chung Shan Institute of Science and Technology. Since 1996, he has been with the computer science and information education, National Tainan Teachers College, Taiwan, ROC, where he is currently a professor and the director of the Library of National University of Tainan. Professor Sun won the Drag Thesis Award (PhD) granted by the Acer Co. in 1992, the Best Paper Award of the International Conference on Computer-Assisted Instruction (ICCAI) in 1998 and 1999, and the Best Paper Award of the Medical Informatics Symposium in Taiwan (MIST) in 2005. He was the editor-in-chief of the *Journal of National Tainan Teachers College* (2002-2004), and the editor-in-chief of the *Journal of Science and Technology* (National University of Tainan)(2005-). His current research interests are neural network, genetic algorithm, fuzzy set theory, computer-assisted instruction/learning design, and cognitive science.

Daniel Tiong Hok Tan is currently the director/Centre for Educational Development, acting director/Centre for Continuing Education and associate professor/School of Electrical and Electronic Engineering at the Nanyang Technological University. He earned a BSc from the University of Aston, Birmingham. He subsequently achieved a PhD from the University of Manchester Institute of Science and Technology and a post-graduate diploma in teaching in higher education from the Nanyang Technological University, Singapore. His research interests cover Internet and computer security; human factors and usability. He is involved in several projects on information warfare, encryption, authentication, intrusion detection systems, and usability. Assoc Prof Tan, as director of the Centre for Educational Development at the Nanyang Technological University, led a team to develop and implement an e-learning campus ecosystem. This environment, comprising a holistic approach towards system design, learning platform, server architecture, coupled with edUtorium — the staff development program and pedagogical design has resulted in a high immersive and adoption rate, by both staff and students. Through this innovative e-learning initiative, the university has won recognition by being a winner of the Intelligent20 Award 2003, Honouree of CIO Asia100 Award 2004, and EMC Best Practice Award 2004.

Chun Yen Tsai is a PhD student at the National Kaohsiung Normal University (NKNU), Taiwan, ROC. He majors in science education at the Graduated Institute of Science Education (GISE). Before entering GISE at NKNU, he earned a Bachelor of Education in mathematics and science education at National Tai-Chung Teachers College, Taiwan, and a master's degree in information and computer education at NKNU. His research interests include e-learning systems, computer-assistant instruction, and the media assistant in science education.

Yuefei Xu is a research officer in the Information Security Group, Institute for Information Technology, National Research Council Canada. Before this, he was a post-doctoral fellow in the University of Calgary (Canada) focused on agent-based re-configurable distributed control systems. He earned a BSc, an MSc, and a PhD from the Northwestern Polytechnical University, China. His research interests include distributed information systems, e-business, and information security and privacy. His current research activities are in privacy protection and trust management for e-learning applications.

Jin-Tan Yang is an associate professor of general education at National Kaohsiung Normal University (NKNU), Taiwan, ROC. Prior to entering NKNU, he received a Bachelor of Science in applied mathematics at National Chung-Hsiung University of Taiwan, a Master of Science in computer science at the State University of New York at Buffalo (SUNYAB), and a PhD in computer education at the University of Oregon (UO). He has been involved in an e-

Learning National Project, supported by the National Science Council of Taiwan, for three years. His research interests include learning content management system of e-learning, intelligent agent, and Semantic Web.

George Yee is a senior scientist in the Information Security Group, Institute for Information Technology, National Research Council Canada (NRC). Prior to joining the NRC in late 2001, he spent more than 20 years at Bell-Northern Research and Nortel Networks. George earned a BSc (mathematics), an MSc (information and systems science), and a PhD (electrical engineering) from Carleton University, Canada, where he is currently an adjunct research professor. He is a senior member of IEEE, and a member of ACM and Professional Engineers Ontario. His research interests include security and privacy for e-services, using software agents to enhance reliability, security, and privacy, and engineering software for reliability, security, and performance.

Pao Ta Yu earned a BS in mathematics from the National Taiwan Normal University (1979), an MS in computer science from the National Taiwan University, Taipei, Taiwan, ROC (1985), and a PhD in electrical engineering from Purdue University, West Lafayette, USA (1989). Since 1990, he was been with the Department of Computer Science and Information Engineering at the National Chung Cheng University, Chiayi, Taiwan, ROC, where he is currently a professor. His research interests include e-learning, neural networks and fuzzy systems, nonlinear filter design, intelligent networks, and XML technology.

Shuichi Yukita earned a BS in physics and an MS in mathematics from the University of Tokyo, Japan (1976 and 1978, respectively). He earned a PhD in information science from Tohoku University, Sendai, Japan (2000). From 1983 to 1987, he was with Toyo University, Saitama, Japan. From 1987 to 1993, he was with Wakkanai-Hokusei Junior College, Hokkaido, Japan. From 1993 to March 2000, he was with the University of Aizu, Fukushima, Japan. In April 2000, he joined the Faculty of Computer and Information Sciences at Hosei University, Japan, as an associate professor, and become a professor in April 2001. His current research areas include cellular automata theory, algorithmic mathematics, and mathematical visualization. He is a member of the IEEE, the IEICE, the IPSJ, the Mathematical Society of Japan, and JSIAM.

Index

N

O

P

R

S

T

U

V

W